THE ENGLISH WOOL

The wool market was extremely important to the English medieval economy and wool dominated the English export trade from the late thirteenth century to its decline in the late fifteenth century. Wool was at the forefront of the establishment of England as a European political and economic power and this volume is the first detailed study of the medieval wool market in over twenty years. It investigates in detail the scale and scope of advance contracts for the sale of wool; the majority of these agreements were formed between English monasteries and Italian merchants, and the book focuses on the data contained within them. The pricing structures and market efficiency of the agreements are examined, employing practices from modern finance. A detailed case study of the impact of entering into such agreements on medieval English monasteries is also presented, using the example of Pipewell Abbey in Northamptonshire.

ADRIAN R. BELL is Director of Teaching and Learning at the ICMA Centre, University of Reading.

CHRIS BROOKS is Professor of Finance at the ICMA Centre, University of Reading.

PAUL R. DRYBURGH is Research Fellow in the Department of History at King's College, London.

THE ENGLISH WOOL
MARKET, *c.* 1230–1327

ADRIAN R. BELL,

CHRIS BROOKS

AND

PAUL R. DRYBURGH

CAMBRIDGE
UNIVERSITY PRESS

CAMBRIDGE UNIVERSITY PRESS
Cambridge, New York, Melbourne, Madrid, Cape Town, Singapore,
São Paulo, Delhi, Dubai, Tokyo, Mexico City

Cambridge University Press
The Edinburgh Building, Cambridge CB2 8RU, UK

Published in the United States of America by Cambridge University Press, New York

www.cambridge.org
Information on this title: www.cambridge.org/9780521187510

First published 2007
First paperback edition 2010

A catalogue record for this publication is available from the British Library

ISBN 978-0-521-85941-7 Hardback
ISBN 978-0-521-18751-0 Paperback

Contents

Acknowledgements

This book (like many books) has been an age in the making, probably about ten years in total – eight thinking about it, and two actually producing it. It exists because two young researchers (considerably aged by the writing process) wanted to combine their interests of finance and history to try to shed light on the early existence of financial markets. We finally decided to put a research proposal to the ESRC, which was successful, and we must first thank them for providing the funding, under grant RES-000-22-0647, to carry out the study, which led directly to the writing of this book.

Jim Bolton, Anne Curry, Richard Dale, Chris Dyer, Richard Goddard, Brian Kemp and Joelle Miffre gave valuable advice both before and during the project. We are also grateful to an anonymous reviewer for Cambridge University Press who made a number of valuable comments on the draft text. Thank you also to David Simpkin for compiling the index. Whilst all of our colleagues at the ICMA Centre were supportive throughout, Hilary Feltham deserves a special mention for her great patience and understanding.

During the period of consultation of original sources, the staff at the National Archives at Kew were always accommodating and we should in particular thank Aidan Lawes, Malcolm Mercer and Pamela Nightingale. We also received constructive criticism from participants at various conferences, namely: Queen Mary, University of London, Conference on Banking, Credit and Finance in Late Medieval and Renaissance Europe, organised by Jim Bolton and Leeds Medieval Congress in a Cistercian Session organised by Terryl Kinder of the journal *Citeaux*, who has also been an encouraging supporter of our work.

Ultimately, responsibility must remain with the authors and as this is a multi-authored book, we must take joint responsibility.

Notes on weights, measures and monetary units

The lack of uniformity in the system of weights and measures employed in England in the thirteenth century renders calculations as to the exact amount of wool at issue in any one contract problematic. A casual perusal of the contracts in this volume reveals a wide range of local sack weights, although for the purpose of the totals given in the following chapters, the predominant denomination of 26 stones of wool to each sack, at 14 lb to the stone (364 lb in total), has been taken. In terms of individual fleeces, again local conditions meant that a sack could vary between around 200 and 260 fleeces of between 1½ lb and perhaps 3 lb each.[1] Generally, prepared fleeces were rolled into bales and stuffed into canvas sarplers containing, depending on their size, either one or, more commonly, two sacks.

The basic currency unit in England was the silver penny (denarius). In more detail:

12d = one shilling (solidus)

240d/20s = one pound sterling (librus sterlingorum).

The most commonly used currency denomination for pricing of individual sacks of wool, however, was the 'mark', a notional sum containing 13s 4d. Presumably, the mark helped facilitate easy calculations between parties of many different nationalities and languages.[2]

---

[1] For details on the environmental, climatic and nutritional factors affecting fleece weight, see M. L. Ryder, 'Medieval Sheep and Wool Types', *Agricultural History Review* 32 (1984), pp. 14–28.

[2] For more detail on monetary units and fluctuations in the value of coinage across Europe, see P. Spufford, *Handbook of Medieval Exchange* (London, 1986).

Glossary of wool terms

Clack	soiled wool[1]
Collecta	wool of small-scale producers and tenant farmers collected by monastic agents and prepared, marketed and sold with the demesne crop
Cot	matted wool
Gard	wool shorn from the top of the animal's legs
Locks	the straggly parts of the fleece which fell from the animal prior to shearing
Tayller	offcuts[2]

---

[1] Thanks to J. A. Bell for advice regarding this term. From anecdotal evidence, it would appear that such wool would be included by twentieth-century British farmers when they were being paid by weight. Later, the Wool Board countered this practice by paying on quality of produce. However, the medieval wool contracts that we describe in the following chapter explicitly ruled this out. It seems that a lesson could have been learnt from the thirteenth-century merchant.

[2] Thanks to Professor D. A. Trotter, University of Wales, Aberystwyth, for advice regarding this term.

CHAPTER I

Introduction

THE CONTEXT

[T]he Wolles growyyn withynne this Reaume, here before have ben the great comodite, enrichyng and welfare of this land.

Petitioners to parliament in 1453, in making an impassioned plea over the depressed state of the wool market at that time, consciously harked back to an era when trade in wool had been *the* backbone and driving force in the English medieval economy.[1] The period which had undoubtedly witnessed the greatest activity, indeed, was the fifty years either side of the turn of the fourteenth century, when the interplay of warfare, governmental interference in the form of taxes, export duties and export bans, epidemics of disease and famine, better marketing practices, and serious competition among some of the most important elements of the European mercantile elite for the superior product of the English wool-grower, created an unparalleled cycle of boom and bust in wool exports and prices.

It should occasion no surprise, therefore, that it is the wool trade of the late thirteenth and early fourteenth centuries that has predominantly attracted the attention of modern scholars. This is particularly the case when the ample volume and rich variety of surviving source material for this period, notably including extensive, if not comprehensive customs accounts,[2] and schedules and treatises of prices and producers, is taken into consideration. Chief amongst these is the raft of contracts for the advance purchase of wool entered into by both monastic institutions and

---

[1] *Rotuli Parlamentorum*, V, ed. J. Strachey *et al.* (London, 1787), p. 274; quoted in T. H. Lloyd, 'The Movement of Wool Prices in Medieval England', *Economic History Review Supplement* 6 (Cambridge, 1973), p. 25. The petition continues: 'and how now late the price of the said Wolles ys so gretly decayed and amenused in the hondes of the growers'.

[2] S. Jenks has recently published a finite list of all English customs accounts from the late Middle Ages: S. Jenks, *The Enrolled Customs Accounts (TNA: PRO E 356, E 372, E 364), 1279–80 – 1508–09 (1523/1524)*, Part I (Kew: List and Index Society, 2004).

lay producers, who bargained for the sale of the produce of their flocks for up to twenty years in advance with mostly foreign and particularly Italian (more specifically Florentine and Lucchese) merchant societies often in return for huge sums of liquid capital. These were employed by E. Power in her seminal study *The Wool Trade in English Medieval History* and by T. H. Lloyd in a number of works which set a standard that few have challenged.[3] The work by Power comprises the text of her Ford Lectures, delivered in January 1939. The book was published posthumously and as such does not contain footnotes or referencing. Lloyd's *The English Wool Trade in the Middle Ages* is a much more substantial body of work. It is a general overview of the wool trade and the chapter 'Marketing the wool' focuses upon its sale. Lloyd does not investigate the advance contracts in great detail – other than discussing briefly some of the terms and amounts present in a few selected examples. While both attest to the importance of such contracts in the functioning and financing of the trade, their intention, however, was mainly to place them within the broader economic context and to examine English involvement in the western European wool and commodity markets. J. H. Munro's research is extremely relevant to this book, particularly on wool pricing, and will provide comparative data concerning the continental markets to aid our analysis.[4] Such general histories, moreover, complement studies of more specific, localised elements of the trade – the Italian merchant societies[5] and the monastic producers themselves[6] – all of which made use of the known body of contracts and brought others to light. As a consequence of this diversity of focus, though, there has been no concerted attempt to explore the fuller extent of the source base, meaning that important details may have been

---

[3] E. Power, *The Wool Trade in English Medieval History* (Oxford, 1941); E. Power and M. M. Postan, *Studies in English Trade in the Fifteenth Century* (London, 1933); Lloyd, 'Movement of Wool Prices'; Lloyd, *The English Wool Trade in the Middle Ages* (Cambridge, 1977).

[4] For instance: J. H. Munro, 'Wool-Price Schedules and the Qualities of English Wools in the Later Middle Ages, c. 1270–1499', *Textile History*, 9 (1978), pp. 118–169.

[5] E. S. Hunt, 'A New Look at the Dealings of the Bardi and Peruzzi with Edward III', *Journal of Economic History* 50 (1990), pp. 149–162; Hunt, *Medieval Super Companies* (Cincinnati, 1995); R. W. Kaueper, *Bankers to the Crown: The Riccardi of Lucca and Edward I* (Princeton, 1973); M. Prestwich, 'Italian Merchants in Late Thirteenth and Early Fourteenth Century England', in *The Dawn of Modern Banking* (Yale, 1979), pp. 77–104.

[6] R. J. Whitwell, 'English Monasteries and the Wool Trade in the 13th Century', *Vierteljahrsschrift für Sozial- und Wirtschaftsgeschichte* 2 (1904), pp. 1–33; N. Denholm-Young, *Seigneurial Administration in England* (London, 1937); R. A. Donkin, 'Cistercian Sheep-Farming and Wool-Sales in the Thirteenth Century', *Agricultural History Review* 6 (1958), pp. 2–8; B. Waites, 'Monasteries and the Wool Trade in North and East Yorkshire during the 13th and 14th Centuries', *Yorkshire Archaeological Journal* 52 (1980), pp. 111–121; E. Jamroziak, 'Rievaulx Abbey as a Wool Producer in the Late Thirteenth Century: Cistercians, Sheep and Debts', *Northern History* 50 (2003), pp. 197–218.

obscured from economic historians and, perhaps more pertinently, historians of the local and monastic economy.

Despite this lack of in-depth discussion, historians do still make statements regarding the early existence of sophisticated financial instruments within the wool market in England. R. Britnell, in his recent survey of the economy and society of Britain and Ireland, relying on Lloyd, comments, 'Being able to control large funds, Italians could lend to monasteries on the security of future wool deliveries'.[7] M. Keen comments, 'great wool producing abbeys, like Meaux in Yorkshire, were selling to Italian exporters futures in their wool crop'.[8] So, historians are happy to accept that these contracts are evidence of loans, or alternatively, as Keen states, evidence of 'futures'. Our study will provide a considered view on these advance wool sales and we will argue that they should be seen as financial instruments combining an element of loan and forward contract characteristics, and certainly should not be viewed as early evidence of futures contracts.

Of course, it must be made clear from the outset that the surviving contracts discussed in this volume represent but a modest fraction of the wool that changed hands in England in the period under consideration. The approximately 5,300 sacks sold by advance contract over more than about 50 years is dwarfed, for example, simply by the 7,654 sacks of wool dispatched from Boston, England's principal wool port, upon which customs were paid in 1280, a year in which around 25,000 sacks were exported from England.[9] It also only just surpasses the *c.* 3,540 sacks admitted as due to the Italian merchants in their submissions to Edward I recorded in the so-called 'Exchequer Schedule' of 1294.[10] On the whole, wool sold by advance contract represented the very best that was on offer in England and could command astronomic prices and attract multiple suitors willing to make significant outlay to fuel the burgeoning

---

[7] R. Britnell, *Britain and Ireland 1050–1530: Economy and Society* (Oxford, 2004), p. 126.

[8] M. Keen, *England in the Later Middle Ages: A Political History*, 2nd edn (London, 2003), p. 142. That these contracts can be considered as 'futures' is a common misconception and is repeated by R. M. Eldridge and R. Maltby, 'On the Existence and Implied Cost of Carry in a Medieval English Forward/Futures Market', *Review of Futures Markets* 11 (1992), pp. 36–49. A futures contract is a standardised agreement to buy or sell a particular quantity of a good or asset on a particular date for a price agreed now. Futures contracts, unlike forward agreements, are tradable on a secondary market. This issue is discussed in detail in Chapter 4.

[9] TNA: E 372/124; Jenks, *Enrolled Customs Accounts*, p. 1. For calculations of annual wool exports in this period see this work and E. M. Carus-Wilson and O. Coleman, *England's Export Trade, 1275–1547* (Oxford, 1963).

[10] TNA E 101/126/7. For a modern edition, see A. R. Bell, C. Brooks and P. Dryburgh, *Advance Contracts for the Sale of Wool c. 1200–1327*, vol. 315 (List and Index Society, 2006), Appendix 1. This source will be referred to subsequently as *Advance Contracts*.

and highly lucrative luxury cloth industry in the Low Countries and Italy.[11] On the economic level, therefore, they are critical in adding to the all-too-scarce information surviving on medieval prices and, more generally, on the operation of the wool trade at the upper echelons.[12] Perhaps equally as importantly, they provide a wealth of detail on diverse matters ranging from sheep husbandry, the effects of disease and developments in market-ing strategy, which were couched within the religious institutions them-selves, to the varying depths of penetration of foreigners into the English wool market. The contracts also shed light on the construction, function and, frequently, collapse of their trading and credit networks on both the local and national stages.

MODERN FINANCE IN THE MIDDLE AGES?

It is widely believed that 'derivative instruments', which derive their value from another ('underlying') asset, such as forward contracts and options, are recent inventions. However, as intimated above, an examination of the appropriate historical documents demonstrates the existence of quite sophisticated financial contracts much earlier.

The first official exchange for trading contracts for forward delivery, the Royal Exchange (which later became the London Commodity Exchange), was formed in 1570 as a place where metal traders could come together. A formal futures exchange occurred in the late seventeenth century in the Japanese rice markets. Whilst the US has now become the world's largest centre for derivatives trading, the first forward contract in the US (on corn) was not written until 1851 following the formation of the Chicago Board of Trade (CBOT) in 1848.[13] A highly developed options market existed for a brief period in New York between 1873 and 1875, although such markets did not gain anything near their current level of importance until the late twentieth century.[14]

Within the historical literature, however, there is an ongoing revis-ionism regarding the sophistication of medieval financial transactions. Recent research has included that by J. H. Munro and M. Kowaleski on

---

[11] J. H. Munro, 'Industrial Transformation in the North-west European Textile Trades, *c.* 1290–*c.* 1340: Economic Progress or Economic Crisis?' in B. M. S. Campbell (ed.), *Before the Black Death: Studies in the 'Crisis' of the Early Fourteenth Century* (Manchester, 1991), pp. 110–148.

[12] See Munro, 'Wool Price Schedules and the Qualities of English Wools', pp. 118–169.

[13] See for example, S. Kroll and M. J. Paulenoff, *The Business One Irwin Guide to the Futures Markets* (Homewood, IL: Business One Press, 1993).

[14] J. P. Kairys Jr. and N. Valerio III, 'The Market for Equity Options in the 1870s,' *Journal of Finance* 52 (1997), pp. 1707–1723.

transaction costs, by J. Masschaele on business partnerships and by P. Spufford on banking.[15] It is suggested that many of the financial instruments employed in the medieval economy were motivated by the illegality of interest payments on loans (usury) at that time, creating a need for relatively complex transactions that paid an implicit interest. J. Gilchrist presents an example of non-existent loans of wheat (where only cash actually changed hands) made at prices below those prevailing and where repayment occurred later at market value.[16] From the middle of the thirteenth century, there was a gradual narrowing of the definition of usury so that it eventually encompassed only loans at exorbitant rates of interest. For example, Gilchrist states: 'a merchant who forgoes a chance to make a profit because he makes a charitable loan can reasonably take interest provided that his intention was honest and that he was not accustomed to make such loans'.[17] Reasonable rates of interest were argued to be of the order 5 per cent–12 per cent, figures far lower than those implicit in most documented transactions of the time.

A further example of a fictitious deal occurred when landowners would sometimes transfer the legal title of their property to a 'financier' in exchange for cash.[18] The financier would earn a profit by collecting any rents or profits that accrued to the holder of the land, and the original landowner had the right to reclaim the land at the original price on a pre-specified date. M. S. Knoll shows that such an arrangement could be viewed as using tools from modern finance known as 'financial options'. These options would pay the holder in certain circumstances, and would artificially create the same contingent pay-offs as a loan secured on property. Both put and call options (giving the holder the right but not the obligation to sell and the right but not the obligation to buy respectively) were written on tulip bulbs in Amsterdam in the 1600s. The existence of

---

[15] Munro, 'Industrial transformation in the north-west European textile trades'; Munro, 'The International Law Merchant and the Evolution of Negotiable Credit in Late-Medieval England and the Low Countries', in D. Puncuh, ed., *Banchi pubblici, banchi privati e monti di pieta nell'Europa preindustriale: amministrazione, tecniche operative e ruoli economici*, Nouva Serie, Vol. XXI (Genoa: Societa Ligure di Storia Patria, 1991), pp. 49–80; reprinted in Munro, *Textiles, Towns, and Trade: Essays in the Economic History of Late-Medieval England and the Low Countries*, Variorum Collected Studies series CS 442 (Aldershot and Brookfield: Ashgate, 1994); M. Kowaleski, *Local Markets and Regional Trade in Medieval Exeter* (Cambridge, 1995); J. Masschaele, *Peasants, Merchants and Markets: Inland Trade in Medieval England, 1150–1350* (Basingstoke, 1996); P. Spufford, *Power and Profit: The Merchant in Medieval Europe* (London, 2002).
[16] J. Gilchrist, *The Church and Economic Activity in the Middle Ages* (London, 1969), p. 107.
[17] *Ibid.*, p. 69.
[18] M. S. Knoll, *The Ancient Roots of Modern Financial Innovation: The Early History of Regulatory Arbitrage* (2004) Mimeo. Wharton School, University of Pennsylvania.

such instruments adds weight to our argument, detailed in Chapter 4, that the pricing formulae used by modern financial market practitioners are not necessary for the instruments to be priced and traded. The put–call parity relationship, which would now be employed to ensure that financial options are priced correctly, was developed only by a study in 1969.[19] E. J. Swan presents a comprehensive account of the history of derivatives markets.[20]

The data on which this monograph is based emanate from the ESRC-funded, one-year research project 'Modern Finance in the Middle Ages? Advance Contracts for the Sale of Wool' based at the ICMA Centre, University of Reading, UK. A multidisciplinary study, which adds to the growing literature highlighting the financial sophistication of the medieval economy, it combines empirical historical and modern financial research methods to examine the nature and extent of the forward selling of one of medieval England and Europe's most highly prized commodities at a period of considerable economic flux. This research documents more comprehensively than before the existence and volume of what are termed 'advance contracts' for the sale of wool in England around 700 years ago. The primary objective of the study was to employ valuation techniques from 'modern' finance theory to analyse a sizeable corpus of such contracts, which are recorded in governmental records from the thirteenth century, investigating whether plausible rates of interest were charged and if the wool market was informationally efficient. To our knowledge, this is the first study in either discipline to examine the information contained in advance contracts for the sale of wool in such volume and the first to consider the efficiency of the market.[21] In order to facilitate this analysis, it was necessary to collect a large body of historical data, much of which, though widely employed by economic and monastic historians before, has not been published *in extenso*.[22]

The advance contracts for the sale of wool that will be examined and discussed in great detail in the following chapters demonstrate that not only options, but also instruments akin to forward contracts, were in widespread use throughout the thirteenth and fourteenth centuries.

---

[19] H. R. Stoll, 'The Relation between Put and Call Prices', *Journal of Finance*, 44 (1969), pp. 801–824.
[20] E. J. Swan, *Building the Global Market: A 4000 Year History of Derivatives* (Dordrecht, 2000).
[21] The financial aspects of the contracts are discussed in Chapter 4.
[22] The contracts investigated in this project and drawn upon in this current study have been published in *Advance Contracts*.

English monasteries frequently sold their wool to Italian merchant societies for up to twenty years in advance for prices agreed on the date that the contract was signed. Lloyd states that 'Italian firms were desirous of exporting the best wools and were prepared to pay very high prices and to make long term contracts to get them . . . The Italians, for instance, took the lion's share of Cistercian wool and in 1294 were buying from 49 out of the 74 monasteries'.[23]

It also appears that Italian merchant societies, most notably the Bardi and the Peruzzi of Florence, engaged in forward exchange rate agreements for papal taxes collected in England.[24] The contracts specified the precise exchange rates and dates of exchange for a year in advance.[25] The Italian merchants were at the forefront of the development of these early derivatives markets. Forward agreements for the sale of glass and grain have also been documented, and in both cases the purchasers were Italian merchants. The Medico of Genoa contracted on 24 July 1215 to purchase four '*centenaria* of good and fine glass' for £3 Genoese, while Ser Ottonio paid £200 Veronese on 12 June 1236 for 500 '*modii* of cereals' over the next two years.[26] More evidence of financial sophistication exists in the Middle Ages. For example, M. Kohn suggests that risk transfer instruments were already in existence at that time. Marine insurance ('sea loans'), for instance, were employed in Genoa as early as the twelfth century and were in widespread use by 1200 in large ports such as Venice. Sea loans were debt contracts that were only repayable contingent upon safe arrival of the ship. There is also evidence that these early insurers were far from naïve in their use of the instruments. Indeed, they appeared to have been aware of moral hazard[27] problems, only permitting a fraction (e.g., 25 per cent–30 per cent) of the value of a cargo to be insured.[28]

The needs for derivative instruments and insurance were arguably much greater then than they are now: the processes of trade and sale were far more risky; transportation was fraught with dangers including piracy or shipwrecks at sea and theft or confiscation by corrupt officials on land. Born of

---

[23] Lloyd, 'The Movement of Wool Prices in Medieval England', p. 10.
[24] R. A. Goldthwaite, 'Local Banking in Renaissance Florence', *Journal of European Economic History*, 14 (1985), pp. 5–55.
[25] Kohn, 'Risk Instruments in the Medieval and Early Modern Economy', Department of Economics, Dartmouth College (1999), Unpublished, Working paper 99-07.
[26] R. S. Lopez and I. W. Raymond, *Medieval Trade in the Mediterranean World* (New York, 1955).
[27] This is a tendency for those who are insured to take greater risks than they otherwise would have done, thus increasing the probability of an insurance claim.
[28] Kohn, 'Risk Instruments in the Medieval and Early Modern Economy'.

this need for some certainty in a highly uncertain world, wool-growers were willing to forgo some of their revenue for the future sale of their product in order to receive an up-front payment. The merchants with whom the wool producers did business, by contrast, had the financial resources to be able to bear these risks and to diversify them substantially away by transacting with a large number of different producers.

THE MEDIEVAL ENGLISH WOOL MARKET

The wool market was extremely important to the English medieval economy. Wool dominated the English export trade from the late thirteenth century to its decline in the late fifteenth century. Even contemporary comment noted the significance of the wool trade – naming it 'the jewel of the realm' and demonstrated in the often quoted statement by Postan that, 'The barons of England, sitting in Parliament, asserted in 1297 that wool represented half of England's wealth or, as they put it, "half the value of the whole land"'.[29] Wool was at the forefront of the establishment of England as a European political and economic power and the importance of wool is highlighted in many well-known historical episodes: the letter from Charlemagne to King Offa, complaining that the standard of English woollen cloaks had slipped; the massive ransom of Richard the Lionheart, paid with 50,000 sacks of English wool; and the anachronism of the Lord Chancellor sitting on the Woolsack as a symbolic recognition of his power.

By the end of the thirteenth century, the heavily industrialised areas of Europe could not have existed without the export of English wool. A halt in the export trade could bring whole areas to the brink of starvation and economic ruin. The trade in raw wool, and the taxes charged on its export, financed the wars of Edward I and allowed the English to compete with the larger resources of France during the Hundred Years' War. Indeed, it is possible that this protectionist policy, introduced to finance war, ended the sophisticated and early use of forward contracts in the late thirteenth century. Fiscal control of the wool market helped finance Edward III's successful campaigns against the French during the first phase of the Hundred Years' War.[30] That some of the Italian bankers subsequently

---

[29] A common way of referring to the wool trade from the middle of the fourteenth century, cited in M. M. Postan, *Medieval Trade and Finance* (London, 1973), p. 342.

[30] For instance, Edward III's extraordinary indenture with his merchants in 1337 in a speculative structured wool deal to finance his alliance strategy to the tune of £200,000, *Calendar of Patent Rolls 1334–38*, pp. 480–2. For the best treatment of this 'English Wool Company', see E. B. Fryde, *William de la Pole, Merchant and King's Banker* (London, 1988), chs. 6 and 7.

went bankrupt has been widely documented and some of the blame has been levelled at Edward III. This is a misconception, and the failure of these houses has been shown to have been a much more complex affair and little to do with the actions of the English Crown.[31]

England began the period as an exporter of wool as a raw material and was transformed into an exporter of mainly manufactured woollen cloth. The peak in exports in raw wool was during the thirteenth and early fourteenth centuries with perhaps 40,000–45,000 sacks exported each year,[32] and this gradually declined with the export of 33,000 sacks in 1355 and only 9,706 sacks in 1476.[33] The Crown's decision to tax the export of wool encouraged (deliberately or not) the development of a domestic cloth industry and thus a move to the export of cloth. The increase in cloth export is seen to rise from fewer than 10,000 cloths per year in 1349–50 to 60,000 cloths in 1446–7 and around 140,000 annually by 1539–40.[34] This domestic cloth industry was further strengthened by the immigration of Flemish cloth weavers, who perhaps facilitated the growth of the textile industry in England. It can be clearly demonstrated by the export figures that the wool export market may have declined, but in its place a textile industry was born.

OUTLINE OF THIS BOOK

It might be perhaps pertinent to begin by explaining what is not covered in this book. This volume is not an attempt to write a history of the wool trade in medieval England, for this task has been more than amply completed by Lloyd, Power and the like. Rather, this book is an attempt to provide a detailed insight into an extraordinary body of evidence regarding the early use of advance contracts. This is primarily and unapologetically a study focused upon the use of an early form of financial instrument in medieval England. We will demonstrate that this important source material justifies this concentrated study and discuss how our research into this sophisticated market in wool will alter our understanding of modern finance. Financial specialists may have to accept that advances in asset pricing techniques were developed very early in Europe and that we should be cautious when ascribing such financial tools to the twentieth century.

---

[31] See for instance: Hunt, 'A New Look at the Dealings of the Bardi and Peruzzi with Edward III'.
[32] Postan, *Medieval Trade and Finance*, p. 350.
[33] Lloyd, *English Wool Trade*, p. 311, Table 19. For a summary of exports, see Carus-Wilson and Coleman, *England's Export Trade*, especially pp. 122–123, England: Raw Wool Exports.
[34] *Ibid.*, pp. 138–139, England: Cloth Exports.

The book is split into five chapters, including the current introduction. Chapter 2. 'Advance contracts for the supply of wool', will discuss the unique existence of advance contracts for the supply of wool from *c.* 1200 to 1327. These contracts are preserved at the National Archives and demonstrate that some of the monastic orders in England had developed a sophisticated method of financing their wool sales with continental and, primarily, Italian merchant societies. We will discuss: the sources; the contracting parties; the volume, structure and nature of the contracts; why advance contracts were written; what happened following default; the practicalities of the trade, including wool standards, delivery and distribution and local variations. Chapter 3: 'Case study – Pipewell Abbey, Northamptonshire', will focus upon one particular abbey, the Cistercian monastery of Pipewell in Northamptonshire and a series of contracts drawn up for the forward sale of its wool production. What were the monks doing with all the money? What mechanisms were used to ensure that both parties kept to their side of the bargain and what happened when such mechanisms broke down? The story of the wool contracts entered into by the abbots of Pipewell ended in dispersal, but was it greed or optimism that led the monks into this circle of indebtedness? Chapter 4: 'Modern finance in the middle ages?', will look at the structure of the forward agreements for the sale of wool, what was included and why they exist. We will also investigate from a modern finance perspective whether the wool market was efficient. Were the monks making effective deals – were reasonable interest rates charged? Did the monasteries or counterparties default on the agreements and what systems existed to deal with the aftermath? The chapter will look in detail at how the contracts were structured and priced and compare the pricing against the prevailing wool prices. Finally, Chapter 5: 'Conclusions' will summarise the main findings of this study.

We have also included three Appendices to support this volume. Appendix 1 is an example of an advance contract for the supply of wool and includes a photograph of the contract, a Latin transcription and an English translation. This is perhaps the earliest known indenture for the forward sale of wool and has been previously overlooked in other studies on the wool market. Appendix 2 is a summary of facts and figures drawn from the body of contract evidence that we have collected and Appendix 3 is a listing of the contracts we have drawn upon throughout this study.

CHAPTER 2

Advance contracts for the sale of wool

This study is focused upon the use of forward agreements for the purchase of wool. It would therefore make sense to discuss our source material in more detail at the outset. We have been able to identify, transcribe and translate, from both Latin and Anglo-Norman French, over two hundred contracts, ranging in date from 1200 to 1327, which deal with the advance purchase of wool.[1] These contracts survive principally among the records of central government housed at the National Archives, Kew, and particularly among series where commercial debts were registered and disputes addressed and settled. The system for commercial debt registration as a whole was well developed by this time in England, and the debt recognitions for wool take their place alongside more general debt negotiations and governmental finance.[2]

In their most basic form, the wool debt recognitions constitute an acknowledgement by the vendor that he has received a sum of money in advance of the delivery of a certain amount of wool, enumerated by the sack, to the buyer at specified terms in the future, whether in the following season or spread over any number of years, the producer further binding himself and his possessions for the faithful repayment of this sum either in cash or wool in the event of his default by a writ of *fieri facias* to the barons of the Exchequer.

THE SOURCES

Memoranda Rolls (E 159, E 368)

The contracts are primarily located in the section concerning private recognisances of debt in the parallel series of Memoranda Rolls of the

---

[1] *Advance Contracts*. We discovered one contract dated 1200, but this appears to be an outlier as the bulk of our data are drawn from contracts written between 1230 and 1327.

[2] For a recent discussion of the development of the Exchequer in the thirteenth century see, N. Barratt, 'Finance on a Shoestring: The Exchequer in the Thirteenth Century', in A. Jobson (ed.), *English Government in the Thirteenth Century* (Woodbridge, 2004), pp. 71–86.

Exchequer, a survey of which has been undertaken covering the years 1216–1326 [TNA E 159/1–102 and E 368/1–98], producing 128 examples.

Written contracts for the advance purchase of wool have a long history. Among the records of William Cade, a disgraced Flemish financier of the mid-twelfth century, there are debts of wool sold in advance by the Cistercian abbeys of Louth Park (Lincs) and Roche (Yorks).[3] Indentures of purchase and sale also survive from fairly early in Henry III's reign.[4] But, with the increase in the amounts of capital and wool at stake and with it the volume of credit, it was more frequently in the interests of one or both parties to secure a record of their bargain before the king's ministers, who could bring royal sanction to bear in the regulation of such transactions. From their inception, perhaps as early as 1177, it had become common practice that the enrolment of debts entered into between private individuals in the Exchequer would be made primarily in the memoranda rolls, the principal records of the business of the Exchequer and its court. Originally, such enrolments appeared among the *communia* section of the rolls, which was generally concerned with day-to-day business, dealing with decisions taken over disputed liabilities for payments charged to sheriffs on their account.[5] However, as the weight of business grew heavier, a separate section to record acknowledgements of indebtedness – *Recogniciones* (Recognisances) – was created in 1262.[6] This corresponds with a tangible rise in the incidence of recorded debts in wool and the following two decades witnessed a real explosion as, particularly, foreign creditors began to exploit their increasingly privileged status to use Exchequer procedure to make recoveries against defaulters. By 1280, indeed, they apparently threatened to become an 'institution'.[7] This, though, was ultimately not the case and by the turn of the fourteenth century the incidence of advance wool contracts recorded in the memoranda is practically negligible as the government introduced other measures to tackle the rising tide of credit and indebtedness. Moreover, while the

---

[3] H. Jenkinson, 'William Cade, a Financier of the Twelfth Century', *English Historical Review* 28 (1913), pp. 221–222.

[4] E 327/541. *Advance Contracts*, no. 221. This is the earliest surviving indenture to have been identified.

[5] E 159/10, rot. 6d; *Advance Contracts*, no. 1. Although the majority of wool contracts are recorded among the Recognisances, perhaps the most detailed, those concerning the dispute between Pipewell abbey and a group of Cahorsins, were enrolled among the *communia*, as well as in the Close Rolls of Chancery: E 159/62, rot. 4; C 54/108, mm. 8d–99d; E 159/64, rot. 10, E 368/62, rot. 14. *Advance Contracts*, nos. 110, 133.

[6] E 159/37, E 368/37. For more detail see the relevant TNA series lists.

[7] Lloyd, *English Wool Trade*, p. 293.

Memoranda Rolls of the reign of Edward II (1307–27) are saturated with explicitly monetary 'loans' from foreign financiers to monastic institutions, the collapse of several leading Italian merchant banking houses either side of 1300 and the introduction of greater regulation in the export trade with the staple ordinances of 1313, 1319 and 1326 provided an opportunity for English merchants to drive the domestic wool market and all but eliminated the advance contract from the record.[8]

There has been some contention over the meaning and importance of the advance contract, especially when its ephemeral nature is taken into account. On the one hand, it may be little more than a simple, official registration of business obligations entered into either within the monastic precinct, at market, or perhaps during a visit to Court. The monastic or lay producer appeared in person at the Exchequer, or sent his representatives, and had his debt enrolled for the payment of a fee perhaps as part of the original sale agreement. Both sides could then be sure that an official record had been kept, facilitating recovery against the seller in case of default, or ensuring payment from the Crown for bargained produce in the event of the buyer's ruin or default on his part. Assiduous record would also be kept of the often drawn-out process of repayment. The height of its popularity came in the late 1270s and 1280s, years of rapidly expanding credit coinciding with Italian predominance in banking, diplomacy and in household and military supply to Edward I.[9] The proximity to the Crown of several merchant societies of Florence, Lucca, Piacenza and Siena enabled them to obtain a prime position in royal financial affairs, becoming privileged suitors at the Exchequer court, their debts being treated as those of the king. Access to Exchequer process ensured a more rapid judgement and recovery in cases of default, which in turn cemented their supercession of Flemish, French and German competition in the English (and Welsh) wool market gained during the Anglo-Flemish trade disputes of 1270–4 when numerous advance contracts passed from Flemish into Italian hands[10]; hence the predominance of the Exchequer in recording such transactions.

Contention has even arisen as to whether wool ever changed hands by means of advance contract. The upfront payments may rather have been

[8] Kaueper, *Bankers to the Crown*, pp. 209–44; Lloyd, *English Wool Trade*, pp. 106–20.
[9] For a detailed analysis of the Riccardi of Lucca's bankrolling of Edward I and the rewards they garnered, see Kaueper, *Bankers to the Crown*, pp. 46–48, 76–131.
[10] E. von Roon-Bassermann, 'Die Handelsperre Englands gegen Flandern 1270–1274 und die lizenzierte englische Wollausfuhr', *Vierteljahrsschrift für Sozial- und Wirtschaftsgeschichte* 50 (1963), pp. 71–82; Lloyd, *English Wool Trade*, pp. 28–39.

loans on the security of wool thinly disguising the levy of interest and the crime of usury.[11] This fits the widespread pattern of large loans made by both Italian merchants to layman and religious during the period and there was, after all, a myriad of charges on the monastic and aristocratic purse alike.[12]

Such charges multiplied inexorably at this time as scab, a skin disease rendering fleeces useless, which had previously been a sporadic visitor to her shores, ravaged England's sheep flocks throughout the 1270s.[13] Not only were producers deprived of a steady, reliable source of income for the immediate future over a number of years, but at a stroke they also found themselves incapable of fulfilling agreements with merchants which in the past had proved lucrative and, to some sellers no doubt, indispensable. For buyers, who might have vast sums of capital tied up in such enterprises and themselves have innumerable credit obligations across northern Europe and beyond, it was paramount that they could secure their investment. The preponderance of advance wool contracts, then, might rather reflect the resort to legal means to this end. T. H. Lloyd suggests that several are, in fact, the consequence of the buyers' victory in the Exchequer court, whereby the recorded Recognisance represented the loser's acceptance of his debt, terms for repayment and the possibility of distraint after further default.[14] They are certainly indicative of an inability to fulfil commitments. Equally, disease provoked uncertainty as to when and if recovery might occur in the near future. It is possible that some contracts, in their proffer of money in advance, aimed both to help producers restock or combat the effects of disease and to gain first refusal upon, or at least stake a claim to, dwindling and endangered wool stocks.

Plea Rolls (E 13)

There is little question as to the legal character of many of the advance contracts that have been identified and that these can only be related to default on the terms of contracts, which increased during the times of severest dearth and disease. Ensuing litigation produced 64 examples entered onto the Plea Rolls of the Exchequer in the period 1269–1326

---

[11] E 13/1E, m. 14d; E 159/51, rot. 20d, E 368/51, rot. 13d, and schedule; E 159/62, rot. 4; C 54/108, mm. 8d–9d, E 159/64, rot. 10, E 368/62, rot. 14; E159/69, rot. 62. *Advance Contracts*, nos. 11, 23, 110, 133, 153.

[12] See the table of recipients in Kaueper, *Bankers to the Crown*, pp. 56–59.

[13] I. Kershaw, 'The Great European Famine and Agrarian Crisis in England, 1315–22', *Past and Present* 59 (1973), p. 27.

[14] Lloyd, *English Wool Trade*, p. 292.

(E 13/1E-52). While the Memoranda Rolls might simply register obligations or reproduce the result of litigation, the Exchequer court presided over by the barons heard and settled the disputes between wronged creditor and defaulting debtor and, very occasionally, vice versa.[15] In terms of jurisdiction, the Exchequer of Pleas dealt with cases concerning the king's revenue, which, as said, included that of his financiers, though not of the person of the king himself, and those associated with Exchequer or local royal officials. They certainly provide the best evidence of the privileged status enjoyed by foreign merchants. In several examples merchants act as plaintiffs in pleas of debt and are described as *valettus Thesaurarii*.[16] Numerous entries, moreover, begin by stating that the plaintiff 'offered himself on the fourth day' ('optulit se quarto die'), shorthand for the non-appearance of the defendant and the continuance of the plea in his or her absence. Cases enrolled among the pleas of the Exchequer also display rather more variety and intimacy of detail than their counterparts among the memoranda, particularly with regard to the actual behaviour of the contracting parties towards each other and the reasons for the failure to comply with the terms of their bond.

Whatever their motivations for bringing their plight before the king's fiscal ministers, it is remarkable how few pleas ended in punishment for one or other party. Compromise and settlement appear to have been the order of the day. Neither party, it seems, was willing to forsake the potential profits and connections they had negotiated or their hopes for future financial security and/or prosperity. For the merchants, indeed, when the prize was the richest pickings from the cream of the crop, this was hardly surprising. Many cases, too, were patently far from clear cut and a few were clearly insoluble, petering out after multiple adjournments, perhaps as a result of an interim settlement with such thoughts in mind.

Close Rolls (C54)

Another eleven contracts were specifically enrolled on the Close Rolls of the Chancery. With the notable exception of the settlement brokered between John de Hillun, abbot of Pipewell, and Arnaud de Soliz and

---

[15] E 13/22, m. 13; 26, m. 23. *Advance Contracts*, nos. 158, 171.
[16] E 13/22, m. 27; m. 37; m. 70d; E 159/73, rot. 35; E 13/25, m. 15; m. 27; m. 47d; 26, m. 23; m. 69; 27, m. 69; 29, m. 40; 36, m. 45d. *Advance Contracts*, nos. 159, 161, 162, 163, 168, 169, 170, 171, 172, 174, 177, 191.

William Servat of Cahors in January 1291, the result of the intervention of royal arbiters, they are generally as limited in form and content as those on the Memoranda Rolls.[17] Whether their enrolment in Chancery is a sign of particular favour or of the importance granted to their resolution is difficult to say, though from their content this is questionable. The Exchequer still exercised jurisdiction over disputed debts and the enrolment of a majority of obligations through to the fourteenth century.

The Exchequer Schedules (1294)

Implicit evidence of around another 220 contracts survives in schedules of submissions made by the leading Italian merchant companies in England in 1294.[18] Anxious to accumulate enormous reserves with which to finance his impending campaign in Gascony, in June Edward I forfeited and cast into exile foreign merchants then active in England, simultaneously sequestrating their assets.[19] In so doing, he hoped to be able to exploit their vast wool stocks on the continental market. As a result, representatives of these societies were called before the Exchequer to submit details of the wool they expected to receive in that year and of what they had received in the previous season. These schedules are invaluable for historians of the medieval wool trade, as in effect they provide a list of spot prices of wool throughout England for this particular year. In terms of the operation of the trade, they also contain information regarding local locations for delivery, unparalleled evidence of the costs of dressing, packaging, carriage and brokerage of the wool, and one of the fullest lists of producers, lay and secular, in the medieval period. T. H. Lloyd tabulated the data contained within for his comparative study of commodity values *The Movement of Wool Prices in Medieval England*, which supersedes an earlier synopsis by G. Bigwood.[20]

---

[17] C 54/108, mm. 8d–9d, E 159/64, rot. 10, E 368/62, rot. 14. *Advance Contracts*, no. 133. For analysis of the remarkable dealings of successive abbots of Pipewell with the Cahorsins, and the consequences of their relationship, see Chapter 3.

[18] E 101/126/7, mm. 11–25; *Advance Contracts*, nos. 204–16.

[19] M. Prestwich, *Edward I* (New Haven and London, 1997), pp. 378–379.

[20] A full edition of these schedules now appears in *Advance Contracts*, Appendix I; Lloyd, 'Movement of Wool Prices', Table 5, pp. 52–61; G. Bigwood, 'Un marché de matières premières: laines d'Angleterre et marchands italiens vers la fin du XIIIe siècle', *Annales d'histoire économique et sociale* II (1930), pp. 196–211. For a discussion of the relative importance of the Exchequer Schedules see Munro, 'Wool Price Schedules and the Qualities of English Wool', pp. 126–129.

Miscellaneous documents

We believe that we have only begun to scratch the surface of the potential surviving evidence and our analysis is largely restricted to series long identified as containing the more important and voluminous material. Furthermore, we have not explored the fruitful series of certificates of Statute Merchant and Statute Staple in the records of Chancery (C 131, 241). Inundated by the flood of mercantile debts in the 1280s and the desire for their registration, by the Statutes of Acton Burnell (1283) and Westminster (1285) Edward I introduced a more rigid system for the registration of merchants' debts before mercantile borough courts. This localised and attempted to speed up the process of debt recovery, for if the defaulter's goods could be found locally, recompense might be more immediate. If not, certificates were to be delivered into Chancery to initiate further process.[21]

Nonetheless, a brief search of series outside the main body of material, which have remained largely untapped, has made it clear that there is likely to be more varied evidence of advance wool contracts across a broader spectrum of records, examples of which are described here. A handful of contracts which may not yet have reached the public domain have been located, for example, in three series of Ancient Deeds (E 210, E 326, E 327), artificial collections constituted primarily of conveyances of property, particulars of account and sales of produce.[22] Likewise, intimate details of the struggles of the Riccardi to hold the Yorkshire Cistercian abbey of Meaux to a large wool debt, and the methods and contacts they employed to expedite this business, survive in the equally artificial collection of private correspondence (SC 1).[23] The series which present the greatest potential, but also the biggest headache, however, are the unfathomably extensive series of national and local legal records preserved in the National Archives. Nationally, the rolls of the King's Bench (KB 26) in the early thirteenth century provide a handful of examples which can be accessed in calendar form. A random selection from the rolls of the proceedings of the Court of Common Pleas (CP 40) produced four entries for Michaelmas

---

[21] P. Nightingale has identified some eighty-seven certificates of Statute Merchant concerning purchases of wool in the period from 1284 to 1311, and she is presently finalising her survey of these enormous series to enhance TNA's catalogue. P. Nightingale, 'Knights and Merchants: Trade, Politics and the Gentry in Late Medieval England', *Past and Present* 169 (November 2000), p. 38. The authors would like to express their gratitude to P. Nightingale for her insights into the medieval credit system and her willingness to share her research findings.

[22] E 327/541; E 210/7015; E 326/8934; E 326/11541. *Advance Contracts*, nos. 221–224.

[23] SC 1/10/116, SC 1/30/101, SC 1/8/81. *Advance Contracts*, no. 228.

term 1280 alone, admittedly a time of increasing foreign credit in the wool trade, but nevertheless an important indicator of what might be found in a broader search. What lurks, however, among the rolls of the proceedings of Justices in Eyre (JUST 1) has been more difficult to quantify, but it is certainly a potential avenue of further research.

Foreign Sources

Some 23 further contracts are recorded by Gian-Francesco Pagnani della Ventura, an eighteenth-century Florentine Chancellor of the Tithe, whose examination of the trading history of his city contains evidence of a transfer of contracts for the purchase of wool made by the society of the Cerchi of Florence in 1284 to Simone Gerardi, an agent of their competitors, the Mozzi, in England.[24] Further detail on this international trade is provided by the treatise *La Pratica Della Mercatura* compiled by Francesco Balducci Pegolotti, a member of the Bardi company who spent three years as its agent in England from 1318 to 1321.[25] Pegolotti lists a similar number of religious houses to that in the Exchequer Schedules, noting both prices and annual output.

THE CONTRACTING PARTIES

The sellers

Although most scholars have quite naturally concentrated on the contracts entered into by monastic producers, as many of these are concerned with vast quantities of wool, there is actually a fairly even division between the monastic (113) and lay (102) producers in the contracts we have analysed.

Many, if not all, of the monastic orders in England are represented to some extent in the advance contracts. By far the most active in the wool trade on this evidence were the Cistercians with 73 contracts for around 2,900 sacks of wool and five whole crops for an unspecified amount of wool. The White Monks are accompanied by: the Augustinian canons who entered into 13 contracts for a total of 372 sacks and one whole crop; the Benedictines with 7 contracts containing 403 sacks and one whole crop; the Cluniacs with 8 contracts for 963 sacks and one whole crop; the

---

[24] *Della Decime e delle altre gravezze imposte dal Commune de Firenze, della moneta, e della mercatura dei Fiorentini fino al secola XVI*, ed. G-F Pagnini, III (Lisbonne-Lucques, 1766), pp. 324–327.

[25] *La Pratica della Mercatura*, ed. Allan Evans (Cambridge, MA: 1935), pp. 256–269.

Premonstratensians with three contracts for 5 sacks and two whole crops; the Knights Templar involved themselves in two contracts for wool valued at £571 6s 8d.

While Hospitaller and Gilbertine houses are recorded among the Exchequer Schedules of 1294 and are mentioned in Pegolotti, none was involved in any of the main body of contract material.[26] In total, the religious houses examined here made contracts involving just over 4,600 sacks, 21½ stones, ten whole crops and wool worth £571 6s 8d. This far outstrips the wool sold in advance by lay growers who contracted for the sale of 983 sacks and 21½ stones of wool.

The buyers

In dealing with the credit side of the relationship, distinctions can be made in terms both of nationality and, in the case of Italian merchants, by city of origin and merchant society. It might be natural to suppose that, given their familiarity with legal processes and access to a wider variety of markets and producers, English merchants would appear rather frequently in the contracts. This is not entirely the case as only 38 contracts for 1,138 sacks, 6 stones of wool and two whole crops have been identified and of these, several may merely be purchases on behalf of foreign merchant companies by middlemen. Moreover, despite their dominance of the English wool trade in the first three-quarters of the thirteenth century, as outlined most voluminously by Lloyd,[27] only 3 contracts made by Flemish merchants seem to have survived, encompassing just 18 sacks of wool. Northern French merchants, too, appear infrequently, on only five occasions, contracting for 50 sacks and 12 stones of wool. Finally, German merchants entered into two contracts for just one sack and one whole crop altogether. As a result, the evidence for northern European merchants as a whole contracting for wool with producers in England is rather scanty, but, as outlined above, evidence from advance contracts concerns a fraction of the national export.

On the other hand, southern Europeans dominate the body of existing contracts. Cahorsin merchants led by Arnaud and Jean de Soliz and William Servat, for instance, appear as buyers in 20 separate contracts for 600 sacks and one whole crop of wool. An overwhelming number of

---

[26] It should be noted that all religious orders are listed in a much broader range of houses by both the Exchequer Schedule and Pegolotti.

[27] Lloyd, *English Wool Trade*, chs 1 and 2.

contracts, about 150 in all, were drawn up in favour of merchants of the Italian peninsula, who as a whole purchased slightly under 4,000 sacks and six whole crops of wool, along with the contracts with the Templars.

Leading the way with 87 recorded contracts are the Riccardi of Lucca, who purchased just under 1,400 sacks of wool. A further 10 contracts were made by merchants of the same city: the Bellardi purchased 20 sacks over 2 contracts; the Bettori, 31 sacks in a single deal; the Gotele, two whole crops; and the breakaway faction from the Riccardi, established by Baroncino Gualteri, 450 sacks over 5 contracts. Lucchese merchants, then, dealt for approximately 1,900 sacks and two unspecified whole crops of wool over 97 contracts. Although merchants of Florence appear to have entered into a smaller volume of contracts, some 47 in all, they seem to have purchased a greater volume of wool during the entirety of the period in question – just over 2,000 sacks, four whole crops and the Templar wools. These figures can be further broken down by society. Due probably to the earlier nature of the bulk of the contracts, on the whole drawn up before 1291, only 5 contracts for 13 sacks and wool worth £475 6s 8d can be found involving the Bardi, a society which enjoyed phenomenal success under Edward II and his son.[28] Most prolific in terms of wool purchased are undoubtedly the Frescobaldi, whose 28 contracts cover a massive 1,258 sacks, 13½ stones, four whole crops and Templar wool valued at 1,100 marks. Neither the Cerchi with 249 sacks over 5 contracts, the Falconieri with 38 sacks, 20 stones in 4 contracts, the Mozzi with 229 sacks in 2 contracts, the Peruzzi with 8 sacks in just 1 contract, the Pulci-Rembertini with 69 sacks over 3 contracts, nor the Spini with just 1 contract for 50 sacks, should be assumed to have taken a lesser role in the trade, however, as the 1294 schedules amply demonstrate their widespread buying up of English wool.[29] Of other Italian cities, only the Ammanati of Pisa, contracting for 2 sacks, and the Scotti of Piacenza, with 5 contracts for 57½ sacks, appear among the Recognisances. Between them, the Riccardi and Frescobaldi dominate our material, accounting for just over half of all of the contracted wool. This may be a result of better access to the king's favour, a willingness to take on riskier contracts, greater mistrust of debtors leading to legal registration of their Recognisances, or simply a larger involvement in this trade meaning that their activities are easier to trace.

An in-depth examination of the body of contract evidence necessarily requires some de-contextualisation from the bulk of other data relating to

---

[28] Hunt, 'A New Look at the Dealings of the Bardi and Peruzzi with Edward III'.

[29] E 101/126/7, mm. 11–25. Of course, as the 1294 schedules demonstrate, both the Cerchi and Frescobaldi split into white and black factions.

the medieval English wool trade in all its many forms. The total sum of 5,330 sacks contracted by means of advance purchase only just surpasses the *c.* 3,540 sacks admitted as due to the Italian merchants in 1294, a time at which annual exports of wool had reached somewhere around 25,000 sacks.[30] It is clear therefore that the recorded contracts represent only a tiny fraction of the wool that changed hands in England in the period from 1265 to 1315.

ADVANCE CONTRACTS

Advance payments?

One unusual aspect of the advance contracts is the advance payment associated with the bargains paid in 78 of the main body of 215 contracts we found during our research. Of course, as can be seen from these figures, advance payments were not always made. In one of the largest contracts undertaken during the period of Italian predominance in the English wool market, for example, James of Lissington, a royal clerk with interests in Yorkshire, and his wife, Agnes, contracted with the Augustinian priory of Newburgh in the North Riding for some 123 sacks of wool to be delivered to him in parcels of 10¼ sacks at Trinity in each year from 1283 to 1294. The total value of such was £584 and James committed himself to payment of £49 a year only upon delivery of the prior's bargain. It does not appear in this case that an advance had been forwarded.[31]

Extrapolating further from this evidence, it is clear that foreign merchants were particularly willing to make considerable financial outlays to guarantee a constant supply of English wool often over a number of years, while relatively small advances might be made – as, for example, in the case of the Frescobaldi's contract with Margaret, prioress of the Benedictine nunnery of Arden in the North Riding of Yorkshire, who received just £10 in advance for the entire crop of her house,[32] or in the case of Godfrey, prior of the Cluniac house at Pontefract in the West Riding, who received an initial advance of 80 marks on a contracted crop worth 800 marks.[33]

---

[30] E 101/126/7, mm. 12–25; *Advance Contracts*, Appendix I; Lloyd, *English Wool Trade*, p. 63.

[31] E 13/10, m. 7. *Advance Contracts*, no. 70.

[32] E 13/26, m. 23. *Advance Contracts*, no. 171. It should be noted, however, that the figures produced in 1294 and by Pegolotti give annual crop totals for this house of only 10½ and 10 sacks respectively: E 101/126/7, m. 21; *Advance Contracts*, no. 212; *La Pratica della Mercatura*, p. 266.

[33] E 368/53, rot. 14d. *Advance Contracts*, no. 46.

A startling 53 of the 78 sellers in surviving contracts where an advance is given received *full payment* for their crop in advance. In some instances this amounted to a relatively minor financial outlay. On two separate occasions Reginald Maniward, a Hereford wool merchant, contracted to deliver parcels of two and five sacks of marcher lambswool to the Riccardi and received £8 and 42½ marks respectively.[34] At Michaelmas 1282 Thomas Luard, vicar of Wellington in Shropshire, acknowledged he was to deliver three sacks over two years to Richard Borrey at the Shrewsbury fair, having received an advance payment in full of £16.[35] Roger de Toftes, lord of the manor of Bircham Tofts in Norfolk, acknowledged his debt of three sacks worth 33 marks during Michaelmas term 1281, having received full payment in advance.[36] As we shall see, more commonly, advances amounted to rather larger sums of money.

In one of the two significant contracts entered into by Anglo-Irish aristocrats, Richard de Burgh, earl of Ulster, and Nicholas de Segrave agreed to provide 50 sacks of Irish wool to the Riccardi, for which they had received £200 in advance at the rate of £4 per sack.[37] In the other, John fitz Thomas, lord of Offaly, contracted with the Riccardi to provide 15 sacks of *collecta* from the counties of Dublin and Kilkenny, having received an advance of £70.[38] John and Richard de Bolmere of Bulmer in the North Riding of Yorkshire similarly received £200 in advance for 30 sacks valued at £6 13s 4d each. Indeed, it is noticeable that lay producers frequently received full payment for their crop in advance, this being the case in over one fifth (22/99) of the contracts involving non-monastic growers. In the case of de Burgh and fitz Thomas, problems of distance, travelling and transport arrangements may have necessitated full delivery upfront, but with regard to English lay producers, there may be other explanations.

It is known, for example, that John de Reddemere of Appleby in Lincolnshire contracted with Baroncino Gualteri during Easter term 1280 for thirty sacks of his wool.[39] Gualteri was the chief member of the society of the Riccardi in England throughout most of the late thirteenth century and acted as the Riccardi's agent at that time.[40] It may well be that a number of the laymen involved with such advance purchases were agents of

---

[34] E 159/60, rot. 20d; 61, rot. 13. *Advance Contracts*, nos. 98, 102.

[35] E 159/56, rot. 4; E 368/56, rot. 4. *Advance Contracts*, no. 69.

[36] E 159/55, rot. 9; E 368/55, rot. 8. *Advance Contracts*, no. 61.

[37] E 159/58, rot. 14d. *Advance Contracts*, no. 77.

[38] E 159/65, rot. 33; E 368/63, rot. 26d. *Advance Contracts*, no. 140.

[39] E 368/53, rot. 15. *Advance Contracts*, no. 48.   [40] *CPR, 1281–92*, p. 17.

the various merchant societies, though nowhere is this specifically outlined within the contracts themselves, and so enjoyed preferential treatment or, at least, were more reliable and thus received more fulsome payment.

More spectacular, however, are examples of monumental full payments made to the heads of religious houses in Yorkshire. During the Easter term of 1287 Henry Otley, abbot of the Cistercian house of Fountains, acknowledged receipt of £732 in advance of delivery in the following July of 61 sacks of good wool of his house valued at £12 a sack.[41] At the following Michaelmas Thomas, abbot of Rievaulx recognised he had received two advances for a delivery of 26 sacks, 16 of good wool priced at £10 13s 4d per sack and 10 of the *collecta* of his house worth £8 each, totalling some £250 13s 4d., which represented the full value of this wool.[42] It would seem then that a majority of contracts in which an advance is detailed with a monastic producer lead to full payment of the whole value of the wool in advance, this holding true in over half of the cases (31/56).

Perhaps the most immediate explanation for this phenomenon, in Yorkshire at least, is the apparent battle which raged in the mid-1280s between the established Riccardi of Lucca and the up-and-coming Mozzi of Florence, following the latter's decision to take up more direct involvement in the English wool trade upon receipt of a competitor's interests in 1284.[43] In 1286 the Mozzi contracted to take 168 sacks of the best wool the abbey had to offer and thus staked the monks to a 9-year commitment of 18 sacks and 20 stones of wool a year.[44] Whether this effectively attempted to squeeze out the Riccardi is difficult to say, no conclusive evidence having yet been identified to demonstrate that they enjoyed an earlier financial relationship with the monks. Nevertheless, in 1287 the Riccardi contracted for 24 sacks – 18 of good wool, 2 of middle-grade and 4 of locks – although on this occasion they may not have paid in advance.[45] A year later, as shown above, they contracted for 26 sacks of good wool and *collecta* to be delivered over the following 2 seasons. A series of Recognisances enrolled during the Michaelmas term of 1289 highlighted the multiplicity of financial connections the abbey had created, the abbot owing the Mozzi a massive £1,582 which was to be repaid over 9 years, the Frescobaldi 250 marks, and the Cerchi Bianchi £1,600.[46] The depth and breadth of such connections is further revealed by the 1294 exchequer schedules in which Rievaulx was

---

[41] E 159/60, rot.16d; E 368/60, rot. 14d. *Advance Contracts*, no. 93.
[42] E 159/61, rot. 11d. *Advance Contracts*, no. 99.
[43] For more details of which, see *Della Decima*, pp. 324–327.
[44] E 159/59, rot. 9d; E 368/59, rot. 19d. *Advance Contracts*, no. 86.
[45] E 159/61, rot. 11d. *Advance Contracts*, no. 99.   [46] E 159/62, rot.14.

apparently committed to the Riccardi, the Spini and the Cerchi Neri, the latter of whom were to take 54 sacks.[47]

The Cistercian houses of Yorkshire produced some of the highest quality wool in England and prepared their product on what might be termed a professional basis. The monks could always hope to find a ready market for their wool. On the other hand, E. Jamroziak, in examining the motivations of the monks at Rievaulx, tentatively concludes that they may have been playing a duplicitous game with the aim of obtaining the highest possible price for their wool and thus the most possible capital to service the debts of their house.[48] This was presumably not an experience peculiar to Yorkshire, as the Exchequer Schedule of 1294 amply demonstrates. The submissions of the main Italian merchant societies highlight a considerable number of houses which had contracted with two or more companies in the hope of selling their wool and, presumably, creating competition for their business, or even a larger market for their produce. This, then, may be one of the primary factors involved in the creation of the body of advance contract material in the late thirteenth century.

The contract bearing the single largest advance payment, however, may hint at more underlying reasons for the proliferation of such contracts in the 1270s and 1280s. During the Michaelmas term of 1277–78 John of Avignon, prior of the Benedictine house of Lewes in Sussex, sold 400 sacks of wool to the Riccardi for the enormous sum of £1,666 13s 4d.[49] Revealingly, the wool concerned was the house's *collecta* to be gathered from lay producers on the estates of the priory and in the surrounding area.[50] The potentially varying standards of *collecta* wool as compared to that produced from the prior's own sheep, generally, though not exclusively, commanded a lower price than good wool. This may have persuaded the merchants to pay more upfront in an attempt to induce and enable the monks to produce a delivery of higher quality. Perhaps, more pertinently, the prevalence of disease in the 1270s and 1280s, which had a catastrophic affect on the availability of wool of good quality, forced merchants into buying as much wool of lesser grade as possible which might have escaped the ravages of scab in order to maintain a steady level of profits. Large full payments for *collecta* wool are, in fact, surprisingly common.

---

[47] E101/126/7, mm. 12, 18, 23. *Advance Contracts*, nos. 205, 209, 214.
[48] Jamroziak, 'Rievaulx Abbey', pp. 216–218.
[49] E 159/61, rot. 14. *Advance Contracts*, no. 104.
[50] An earlier contract of Easter term 1286 involved the gathering and processing of the abbey's wool from lands in Grantham, Leicester and Melton Mowbray: E159/59, rot. 12d. *Advance Contracts*, no. 87.

On 15 October 1276, Dunelinus Jonte, on behalf of his fellow merchants of Florence, paid some £465 upfront for 62 sacks of Fountains *collecta* valued at £7 10s per sack.[51] During Hilary term 1280, Robert of Skerne, abbot of Meaux in the East Riding, acknowledged that he had received full payment of £441 13s 4d for 53 sacks of *collecta* of his abbey valued at £8 6s 8d a sack.[52] Overall, at least 28 of the sampled contracts deal exclusively with wool produced outside the strictly seigneurial or monastic environment, though others where the grades are not specified may also conceal such wool, a sign perhaps of the crisis in sheep husbandry in the late thirteenth century.

Why advance purchases?

Advance purchases of wool had been made over at least the previous century, little evidence of which now survives. Only when Henry II ordered an examination of the debts of the ubiquitous merchant William Cade, in 1166, did his advance purchase of wool from the Cistercian abbeys of Roche (Nottinghamshire) and Louth Park (Lincolnshire) come to light.[53] The development of the machinery of the advance contract, which has been identified as *the* significant change in the English wool trade in the final quarter of the thirteenth century, demystified important aspects of the sale, marketing and purchase of wool.[54] Without doubt, to a greater extent, the enrolment of such contracts became a key weapon in the legal armoury of merchants.

As the figures previously discussed abundantly express, the development and proliferation of advance contracts must have been largely influenced by the Italians. Their predominance in the contracts he had examined prompted M. Prestwich to argue that only the Riccardi made regular use of the machinery of the contract on the Memoranda Rolls.[55] Certainly, they enjoyed the privileged status of being named the king's merchants and from 1275 to 1294 controlled English customs revenues. Such advantages gave them sufficient capital to reinvest in the purchase of wool and put them in an excellent position to try to maximise their profits. Kaueper even

[51] C 54/93, m. 3d. *Advance Contracts*, no. 19. This contract appears in transcription in *Memorials of the Abbey of St Mary of Fountains*, ed. J. R. Walbran (Durham: Surtees Society vol. XLII, 1867), pp. 177–179.
[52] E 159/53, rot. 12d; E 368/53, rot. 14. *Advance Contracts*, no. 42.
[53] Jenkinson, 'William Cade, a Financier of the Twelfth Century'.
[54] Lloyd, *English Wool Trade*, pp. 289–295.
[55] Prestwich, 'Italian Merchants in Late Thirteenth and Early Fourteenth Century England', p. 91.

suggests that the Riccardi may have been able to leverage their position in the wool market as a way of profiting indirectly from their strong relationship with Edward I.[56] However, as has been seen, the Mozzi and Frescobaldi, as well as Cahorsin merchants, also frequently appear among surviving contracts. As all scholars of the wool trade in this period have copiously stressed,[57] the liquid capital available to Italian firms made them attractive business partners for monastic sellers whose 'participation in commercial exchange was crucial for the normal functioning of the monastic economy'.[58] Abbots and priors who needed 'to sell produce which was not consumed internally' were apparently content to register their obligations centrally in return for ready cash with which to purchase necessary items for the house at the numerous fairs at which wool was marketed and also to fund expensive and expansive building projects, such as those at Thornton Abbey in Lincolnshire which were undertaken in the final quarter of the thirteenth century.[59] Indeed, as T. H. Lloyd has argued, it is most likely that a substantial proportion of the surviving contracts merely registered a sales agreement between the two parties.[60] They may also be considered as banking agreements for these same reasons.

Problems

The Italians' supercession of the Flemings' predominance in the English wool market coincided with an epic crisis in sheep husbandry. From about 1272, England was beset by sheep scab which, while not killing sheep outright, detrimentally affected the quality of their fleeces, as it spread from its first outbreak in Lincolnshire and possibly endured for over two decades.[61] By 1284, for example, when the scab was still affecting the West Riding, Kirkstall abbey's flocks had dwindled completely to nought as the monks tried to cut their losses.[62] Wool producers across large areas were threatened with the almost spontaneous elimination of their major means of income, while for merchants who had invested huge sums of money on

---

[56] For a full review of the Riccardi's activities, see Kaueper, *Bankers to the Crown*.
[57] The extent of which has most recently been examined by Edwin Hunt in his 'A New Look at the Dealings of the Bardi and Peruzzi with Edward III'.
[58] Jamroziak, 'Rievaulx Abbey', p. 202.
[59] Observed by one of the authors on a flying visit in August 2004.
[60] Lloyd, *English Wool Trade*, p. 292.
[61] J. P. Bischoff, 'Pegolotti: An Honest Merchant?', *Journal of European Economic History* 6 (1977), p. 106; Donkin, 'Cistercian Sheep Farming and Wool Sales', p. 6. For the effect the disease had on Pipewell's flocks see below, p. 83.
[62] Denholm-Young, *Seigneurial Administration*, p. 61.

the security of wool, the prospects of any return on their investments, let alone an adequate supply of high-quality wool, were in considerable jeopardy. It is in this light that the advance contracts should perhaps best be viewed whatever other interpretations might be put upon them. For both sides, the contracts were part of this broader attempt to create security of finance and supply.

Much of the contract evidence emanates from the period 1279–91 and, while acknowledging Lloyd's view that the majority were simply registrations of debt, his contention that a significant number represented the outcome of a legal dispute over the non-delivery of wool is equally attractive. In essence, those 94 contracts registered among the Recognisances of the rolls of the remembrancers of the Exchequer represented a recent administrative development at the heart of English royal government whereby creditors could now recover debts by using exchequer procedure against defaulters.[63] Set formulae were employed whereby a debtor authorised the Exchequer barons to levy the debt from his lands, tenements, goods and chattels, by a writ of *fieri facias*.[64] It is noticeable that the Italians, who were privileged suitors at the Exchequer court, continued to employ the machinery of the Recognisance after the advent of more rigorous mechanisms for the registration and recovery of merchants' debt introduced via the Statutes of Acton Burnell and of Merchants in 1283 and 1285.[65] Several of the contracts may, as Lloyd suggests, therefore reflect the outcome of a judicial inquiry into the vendor's obligation in the merchants' favour.[66] Their very survival, indeed, points to an inability of producers to deliver, or, equally as likely, the merchants' fear that their investment would see little or no return. Merchants desired recognition of the money they had invested and an official channel through which payment could be induced, if it had not initially been forthcoming.

There can be no doubt, though, that many merchants fully recognised the problems with which the producers were being faced and some took steps to address them, thereby attempting, often in vain, to ensure that any losses would be kept to a minimum or compensated at a later date. Several of the contracts make it clear that the advance was to be put towards the

---

[63] Recognisances first appear in a separate section on the Memoranda Rolls in 37 Henry III [1263–4]: E 159/37; E 368/37.

[64] The standard formula runs: '*Et nisi fecerit, concessit quod barones de scaccario de terris, tenementis, bonis et catallis suis dictam lanam, ad quorumcumque manus devenerint, fieri faciant*'.

[65] Lloyd, *English Wool Trade*, p. 293.

[66] It is not, however, possible to make any significant differentiation between the two, if indeed any was made at the time.

good of the house. John Champneys, abbot of the Cistercian house of Darnhall in Cheshire, acknowledged he had received £53 6s 8d from Giles de Ayre, attorney of John Wermond of Cambrai, in advance of delivery of 12 sacks of *collecta*, so that he might put such a sum 'to the common profit of his house'.[67] On 29 November 1283, William de Basing, prior of St Swithun's, Winchester, acknowledged a loan of £310 made to him by merchants of the Riccardi, 'for great and difficult business of the prior, convent and church and to be spent on serious necessities there'.[68] On 18 March 1298, the Cistercian abbot and convent of Byland recognised they had received 950 marks from the Frescobaldi for 161 sacks of good wool of their house, 'the said monks promising that all of this money is to be put towards the use of the said house'.[69]

It had been only comparatively recently, in the case of the Cistercians at least, that mortgaging wool for the good of their house had been permitted. The original statutes of the Order had outlawed advance sales of wool, the first weakening of that position to recognise the situation in reality coming in 1181, when the General Chapter licensed sales of wool crops one year in advance but only in cases of dire necessity.[70] This having been initially repeated as late as 1277, in the following year, sales over a longer period were allowed, but advances could only be paid for one year's crop. By 1279, this had been lengthened again, but only so that urgent debts could be paid off.[71] Could this have been a contributory factor in motivating Italian merchants to seal long-term deals with Cistercian monks in England in the 1280s?

The relaxation of restrictions upon Cistercian involvement in the advance sale of wool had been forced upon the General Chapter by the financial difficulties in which many of their houses had entangled themselves. Monastic expenditure on expensive building projects might be blamed for the penurious state many abbeys found themselves in towards the end of the thirteenth century.[72] Emilia Jamroziak, however, has demonstrated that, at least in the case of Rievaulx, building expenditure played a lesser part in the bankruptcy of the house in 1276 and 1288.

---

[67] C 54/92, m. 2d: '*resconant por sei et por son convent e por commeun preu de lor meson fere*'. *Advance Contracts*, no. 13.

[68] E 159/57, rot. 9; E 368/57, rot. 9d.

[69] E 159/72, m. 45d.: '*confitentes dicti religiosi predictam pecuniam in utilitatem domus sue esse conversam*'. *Advance Contracts*, no. 157.

[70] Lloyd, *English Wool Trade*, p. 289.

[71] Denholm-Young, *Seigneurial Administration*, p. 55.

[72] For a striking example, see Chapter 3.

Her research has instead pointed to the abbey's contribution to governmental taxation of the Order in 1278 and an accumulation of debts to merchants through advance sales of wool, the delivery of which the scab curtailed.[73] Throughout the 1280s, unable to create income to service increasing debts, and therefore attempting to stretch their arms out to more and more sources of liquid capital, many English monasteries stumbled into a horrific 'Catch-22' situation, from which the only escape was temporary bankruptcy.

The list of bankrupt monastic houses in England in the 1280s is a long one and includes large establishments such as Rievaulx and Fountains, Woburn and Glastonbury alongside smaller, less wealthy houses such as Flaxley and Missenden, Roche and Lewes. This should hardly occasion surprise when the amount of debt some houses had managed to acquire is considered. Fountains's debt in 1291 reached £6,473 10s 6d before dropping to £3,533 12s 1½d by 1294. Lewes had racked up 700 marks at a similar period and Roche £300.[74] Rievaulx in 1288 was committed to the tune of £3,300 to a combination of the Mozzi, Frescobaldi and Cerchi Bianchi.[75] Kirkstall endured debts of some £5,248 15s 7d and 59 sacks of wool in 1284, forcing its estates to be sold off to Henry de Lacy, earl of Lincoln, for 10 years in 1287.[76] Traces of the roots of such debts can be found in the contracts. Successive abbots of Fountains committed their flocks to the production of 229 sacks from 1276 to 1284 and a further 61 sacks in 1287, of which only 31 sacks are recorded as having been delivered.[77] By 1294 they apparently owed their entire annual crop to the Riccardi, which by Pegolotti's time had perhaps reached 76 sacks.[78] While no contracts concerning Kirkstall's wool sales are enrolled among the Exchequer Recognisances, evidence of a series of debts totalling just under £1,000 has been located.[79] Moreover, at Easter 1286 the prior of Lewes committed himself to delivering 23 sacks to the Riccardi, and a year later made the biggest single contract of 400 sacks costing 2,500 marks, demands which must have been incredibly difficult to fulfil.[80]

[73] Jamroziak, 'Rievaulx Abbey', pp. 206–207.

[74] Denholm-Young, *Seigneurial Administration*, p. 55, n. 8.

[75] Jamroziak, 'Rievaulx Abbey', p. 207.   [76] Denholm-Young, *Seigneurial Administration*, p. 61.

[77] C 54/93, m. 3d. (62 sacks); E 159/52, rot. 13, E 368/52, rot. 13 (27 sacks); E 368/53, rot. 12 (130 sacks); E 159/60, rot. 16d., E 368/60, rot. 14d. (61 sacks). *Advance Contracts*, nos. 19, 26, 37, 93.

[78] E 101/126/7, m. 12; *Advance Contracts*, no. 205. *La Pratica Della Mercatura*, p. 260.

[79] E 13/4, m. 6 (406 marks, 2 sacks and 3 stones – Siennese, 1276); E 159/53, rot. 9 (£100 – Cahorsins, 1279); E 159/54, rot. 16 (450 marks – Florentine, 1281); E 13/9, m. 17d., 10, m. 5 (364 marks – Siennese, 1282); E 159/56, rot. 4d. (670 marks – Pulci-Rembertini, 1282–3). *Advance Contracts*, no. 16, Pegolotti claimed 25 sacks could be bought from the abbey: *La Pratica Della Mercatura*, p. 260.

[80] E159/59, rot. 12d.; E 159/61, rot. 14. *Advance Contracts*, nos. 87, 104.

Nevertheless, fulfil them the monks of Lewes apparently did, the Riccardi acknowledging full payment before 6 June 1289, only two years into a five-year contract. Indeed, the number of houses managing to meet their obligations during this period is unexpectedly high. Out of the 226 contracts recorded 49 (22 per cent) bear declarations from the merchants that they have received full delivery of the wool they had been promised. This small proportion disguises the fact that they include some of the largest contracts made – that of Lewes for 400 sacks, as mentioned, the Mozzi deal with Rievaulx for 168 sacks, that made by Florentine merchants with Adam, abbot of Byland for 130 sacks in 1278, and that for 53 sacks made by Robert of Skerne, abbot of Meaux, in 1280.[81] Amid pervasive evidence of bankruptcy and default, it may generally appear that the wool trade had come to a grinding halt in the late 1270s and 1280s and was altogether staggering that so many merchants had been willing to risk frittering away large advances on such an obviously risk-laden investment. Perhaps, however, such figures for full delivery imply that faith in the monks' capacity to fulfil their side of the bargain was not necessarily misplaced. Indeed, in the five-year period from 1286–91 a total of 45 contracts have been discovered in the Exchequer Memoranda Rolls. Of these, 16 were apparently paid in full.[82]

While it might be suspected that the proliferation of contracts in the mid-to-late 1280s and early 1290s could be ascribed to a rather panicky scramble to secure as large as possible supplies of wool, provoked by unrealistic monastic promises of huge quantities of wool of a higher quality which might then have been rarer to find, it is possible that the phenomenon can, however tentatively, be put down to a gradual but visible recovery from scab among sheep flocks. Indeed, there is evidence to suggest that some merchants and monks tried to redress the natural disaster then occurring amongst their greatest assets. At Kirkstall, where flocks had been virtually wiped out by 1284, a flock boasting some 4,000 animals roamed its estates in 1301, the abbey's enormous debt having fallen to just £160. Such a turnaround should be attributed to the custodial management of Henry de Lacy from 1287 to 1297, but the monks may also have used some of the advance payments on restocking their sheep-stations.[83]

---

[81] E 159/59, rot. 9d, E 369/59, rot. 19d (Rievaulx); E 159/52, rot. 13, E 368/52, rot. 12d. (Byland); E 159/53, rot. 12d., E 368/53, rot. 14 (Meaux). *Advance Contracts*, nos. 86, 27, 42.

[82] It is important to note, however, that many of the contracts that do not mention explicit payment in full were probably still fully honoured.

[83] Denholm-Young, *Seigneurial Administration*, p. 61. Robert Wright, in a paper entitled 'Cistercians and the Wool Trade in Medieval Yorkshire' delivered at the IMC in July 2004, intimated that he

The Cahorsin merchants involved with Pipewell abbey, though, went further than any of their contemporaries in ensuring a sufficient resource existed for fulfilment of their contracts. On 12 November 1288, John de Hilliun, abbot of the Northamptonshire Cistercian house, came before the Exchequer barons and acknowledged his debt to Arnold de Soliz, John de Redole and William Servat, of 360 sacks of wool to be delivered over 15 years.[84] The merchants appear to have realised such a burden would be excessive under normal circumstances and contracted with the abbot to deliver to him 733 sheep, half of which were to be maintained at their costs and half at the abbot's. When this contract was renegotiated in 1291, 900 sheep (it is not clear whether these were new sheep or the original 733 with their offspring) were to be set aside and maintained at like costs until a sustainable flock of 2,000 beasts could be achieved.[85] As will be discussed later, this experiment was not entirely successful and litigation re-ensued. Nonetheless, the merchants should be given credit for showing considerable initiative in trying to offset the ravages of disease and indebtedness among the monastic community with their own capital.

Ultimately, however, despite evidence of recovery and some buoyancy in wool production, the facts remain that the majority of contracts did not result in delivery, monastic debts spiralled and litigation spread as merchants attempted to recoup their losses. There is also a lingering suspicion that even in cases where the monks are described as fully quit, all is not necessarily as it seems. During Michaelmas term 1308–9, William de Lee, abbot of Combermere, recognised before the Exchequer barons that he had promised to deliver to Pietro di Frescobaldi and his fellows of the company of the Frescobaldi of Florence 110 sacks of wool, 80 of which were to be of good wool valued at 14 marks per sack, 20 of middling value at 9 marks each, and 10 of locks worth 46s 8d per sack, over a term of 20 years. At the foot of the entry on the Memoranda Roll, a later insertion records that the abbot had satisfied the merchants of this Recognisance.[86] During Hilary term 1315, however, in a writ to the Exchequer barons concerning the debts owed to him by the exile and forfeit of the Frescobaldi at the behest of the

---

believed merchants' lucre had played some role in restoring the abbey to its pristine status. The practicalities of achieving this feat are not clear; see also R. Wright, '"Casting Down the Altars and Levelling Everything before the Ploughshare"? The Expansion and Evolution of the Grange Estates of Kirkstall Abbey', in M. Prestwich, R. Britnell and R. Frame (eds.), *Thirteenth Century England IX* (Woodbridge, 2003). J. P. Bischoff has demonstrated that houses often bought in sheep from elsewhere to breed with their own flocks or even to restock their estates with animals producing a higher-quality wool: Bischoff, 'An Honest Merchant', p. 106, n. 8.

[84] E 159/62, rot. 4. *Advance Contracts*, no. 110.

[85] C 54/108, mm. 8d.–9d.; E 159/64, rot. 10; E 368/62, rot. 14. *Advance Contracts*, no. 133.

[86] E 159/82, rot. 81. *Advance Contracts*, no. 182.

Ordainers in 1311, most of which had been granted to John de Sandale, a long-standing royal official, Edward II noted this earlier Recognisance, but informed them he had heard that a great part of the bond was still in arrears.[87] A subsequent inquiry involving John Canizan, an imprisoned member of the Frescobaldi company, revealed that, in fact, the abbey had delivered only 11 sacks up to 1311 when the contract had, not unnaturally, been temporarily suspended due to their exile. There remained a debt of £182 13s 4d to Sandale, though. When full account had been made of the abbey's debts in wool, which perhaps stretched back to the contract made in 1298 with the Frescobaldi for 140 sacks,[88] the total debt owing on wool came to £689 8s 11d. While the abbot of Burton-upon-Trent, acting for the abbot of Combermere, was able to provide £45 13s 4d, a debt of £643 15s 7d remained payable by the abbey. How far such arrangements represented the experience of other monastic houses across England who are described in the sources as quit is difficult to say, but there is ample evidence of further substantial restructuring of debts, meaning the cancellation of vast sums of debt, as the king attempted to come to terms with merchants and ensure monasteries survived.

Restructuring

The aforementioned contract made on 29 September 1298 by the abbot and convent of Combermere for 140 sacks, indeed, came two weeks after a mutual agreement had been brokered before the Exchequer court then at York. Herein, all agreements, contracts, sales, or other manner of debts in which the abbey had been bound to the Frescobaldi and *vice versa*, whether in wool or specie, were quitclaimed so that neither party could lay claim to them. Presumably, the merchants had tired of the abbey's failure to deliver on an earlier promise to provide wool. After Easter 1279, Abbot Richard had contracted with Guido Chuffanatalis and Guido Amaduri to deliver 300 sacks over 20 years.[89] No record survives of it having been delivered and the date of the final term at which wool would have been due (9 July 1298) is suggestive of an attempt in the contract of September 1298 to renew an association and restructure an earlier commitment at more manageable levels, an arrangement in which the abbot seems happy to demur. Of course, as shown above, such efforts were once more in vain, but faced

---

[87] E 159/88, rot. 140. *Advance Contracts*, no. 193.
[88] E 159/72, rot. 45 (29 September 1298). *Advance Contracts*, no. 156.
[89] E 159/52, rot. 15; E 368/52, rot. 15. *Advance Contracts*, no. 28.

with the prospect of losing out on their investment, merchants could be willing to throw even greater sums at the problem.

Events concerning the Benedictine priory of St Swithun in Winchester further highlight the determination of both sides to come to agreement. During the Easter term of 1293, William de Basing, prior of St Swithun's, acknowledged before the Exchequer that he had made his final account with the king for his debts to the Riccardi, an arrangement having been made by which they now acquitted him of all previous deals made between them whether for wool or for sums of money.[90] This must have included four prior Recognisances, one made on 15 April 1285, two others during Hilary term 1286 and a final one during Michaelmas term 1290–1, for a total of 470 sacks of wool.[91] In return, the prior now submitted himself to a restructuring and rationalisation of his debt. All debts were to be invalidated save for 30 sacks remaining on that year's account and a sum of 200 sacks of wool, which the merchants were unwilling to surrender. This arrangement does seem to have borne some fruit. On 15 February 1296, Edward I wrote to the Treasurer and barons of the Exchequer informing them that on Christmas Eve, Henry, prior of St Swithun's, had delivered 62 sacks of wool worth £289 17s. to Orlandino da Poggio and Frecherico Venture, merchants of the society of the Riccardi.[92] As the merchants had been exiled and their debts were due to the king, Edward seized the wool and ordered the Treasury to deliver the sum due to the prior out of the Exchequer, although deductions were to be made for their arrears on a clerical tax owed to him. Whether this entirely satisfied the king in the long term is doubtful, but it certainly set in train measures to ensure that he recouped the merchants' investment and by 1305 he was able to record that Henry, who was at that point bishop-elect of Winchester, had made good on all debts owed to them for wool.[93] To what extent this was a genuine pay-off or a further restructuring on the lines suggested for Combermere is, however, still open to question.

The rationalisation of monastic debt in many instances sprang from royal desire not to see houses go under, so losing for the Crown valuable sources of taxable and, of course, spiritual wealth, in whose foundation their predecessors had placed so much faith. In a handful of cases, individual merchants come into the Exchequer apparently under pressure from

---

[90] For what follows see E 159/66, rot. 49d.; E 368/64, rot. 43.

[91] E 159/58, rot. 16, E 368/58, rot. 19 (240 sacks, 1285); E 159/59, rot. 4, (200 sacks, 1286); E 159/64, rot. 22d., E 368/62, rot. 27 (30 sacks, 1290–1). *Advance Contracts*, nos. 78, 82, 122.

[92] E 159/69, rot. 62. *Advance Contracts*, no. 153.   [93] E 159/78, rot. 45d.

the Crown to broker compromise with a suffering foundation and so assist in the remittance of other debts. On 10 January 1289, for example, Stephen de Cornhulle, a renowned London merchant, came into the Exchequer to have enrolled his remission to Alice de Cobham, prioress of Minster in Sheppey, of a contract by which her predecessor Isabella de Essetestifford and her convent had covenanted to deliver their entire annual wool crop to him each year for life. In return for his quitclaim of rights to debts conferred by contracts, tallies, sureties or any other instruments, the prioress paid him 20½ marks ostensibly to have this quitclaim enrolled.[94] What lay behind this is difficult to say conclusively, but given that Minster in Sheppey does not appear in the 1294 Exchequer Schedules or the list of wool-producing abbeys compiled by Pegolotti, it might be suspected that the nuns wished to relieve themselves of an onerous, perhaps impossible, burden, rather than cast off one patron for another with more capital to invest in their wool.

Perhaps the most revealing series of Recognisances in this regard, though, concern the dealings of Flaxley abbey, a Cistercian foundation in the Forest of Dean (Gloucestershire), with an English wool merchant, Thomas de Basinges, citizen of London. In late June 1278, Abbot William recognised his debt of £210 to Basinges, a sum to be repaid in annual instalments of £20 for the first eight years then following and £50 in the ninth and final year. Such annuities were then to be allowed to the abbot in part payment of this previous debt of the abbey's wool for twelve years, for which Thomas had contracted and had not received delivery.[95] This was accompanied by a renewal of the contract for wool, by which the abbot promised to deliver the entire crop of the abbey, 10 sacks a year (7 of good worth 10 marks a sack, one of middle-grade valued at 6 marks each and 2 of locks worth 5 marks a sack) two weeks from the Nativity of St John the Baptist over the next thirteen years (9 July 1278 – 9 July 1290). Thomas, for his part, paid £160 in advance for the first eight years of the contract and £50 over the next five, and agreed to remit the earlier contract 'at the command of, and in reverence to, the lord king, as well as in order to relieve the estate of the said monks, by his pure and spontaneous will'.[96]

Such apparent generosity and magnanimity disguised some rather telling clauses in Thomas's favour. The monks, first of all, were to receive

---

[94] E 159/62, rot. 4. *Advance Contracts*, no. 111.

[95] E 159/51, rot. 20d., E 368/51, rot. 13d (schedule). *Advance Contracts*, no. 23. Thomas had eight sacks of the abbey's wool seized in Bruges in 1274: E 163/5/17, m. 1.

[96] ' … *idem Thomas ad mandatum et ob reverenciam dicti domini Regis, necnon ad relevacionem status religiosorum ipsorum, [mera] et spontanea voluntate sua* … '

Thomas's dresser and adhere to his will at their expenses in the preparation of the wool. Moreover, they were not to sell any wool to any party without his consent and were to provide him with all extraneous wool produced over and above that contracted.[97] Within three years, however, Thomas had been forced into accepting a renegotiation of this contract on a smaller scale and over a postponed delivery period. Henceforth, the abbey was to deliver six sacks of good wool and one each of middle-grade and locks, not in the quindene of St John the Baptist 1281, as promised, but ten years to that day. Again, Thomas appears magnanimous, agreeing to this postponement 'freely, inspired by thoughts of charity ... in order that our house might be relieved'.[98] Intriguingly, this contract reveals that Thomas has paid a further 63 marks in advance for wool valued at only 56 marks. If the monks made the delivery, they would receive 56 marks, presumably in the form of an allowance on the money already paid, as they acquit him of payment of that sum at the time the contract was drawn up, but if they defaulted they would be due to pay the full 63 marks.

This did not avail Thomas much either, for by 1286, matters had clearly come to a head.[99] At some point during this period, Edward I had granted Thomas custody of the abbey, most probably during its periods of bankruptcy in 1277 and 1281. But, during the Easter term of that year, the king ordered the Exchequer barons to summon the abbot and Thomas before them, he having heard that the numerous Recognisances made for the sale of wool in the past few years had brought 'great oppression upon the house'.[100] He demanded that the barons help broker a compromise in which, by the taking of a fine, the abbey would be relieved without any further tumult being caused[101] and Thomas might be induced to surrender to the abbey 'in the most honourable manner possible'[102] all that he had by colour of the king's commission to him, he having withdrawn some of the abbey's silver. Thomas must have been incredibly frustrated by his connection with Flaxley. Despite repeated attempts to broker a compromise worthy of both parties, success appears to have been elusive and Thomas may have lost his investment. Such failure to recoup losses must have been

---

[97] Whether or not they had actually sold wool, the abbey and convent were bound in 1282 to Siennese merchants in 72 marks: E 13/9, m. 17d.

[98] E 159/55, rot. 6: '*Et idem Thomas, sua liberalitas et caritatis intuitu solucionem predicte lane ad relevationem domus nostre ...*' *Advance Contracts*, no. 64.

[99] For what follows, see E 159/59, rot. 18.

[100] '*... super quibus domus multipliciter est oppressa*'.

[101] Does this imply physical or legal confrontation had been going on apace outside the king's sight? No evidence has come to light yet.

[102] '*... et prefatum Thomam modis quibus honestius fieri potest inducant ...*'

a frequent part of business for those involved in the English wool trade in the late thirteenth century. When kings were ultimately more willing to preserve the estate of monastic producers, what could be done by merchants to try and obtain redress for default?

Redress for the merchants?

Essentially, there appears to have been two approaches which merchants had available. The first, and evidently most common, was to take the legal route. Those contracts enrolled among the Memoranda of the Exchequer were, of course, theoretically legally binding and default clauses, as outlined above, were built in to ensure payment. There were, however, other options. In 1275, in attempting to press for redemption of the value of 14 sacks and 20 stones of wool, 10 sacks of which were of a better grade and valued at 11 marks, and the remainder of locks and clacks valued at only 7 marks per sack, which he claimed had been unjustly detained by the abbot of Louth Park after an initial advance payment, Giles de Ayre, attorney of John Wermond of Cambrai, had originally sued before the court of John de Britannia, then chief justice in eyre, at Boston. Only when he failed to receive a satisfactory verdict did he come before Chancery where a compromise agreement in his favour was drawn up.[103] To what extent litigants used roving justice in disputes over wool is an area which may require further research. The great majority of pleas concerning wool identified thus far can, however, be found in the Plea Rolls of the court of the Exchequer of Pleas.

The Exchequer of Pleas was a common law court principally open only to 'privileged suitors' – accountants and debtors to the Crown and officers of the Exchequer and their clerks and servants. Over time, however, such restrictions were relaxed to facilitate the speedier and more efficient levying of Crown debts. The plaintiffs sued by writ, the original of which was the *venire facias*, the reply to which dictated whether a writ of *distringas* would be issued to the sheriff to distrain the debtor by his goods or whether a writ of *capias* would be issued for his person if he had no goods. The Plea Rolls appear to be restricted to cases where an actual appearance in court was involved. The jurisdiction of the Exchequer of Pleas came to include cases concerning the king's revenue and those relating to Exchequer and local officials, though some foreign merchants were granted the privilege of suing for debts in this court, some even bringing cases by asserting they

---

[103] C 54/93, m. 18d. *Advance Contracts*, no. 14.

were Exchequer officials, as, for example, Bertram Cappedemayle, Bertram de Crusero and Peter de Donde, who are described as merchants of Brother Joseph de Cauncy, the Treasurer.[104]

Many of the cases discovered so far on the Plea Rolls end with judgement against the producer for detaining wool unjustly from the purchasing party. Two outcomes are most prevalent. In keeping with royal wishes to broker compromise where possible, many cases end with the losing party entering into a further Recognisance for the faithful delivery of wool. Towards the beginning of June 1276, William, abbot of Biddlesden, came into the Exchequer to disavow a contract for 21 sacks of wool worth 252 marks which he claimed had been made without his consent with Reginald de Plesance. Reginald was able to produce a bond attesting to a prior contract and, whilst continuing to deny his part in the deal, the abbot agreed to pay and restructured the deal so that 7 sacks would be delivered in each of the next three years.[105] In the first week of October 1279, a group of Banbury merchants likewise acknowledged a debt of 5 sacks of wool to the Riccardi and agreed to its delivery at the quindene before the Nativity of St John the Baptist then next upcoming [10 June 1280].[106] A couple of other cases conclude with the king granting licence to one of the litigants that if he is able to come to an independent compromise before he is due to appear again before the king, then he will be quit of any charge. Thomas, son of Robert, Roger de Shipwrihcte and Andrew Motty, brought before the Exchequer in the last week of March 1276 to answer William de Frescenade on a plea concerning two sacks of wool, were permitted to postpone a future appearance to answer for these sacks if they could satisfy William in the meantime.[107] Early in 1280, William, abbot of the Cistercian house of Dore in Herefordshire, represented by Brother William de Sautebroyl, a member of his convent, was specifically given a day until Easter in the hope of brokering a compromise with Poncio de Mora and John de Soliz, Cahorsin merchants, on a plea concerning 3 sacks of wool worth 36 marks. Were he to satisfy them in the meantime he would be quit of this appearance.[108] It is possible, of course, that such Recognisances should be treated as being similar to those in the Memoranda Rolls, their enrolment among the pleas of the Exchequer perhaps not implying any default at all. No mention is made of unjust detention after all.

---

[104] E 13/5, m. 2; *Advance Contracts*, no. 18.   [105] E 13/4, mm. 8–8d; *Advance Contracts*, no. 17.
[106] E 13/8, m. 3d. See also E 13/8, m. 9d. *Advance Contracts*, nos. 33, 34.
[107] E 13/4, m. 5. *Advance Contracts*, no. 15.   [108] E 13/8, m. 14. *Advance Contracts*, no. 40.

Others, however, definitely suggest default and in such cases distraint is often brought against wrongdoers. Sheriffs, too, are frequently ordered to find mainpernors for a faithful subsequent appearance in court and occasionally mainpernors themselves are brought into trouble for failure to appear.[109] On 14 January 1280, Peter de Mundenard obtained a verdict against the heir of Walter Whyt, Robert de Cestertone and John de Kenilwrthe on a plea that they were to answer him for 5 sacks of wool, and against the prior of Wroxton for 6 sacks. Edward I may have taken a special interest in this debt as Peter had contracted for this wool to help pay off a debt which he owed to Eleanor of Castile, Queen Consort. While Robert appeared, his fellows did not and the sheriff of Oxfordshire was ordered to spare no expense in entering the liberty of Banbury, if necessary, to distrain them. The mainpernors of such defaulters were also put in mercy.[110] On occasion, conversely, sellers, whether merchants or producers, were able to obtain a similarly successful verdict against buyers. When the German John de Brilaunde appeared in court to press his claim for unjust detention of one sack of wool worth 15 marks against Henry son of Henry de Mapeltone, the barons dismissed his claim as false, because the Letter of Recognisance he produced bore a squashed and partly broken seal of authentication. He was thus placed in mercy.[111] Furthermore, on other occasions merchants fell foul of Exchequer procedure in their attempts to gain redress. Henry le Veyl of Monyash, servant of Walter de Kancia, was unable to press his claim against the abbot of Roche for 6 sacks of wool worth £50 13s 4d as fully as he would have desired. The abbot denied his case on the grounds that as the sacks had been delivered to a lay brother of his house he ought not to answer the charge elsewhere than before the Common Law, quoting *Magna Carta* as his authority. This stymied the process long enough at a time when the Treasurer and several of the barons were absent from the Exchequer, the remainder postponing the case until their return. No further trace of their judgement has been identified.[112]

Insecurity of supply must have dovetailed with insecurity of investment and the possibility that redress at law would not be easy to attain for many merchants, particularly those new to English legal procedure. The second

---

[109] See the example of Clement son of Elias of Pontefract, William son of John and Robert Alzun of Pontefract who, having failed to appear in court, are mainperned to answer Reginald Menezaco and Reginald de Plesance for 4 sacks of wool worth 48 marks. None appear and so are mainperned. None of the mainpernors then appear with their charges. All are to be put in mercy: E 13/6, m. 20d. *Advance Contracts*, no. 22.

[110] E 13/8, m. 11. *Advance Contracts*, no. 39.   [111] E 13/18, m. 27. *Advance Contracts*, no. 147.

[112] E 13/10, m. 7d. *Advance Contracts*, no. 71.

stratagem by which merchants might attempt to cover their losses and, perhaps, augment their profits was to ensure that vendors sealed agreements which tied them to financial penalties for failure to comply, as well as, in a number of cases, structuring payments to producers containing a variety of allowances and subtractions from the maximum sum payable to soften the blow of failure in supply. M. Prestwich, indeed, comments that 'profits were taken in the form of damages for late repayment'.[113]

Twenty-five of 78 (32 per cent) contracts containing an advance do not involve payment of the full value of the wool. On average, most of them leave one quarter to one half unpaid and to be rendered upon requisite delivery of the promised wool, although even here advances could be considerable. Giles de Ayre, attorney of John Wermond of Cambrai, paid £53 6s 8d upfront on a contract worth £72 to the abbot and convent of Darnhall.[114] During Hilary term 1280 Nicholas, abbot of Tilty, a Cistercian monastery in Essex, received £450 for wool valued in total by Giacomo Fronte and Guido Amaduri at £653 6s 8d.[115] In 1298, the abbot of Byland received the enormous sum of £913 6s 8d on an even more substantial amount of wool, some 245 sacks, worth a colossal £1,568.[116] Virtually simultaneously, the buyers from Byland, the Frescobaldi, committed themselves to an advance of £784 on 140 sacks of Combermere wool valued at £1,050 13s 4d.[117] Whether partial advances such as these built in a level of interest, in that the merchants did not expect to have to pay the whole amount, is, again, open to question. Certainly, even though not the full amount, to lay out £2618 13s 4d on 385 sacks within a few months of each other, suggests the Frescobaldi were committed to accessing the best wool they could find no matter what the cost. In other cases, payments were proportionately very much smaller. Godfrey, prior of Pontefract, for example, received only one tenth of the value of wool worth £533 6s 8d in 1280.[118]

In at least some examples, merchants do display a real note of caution. Possibly a sign that they anticipated the difficulties which could ensue in their dealings with the cathedral priory of St Swithun's, Winchester, the Riccardi built in a series of subtractions from the money they were due to pay for 240 sacks of wool valued at £960, on top of an allowance to the merchants the monks were bound to recognise for the sum of £300 that had

[113] Prestwich, 'Italian Merchants in Late Thirteenth and Early Fourteenth Century England', p. 95.
[114] C 54/92, m. 2d. *Advance Contracts*, no. 13.   [115] E 368/53, rot. 13. *Advance Contracts*, no. 45.
[116] E 159/72, rot. 45d. *Advance Contracts*, no. 157.   [117] E 159/72, rot. 45. *Advance Contracts*, no. 156.
[118] E 368/53, rot. 14d. *Advance Contracts*, no. 46.

been paid to them in advance on 15 April 1285.[119] In the first year of this six-year contract, a subtraction of £126 13s 4d was to be made, in the second £53 6s 8d, and in the four final years £26 13s 4d, making a grand total allowed of £586 13s 4d, leaving them just £403 6s 8d left to pay over six years, assuming the wool was delivered. Interestingly, the two contracts which followed early in 1286 for a total of 370 sacks of wool valued together at £1,480 included similar allowances to the merchants on sums to be paid for wool at delivery over and above the advances of £562 13s 4d.[120] In the first year of a four-year contract, £200 would be allowed to the merchants. In the following year, this dropped to just £33 6s 8d, but in the third rose again to £106 13s 4d before falling back to a subtraction of £16 in the fourth, making a total deduction from the £1,480 due overall of £918 13s 4d.

St Swithun's was not the only establishment with which the Riccardi agreed allowances in a contract for wool. At Michaelmas 1287, Roger of Driffield, abbot of Meaux in the East Riding, contracted to deliver 65 sacks of good wool worth a total of £650 over five years.[121] Alongside a partial advance of £270, the Riccardi asked for allowances of £44 per annum, a total of £220 over five years. This left the Riccardi with only £160 to pay for delivered wool. Such allowances and subtractions must have made budgeting easier for the merchants and helped anticipate the blow of failure in delivery or, less seriously, default in any sack at any time. It also meant that monks could not just take the money and run. In order to receive the full value of their product, they would have to deliver it at the pre-arranged time and place.

Many merchants also built penalty clauses into contracts to insure themselves against default. Florentine merchants, for example, claimed payments in the case of default expressly to mitigate any damages which might befall them thereby.[122] Some simply imposed a charge, either a set figure or the value of one sack, in the event of any sack being left out of the delivery of the full contracted amount. The Mozzi would charge the monks of Rievaulx £10 a sack, while the Riccardi who contracted with Meaux in 1280 for 53 sacks of *collecta*, charged 12½ marks, the price of one sack.[123] In one extraordinary case, Giles de Ayre, on behalf of John Wermond of

[119] E 159/58, rot. 16; E 368/58, rot. 19. *Advance Contracts*, no. 78.
[120] E 159/59, rot. 4 (schedules). *Advance Contracts*, no. 82.
[121] E 159/61, rot. 14. *Advance Contracts*, no. 103.
[122] C 54/93, m. 3d. *Advance Contracts*, no. 19.
[123] E 159/53, rot. 12d., E 368/53, rot. 14 (Meaux); E 159/59, rot. 9d., E 368/59, rot. 19d. (Rievaulx). Others contracts to include such penalties are: E 327/541 (Pipewell, 10 marks); E 368/53, rot.14d. (Pontefract); C 54/108, mm. 8d.–9d., E 159/64, rot. 10; E 368/62, rot. 14 (Pipewell); E 159/72, rot. 45 (Byland, £10). *Advance Contracts*, nos. 42, 86, 221, 46, 133, 157.

Cambrai, inserted a clause into his contract with Darnhall, charging the monks £20 for each day that they defaulted, £10 of which would go to pay the expenses of any sheriffs or bailiffs making distraint in their favour. Moreover, a further £20 would be donated to the salvation of the Holy Land.[124] Perhaps as importantly, decisions as to whether the producer had defaulted were in some contracts left entirely at the whim of the merchants. Giles de Ayre, Thomas de Basinges, the Riccardi merchants contracting with St Swithun's priory in 1285 and the Frescobaldi who dealt with both Combermere and Byland in the autumn/winter of 1298–9, all insisted that their simple word ('*simplici verbo*') should be held in sufficient good faith for the monks to pay the penalty of default.[125] Similarly, these contracts also forbid the monks from claiming refuge behind clerical privilege, nor to seek the sanctuary of civil or ecclesiastical law or indeed papal sanction.

How far these measures provided a safety net for merchants against defaulting debtors, regardless of whether default had come intentionally or through natural disaster, is not easy to resolve. The survival of over 200 legal documents, most of which do not attest to satisfaction of contracts, suggests they were not a boon against loss. And yet, as Lloyd has so comprehensively demonstrated, English wool producers continued to export in excess of 25,000 sacks of wool for much of the period, implying that although the contracts shed a great deal of illumination on the problems endured by monks and merchants in the late thirteenth and early fourteenth centuries, and some of the solutions they attempted to impose, they tell far from the whole story. Nevertheless, without their survival innumerable elements of the trade would be further obscured from view, and it is some of those elements which now deserve attention.

The practicalities

Dating where and when an advance was paid and the contract drawn up is one of the most difficult problems in their analysis, as relatively few traces of the original bonds have survived. Much of the negotiation may well have been undertaken by merchants' agents scouring the country in a search for available wool of sufficient quality to meet their sales needs. Consequently, many contracts were most probably drawn up in the weeks leading up to the shearing season in late Spring, early Summer, when the crop that was going to be obtained became clearer, or in the weeks after when wool piled

---

[124] C 54/92, m. 2d. *Advance Contracts*, no. 13.
[125] E 159/58, rot. 16, E 368/58, rot. 19; E 159/72, rot. 45. *Advance Contracts*, nos. 78, 156, 157.

up in granges across the country. Certainly, in the wake of Edward I's orders for the seizure of the goods of foreign merchants issued on 12 June 1294,[126] when Italian merchants were asked to provide details of the wool they expected to receive in that year, all of the companies involved could declare, as did the Ponche of Florence, that 'Truly sire, we have *collecta* wools in the North, but we are not able to know how much until our associate, who is in the North, has returned'.[127]

On 24 August 1284, Margaret, prioress of the Benedictine nunnery of Arden in the North Riding, sealed an agreement with the Frescobaldi for the entire annual wool crop of her house in the chapter house of her priory, recognising advance payment of £10.[128] Though no definitive evidence survives, it is likely that the contract was drawn up on the day that the advance was paid, or sometime shortly thereafter. In one of the few other original bonds which appear to have been transcribed onto the Memoranda Rolls, the prior of St Swithun's, Winchester sealed a contract with the Riccardi for the entire annual crop of his house over six years in the chapter house of his priory on 28 April 1285. The original deal had been brokered on 15 April when it had been explicitly stated that 'the aforesaid merchants are to give and deliver to the aforesaid prior and convent £300 sterling in advance for the aforesaid wool of these six years'.[129] Presumably, the bond of 28 April was drawn up after payment had been made, the prior acknowledging his debt on the Memoranda Rolls sometime later during Easter term.

On the other hand, it is inherently unlikely, given the geographical areas some agents must have covered, that they could carry sufficient sums to meet all their multifarious obligations. Many years of experience may have taught merchants what they could expect in an average year and contracts could have been drawn up by agents on site but then the advance paid well before delivery was due at one of the many fairs, the primary places of exchange in medieval England, held over the summer months in England. Potentially, too, payment might have been made in one of the local centres of the wool trade or places of delivery, such as York, Hull, Beverley, Boston, Grantham, Dunstable or Winchester,[130] places where merchants probably had chambers, where producers could receive advances in the

---

[126] Lloyd, *English Wool Trade*, p. 75.
[127] '*Veraiement sire nous avons laines de coillette vers le North, mes nous ne pooms saver combien tant ke nostre compaignon qui est vers le North soit revenu*': E101/126/7, m. 14. *Advance Contracts*, no. 206.
[128] E 13/26, m. 23. *Advance Contracts*, no. 171.
[129] '*Debent insuper predicti mercatores dare et solvere predictis priori et conventui pro predicta lana sex annorum trescentas libras sterlingorum pre manibus . . .*': E 159/58, rot. 16; E 368/58, rot. 19. *Advance Contracts*, no. 78.
[130] See below for discussion of local and regional trading centres.

form of deductions from outstanding debts or discounts on product purchases.

It is tempting, however, to suggest that at least some advances were paid around the time that the contract was enrolled at the Exchequer and that payment was the direct catalyst for enrolment. Enrolment provided an official registration of the debt for both parties and it would clearly be in both parties' interests to have the other's obligations to them recorded officially as quickly as possible after the deal had been made. At some point during Easter term 1286, a contract between the prior of Lewes and the Riccardi for 23 sacks of *collecta* was enrolled.[131] The prior acknowledges he had received an advance of 289 marks by the hands of the merchants not at his priory, but in London. A letter patent dated 8 November 1275, issued by John, abbot of the Cistercian house of Darnhall, states that he had sold 12 sacks of wool of his abbey to John Wermond of Cambrai 'in the city of London'[132] and that he had been paid 80 marks in advance by Giles de Ayre, John's attorney, 'on the day this letter was drawn up'.[133] London, of course, would have been the location where merchants established their business headquarters in England and some exchanges of money may well have taken place in their offices. In January 1292 Master William de Bosco of Leicestershire was attached to appear before the Exchequer Court of Pleas to demonstrate why he should not honour a debt of his father, John, to Peregrino de Chartres and his fellow Lucchese merchants for one sack of wool from his manor of Thorp Arnold. The merchants produced John's bond, in which he admitted that he had received payment in advance from Peregrino in London.[134] Furthermore, as soon as agents did return from the North (or equally the West or Wales) armed with information on the wool for which they had contracted, merchants could make arrangement with religious houses or their attorneys for a convenient time to ensure registration of the debt.

Perhaps more pertinently, London was the political hub of England and home (for much of the period) to the institutions of government and representation. Abbots could be regularly summoned to parliaments, councils, or provincial assemblies and it might make sense for them to register obligations they had recently entered into when it was practically most possible for them to do so. Moreover, many religious houses probably

---

[131] E 159/59, rot. 12d. *Advance Contracts*, no. 88.
[132] '*en la cite de Londres*': C 54/92, m. 2d. *Advance Contracts*, no. 13.
[133] ' . . . *quatre vinz mars esterling en arres sor la leyne avant nomee le jour ke ceste lettre fu feite* . . . '
[134] E 13/17, m. 16d. *Advance Contracts*, no. 139.

maintained a number of attorneys who saw to the house's business in London whenever necessary. Many of the enrolled contracts were registered during Michaelmas or Hilary terms and probably represent deals made in the preceding season. There can, however, be little precision in deciding when and by what methods contracts appear on the Rolls, and this is an area which requires further work.

How were contracts negotiated and by whom? Instinctively, with regard to monastic contracts, it might be assumed that the heads of houses were responsible for negotiating with merchants. The standard formula of Exchequer enrolments almost exclusively begins 'The same abbot/prior came before the barons and recognised for himself, his convent and his successors that he was bound to ... '[135] Of course, in most cases this is unlikely to have been the result of a personal appearance. Most heads of houses must have been represented by an attorney, although throughout the body of contract evidence only a handful of references to attorneys occur. On 17 February 1280, when William de Aylesford, prior of Wroxton, was attached to answer Peter de Mundenard for 6 sacks of wool, he was represented by Brother Richard de Den, a member of his convent.[136] From a Recognisance enrolled on 9 July 1292, it is clear that one Nicholas of Winchester had long acted as an intermediary in deals concerning wool between the Cistercian abbey of Bindon in Dorset and the Riccardi, the merchants having other bonds in his name for 39 sacks of the abbey's wool.[137] Heads of houses could not just make agreements of their own volition, however. John, abbot of Darnhall, claimed that his deal with John Wermond in October 1275 had been made 'with the good will of his convent'.[138] The abbot of the Cistercian house of Bordesley (Worcs.) was condemned by his convent for an apparently usurious contract with the Cerchi in 1275, and his fellow monks prayed to the king that it should be annulled both on the grounds of usury and on lack of conventual consent.[139]

Other monastic officials, too, must have had considerable input to the framing of contracts. The monastic cellarer, whose remit covered all of the stocks and stores of the house, would be in a far better position to know exactly what amount of wool his house would be likely to produce at any given time. Indeed, it may well have been the cellarer with whom

---

[135] '*Idem venit coram Baronibus et recognovit pro se, conventu suo et successoribus suis se teneri ...*';
[136] E 13/8, m. 15d. *Advance Contracts*, no. 44.   [137] E 159/65, rot. 36d. *Advance Contracts*, no. 142.
[138] C 54/92, m. 2d.: '*venda por sey et por son covent, grantant de lor bone volente ...*' *Advance Contracts*, no. 13.
[139] Lloyd, *English Wool Trade*, p. 291.

travelling agents most frequently dealt, rather than the abbot, whose spiritual and business commitments can have given him very little time for the practicalities of estate management. More intriguingly, however, while the contracts reveal nothing of the cellarer's role, the potential importance of the large body of lay brothers who staffed granges where wool would arrive for storage, sorting and packing is highlighted on three separate occasions. The rarity of lay brothers making an appearance in monastic charters implies that some importance ought to be given to the sealing of the earliest identified advance contract by one Brother Robert, 'a lay brother' of Pipewell abbey.[140] The best example of the central role lay brothers might play in negotiation of wool contracts is that of Brother Ralph de Laneria, a lay brother of Biddlesden abbey.[141] Early in June 1276, Reginald de Molin, Janin de Phillipp' and their fellows, merchants of Piacenza, came into the Exchequer to challenge William, abbot of Biddlesden, as to why he had not delivered 21 sacks of wool valued at 252 marks. They displayed a Recognisance asserting that Brother Ralph, with the consent and will of the abbot and convent, had sold the wool to the merchants in advance.[142] While the abbot denied that he had been present at, or party to, the drafting of the agreement,[143] he recognised that Ralph had indeed made it and refused to answer the charge without Ralph's presence in court to advise him on how he had dealt with delivering the wool. His subsequent submission to restructured terms for the full delivery of the 21 sacks suggests that he would not renounce a deal made by a lay brother.

   C. Platt, in an extensive survey of the monastic grange in England, has outlined the role of lay brothers in the thirteenth century as managers of work on the monastic grange. Presumably, they supervised sheep husbandry on the vast estates and roaming hillsides used for pasturing sheep and attended to the preparation and dispatch of wool for the market.[144] It is surely not stretching the imagination too much to see

---

[140] E 327/541, where the witnesses to a contract for the abbey's entire wool crop with John Tolosanus and Adam of Shoreditch are *'fratre Ricardo de Norhampton, monacho, fratre Ricardo de Assele, monacho, et fratre Roberto converso et aliis'*. *Advance Contracts*, no. 221.

[141] E 13/4, m. 8–8d. *Advance Contracts*, no. 17.

[142] *'in quo continetur quod frater Radulphus de Laneria, conversus domus de Betlesden', ex consensu et voluntate dicti abbatis et conventus eiusdem domus vendidit dictis mercatoribus predictam lanam premanibus'*.

[143] *' ... set dixit quod quia dictus convencio facta fuit inter predictum Radulphum conversum suum et predictos mercatores, cui convencioni idem abbas non interfuit nec constabat ... '*

[144] C. Platt, *The Monastic Grange in Medieval England: A Reassessment* (London, 1969), p. 76.

merchants' agents actually dealing predominantly with those whose task it was to ensure that wool reached the market from the pastures and these may well in the main have been the lay brothers. Indeed, at some time, probably in 1282, Henry, son of Robert le Veyl of Monyash, servant of Walter de Kancia, claimed he had delivered 6 sacks of wool worth £50 13s 4d to Roche abbey (Yorks).[145] Whether this was in an attempt to meet a prior obligation to a merchant or simply a delivery of *collecta* wool from the abbey's estates in the High Peak in Derbyshire is not clear, but Henry apparently delivered the wool to a lay brother of the abbey, who probably then attended to its preparation for the market.

The situation is equally confusing when dealing with merchants who used agents in England, although here it is due to a need to extend the survey of primary and secondary sources examined to establish an individual's connection with a particular company. Most of the important Italian merchant societies had dozens of trading bases across Europe, a fact well demonstrated by the career of Francesco Balducci Pegolotti who, as well as serving as the Bardi of Florence's chief agent in England from 1318 to 1321, also served in Cyprus, Flanders and various parts of Italy.[146] Each company rented chambers in London and almost certainly in other leading wool towns, such as York, Boston, Winchester and Hull. A number of names commonly occur in the contracts which point to the prominence such individuals must have enjoyed within their respective societies and may have become a recognisable face in the markets, fairs, courts, manorial estates and monastic houses of England. With regard to the Riccardi of Lucca, the principal agent in the 1270s and early 1280s appears to have been Baroncino Gualteri, who is the most ubiquitous of all Italians in England. He was accompanied by members of the da Poggio family, Orlandino, Enrico and Rolandino, as well as Ricardo Bonefaci and Ricardo Guidiccioni, all of whom occur at least a dozen times throughout the body of contract material. For the Mozzi of Florence, Simone Gerardi, unsurprisingly given his prominence in the transfer of contracts from the Cerchi in 1284, Chino Bosi, Thomas Spiliati, Lapo Hugoni and Ristorio Bonaventure negotiate the majority of bargains. Within the Frescobaldi's two branches in England, Coppus Cotenne appears to have led the way along with Taldus Janiani. Deciding on their actual role is less simple than identifying them, however, and much depends on how the dating of contracts is interpreted. Most of the figures just mentioned

---

[145] E 13/10, m. 7d. *Advance Contracts*, no. 71.   [146] *La Pratica Della Mercatura.*

probably did not stray too far from their company's base, dealing with correspondence with the main company headquarters in Italy or the export trade and sale for profit of wool in the Low Countries or Italy. Much of their contact with producers may have come in procuring enrolment of contracts and arranging for the distribution of credit and liquid capital to centres across England and the Continent. It is possible that they did travel on the occasion of the sealing of particularly large or important contracts, such as perhaps the bargain made by the Mozzi for 168 sacks of Rievaulx's wool in 1286.[147] More probably, though, the principals themselves employed agents in the shires who travelled from house to house, grange to grange buying up what they could and accounting with the principals on their return to the headquarters. Such men are more difficult to identify.

It is probable too, if not wholly possible at present to demonstrate, that Italian merchants widely employed the knowledge and bargaining skills of well-placed and well-selected English wool merchants as middlemen. John de Reddemere of Appleby in Lincolnshire can be identified as having been employed as an agent for the Riccardi.[148] Others, such as John and Richard de Bulmere in the North Riding of Yorkshire or Reginald Maniward in Herefordshire, may have, on occasion, purchased wool for other parties. Reginald Maniward appears in four surviving contracts all with foreign merchants. During 1262–3, he contracted with Peter Berard of Cahors for the delivery of 13 sacks and 16 stones of lambswool over three years. In the winter of 1283–4, he contracted with John Donedeu and William Jon, merchants of Cahors, to deliver 8 sacks of wool. During Trinity term 1287, he promised delivery of 2 sacks of marcher lambswool to Baroncino Gualteri. Finally, six months or so later, he committed himself to delivering 5 sacks of the same product to the Riccardi.[149] Other merchants of wool centres such as Pontefract and Banbury may well have been acting in the interests of a foreign party.[150] Indeed, the raft of pleas made by Baroncino Gualteri in 1278–80 concerning small amounts of wool from merchants in Grantham, Boston, Leicester and elsewhere, could well represent deals made with local middlemen.[151]

Of the 102 contracts identified in which lay producers are concerned only 11 (just over 10 per cent) can possibly be attributed to larger, possibly

[147] E 159/59, rot. 9d., E 368/59, rot. 19d. *Advance Contracts*, no. 86.   [148] *CPR, 1281–92*, p. 17.
[149] E 159/37, rot. 8 (1262–3); E 159/57, rot 13, E 368/57, rot. 12d. (1283–4); E 159/60, rot. 20d. (1287); E 159/61, rot. 13 (1287–8). *Advance Contracts*, nos. 9, 74, 98, 102.
[150] E 13/6, m. 20d.; 8, m. 3d. *Advance Contracts*, nos. 22, 34.
[151] E 13/8. *Advance Contracts*, nos. 30, 31, 32.

aristocratic, producers.[152] The three Anglo-Irish lords, Richard de Burgh, Nicholas Segrave and John fitz Thomas, approach the top ranks of aristocratic society in the British Isles. Others, such as Robert Tateshale, lord of Bocham castle in Norfolk, were clearly important magnates within a local context. The same can be said for Robert Bozon, steward of the High Peak in Derbyshire. Clearly, the merchants were willing to penetrate into every shire and lordship in England and, indeed, across the British Isles in the search for as much wool as possible.[153]

The wool

Essentially, wool was contracted in three main grades – good, middling and locks. Differences in climate and pasture all served to affect the length of fleeces, which were rarely uniform. Colder, wetter climates, though not to extreme, apparently served to form shorter, finer fleeces. Nevertheless, most fleeces bore fibres of varying lengths right up to the straggly, coarser fibres on the fringes of a fleece known as locks, which in some cases could be so straggly as to merit the description of 'secondary locks', the lowest-valued ovine product.[154] It is difficult to be sure whether such differentiations could be standardised across regions, or even within localities, but it is probable that merchants insisted on wool being sorted according to these artificial gradations to assist them in purchasing and marketing wool and to encourage growers to sort and prepare their product better. Of course, the best means of differentiation is by price. In general, good wool better suited to producing finer cloths fetched 25 per cent–50 per cent more than middle-grade wool, which R. A. Donkin described rather

---

[152] E 159/55, rot. 10 (Norman Darcy); E 159/58, rot. 14d. (Richard de Burgh, earl of Ulster, and Nicholas de Segrave); E 159/59, rot. 8d. (John de Columbariis); E 159/60, rot. 12d., E 368/60, rot. 10d. (Robert Morteyn, Robert de Warlingeham); E 159/32, rot. 17; E 159/60, rot. 20 (Robert Tateshale, lord of Bocham in Norfolk); C 54/102, m. 7d.; E 159/61, rot. 17, 62, rot. 16d.; E 159/64, rot. 25d., E 368/62, rot. 29 (Robert Bozon of the Peak); E 159/63, rot. 26d. (John de Mohaut); E 159/65, rot. 33, E 368/63, rot. 26d. (John fitz Thomas); E 159/74, rot. 41d. (Robert Ughtred). *Advance Contracts*, nos. 2, 63, 77, 79, 85, 88, 97, 105, 113, 120, 134, 140, 165. The wool production of Isabella, countess of Forz in Holderness, one of the largest lay estates in England, does not appear in the body of contracts we have identified, though both Lloyd and Denholm-Young have mined documentary evidence to build up a comprehensive picture of developments there: Lloyd, 'Movement of Wool Prices', pp. 37–9; Denholm-Young, *Seigneurial Administration*, pp. 53–5.

[153] Both the 1294 schedules and Pegolotti's list highlight the merchants' connections with religious houses in Scotland and Wales, as well as their wool supply from Ireland: E101/126/7, mm. 13, 18; *Advance Contracts*, nos. 205, 209; *La Pratica Della Mercatura*, pp. 259, 261.

[154] A contract involving the Benedictine priory of Tickford near Newport Pagnell in Buckinghamshire describes locks as strands which fall from the sheep prior to shearing: E 159/66, rot. 48; E 368/64, rot. 41. *Advance Contracts*, no. 146.

arbitrarily as representing 'the average county product'.[155] In turn, middle-grade wool was usually priced at 12.5 per cent–25 per cent more than locks. On a nationwide level, throughout the Middle Ages wool from the Welsh Marches, the Cotswolds and Lincolnshire generally were clearly of higher quality than, for example, East Anglian or Downlands wool, as they regularly top price indices.[156]

Medieval wool was almost exclusively of a shorter staple in contrast to modern sheep. Most of the wool sold came from ewes. Indeed, shortly after Michaelmas 1279, seven merchants of Banbury in Oxfordshire were attached to answer the Riccardi specifically for five sacks of good ewes' wool.[157] Occasionally, lambswool was sold at a lower price, though the examples identified all concern Reginald Maniword and Herefordshire lambswool.[158] Wool was also prone to relatively rapid deterioration and was generally sold within few weeks of the clip in early summer. In 1303, in response to a complaint from Coppus Cotenne and his fellows of the company of the Frescobaldi that the former prioress of Arden in the North Riding had reneged three years into a ten-year contract to deliver the entire annual crop of her nunnery, the present prioress responded that they had, indeed, delivered as promised, but the merchants had failed to appear to dress the wool, whereby the wool had to be stored until it deteriorated beyond use.[159]

Somewhere in the range of 260[160] fleeces were generally packaged either whole or dressed into sacks weighing 26 stone, each stone consisting of 14 lb (364 lb in total). Two sacks would then be packaged into large hessian sarplers for carriage to the delivery point on horse-drawn carts. This general standard, however, conceals an enormous variety of local weights and measures which militates against conclusive assessment of pricing across the country. The custom in Banbury, for example, was for sacks to contain 26 stones of wool, each stone weighing 12 lb.[161] At Hinckley in Leicestershire, the standard was 28 stones.[162] On Norman Darcy's lands in Lindsey (Lincs), the sack consisted of 30 stones.[163] Overall, the range

---

[155] Donkin, 'Cistercian Sheep-Farming and Wool Sales in the Thirteenth Century', p. 2.

[156] Lloyd, 'Movement of Wool Prices', pp. 70–1; Power, *The Wool Trade in English Medieval History*, p. 23.

[157] E 13/8, m. 3d.: '*lana matricia*'. *Advance Contracts*, no. 33.

[158] E 159/37, rot. 8; E 159/57, rot 13, E 368/57, rot. 12d.; E 159/60, rot. 20d.; E 159/61, rot. 13. *Advance Contracts*, nos. 9, 74, 98, 102.

[159] E 13/26, m. 23. *Advance Contracts*, no. 171.

[160] This is the figure agreed upon by Peter de Mundenard and Wroxton priory in February 1280: E 13/8, m. 15d. *Advance Contracts*, no. 44.

[161] E 159/53, rot. 12d., E 368/53, rot. 14. *Advance Contracts*, no. 41.

[162] E 159/54, rot. 12d.; E 368/54, rot. 12. *Advance Contracts*, no. 53.

[163] E 159/55, rot. 10. *Advance Contracts*, no. 63.

identified in the contracts examined stretches from 24 stones per sack, at 14 lb per stone, for the *collecta* wool of Newbury, to the 42 stones at 13lb to the sack for Irish 'great sacks' to be delivered in the contract arranged by the earl of Ulster and Nicholas Segrave.[164] Such regional variety meant that wool was always susceptible to fraudulent weighing. In May 1291, Edward I prosecuted John de Britannia, earl of Richmond and lord of the town of Boston. It appeared that, contrary to the statute to the effect that sacks of wool should contain 28 stones of wool, numerous merchants had been permitted to add 3–4 stones to each sack upon submission for weighing at John's tron in the town, the fraudulent sacks being substituted by those adhering to the regulation in the hands of John de Gisors, the keeper of the tron. John had thus appropriated to himself the half-mark custom due on each sack. John replied that this was not the case, but that merchants had complained to him that they were being unnecessarily delayed in dispatching wool overseas, wherefore he had allowed them to pass to another tron entirely without taking custom.[165]

Dressing the wool

A large number of contracts lay out precise guidelines for the dressing and preparation of wool, which have become standardised in a clause most often reading that wool is to be delivered 'free from cot, gard, black or grey wool, scab, and all manner of coarse fibres'.[166] 'Cot' can be described as clotted or matted-together wool and 'gard' as wool from the animal's legs. Further poorer-quality elements of a fleece, such as 'clack', were also frequently to be omitted from delivery. Moreover, merchants often requested that wool arrive washed, fully cleansed and dried, dressed and faithfully weighed before being packed into sacks and sarplers. An improvement in the methods of sorting, preparing and delivering wool was clearly in all merchants' interests, so much so that a handful of contracts actually dictate that the monks were to entertain the merchants' dresser, who was then to attend to preparing wool unsupervised and that the merchants were to be given unfettered access to his work. In 1280, for example, two of the Riccardi's dressers were to be sent to Meaux, while two years earlier Thomas de Basing insisted that the defaulting monks of Flaxley entertain his dresser and adhere to his demands in preparing the

---

[164] E 159/58, rot. 14d. *Advance Contracts*, no. 77.   [165] E 13/16, m. 7d.

[166] '*sine coch, garth, nigra, grisa, scabie et omni vili vellere*'. This is the case in about 60 contracts, just under one third of the total.

wool he had contracted to buy.[167] It was important to get wool preparation right, for as the 1294 Exchequer Schedules show, dressing expenses could be considerable. At Garendon in Leicestershire, for example, dressing cost the Frescobaldi 43s per year.[168]

Collecta

An emphasis on improved standards might be said to relate to the proliferation, and necessity of producing, wool not emanating directly from the monastic estate, but from surrounding farmers and tenants. Some merchants were evidently concerned enough about the standard of the product they would receive that they stressed the wool should only come from the pastures of the monastic estate from which they had purchased. The Augustinian priory of Thetford in Norfolk, for example, had to find 59 sacks of wool between 1282 and 1291 for the Pulci-Rembertini from the pastures of the new market of Thetford. Interestingly, the wool was to be washed in *aqua dulce*.[169] Master William de Bosco, in fulfilling a contract entered into by his father with Peregrino de Chartres, a Lucchese merchant, had to provide his sack from his own sheep on the manor of Thorp Arnold.[170] Nevertheless, to judge from the relatively large number of contracts for *collecta* – wool drawn from sources outside the monastic environment which were gathered and prepared along the same lines as monastic produce ready for joint dispatch to the merchants – most Italians at least were generally content to accept such wool.[171]

This should perhaps not be greeted with a great deal of surprise. In his treatise on the art of mercery, Francesco Balducci Pegolotti runs through the regions from which *collecta* can be purchased, all of which are in Yorkshire and the East Midlands.[172] Both in the treatise and in a number of the contracts thus far identified, *collecta* is regularly priced above middle-grade wool and should perhaps be seen as the true middle-grade. Pegolotti's northern *collecta* averages out at about 12 marks per sack, which compares favourably with other values paid throughout the period. The abbot of Byland contracted in 1299 to provide the Frescobaldi with 161

---

[167] E 159/53, rot. 12d., E 368/53, rot. 14 (Meaux); E 159/51, rot. 20d., E 368/51, rot. 13d. and schedule (Flaxley). *Advance Contracts*, nos. 42, 23.

[168] E 101/126/7, m. 21. *Advance Contracts*, no. 212.

[169] E 159/55, rot. 14, E 368/55, rot. 13d. *Advance Contracts*, no. 66.

[170] E 13/17, m. 16d. *Advance Contracts*, no. 139.

[171] There are thirty-two contracts which involve *collecta* within the data we have collected.

[172] *La Pratica Della Mercatura*, p. 259.

sacks of good wool priced at 12 marks, 42 sacks of middling and locks valued at 8 marks and 7 marks respectively, and 42 sacks of *collecta* worth 10 marks per sack.[173] The monks of Fountains who contracted with Florentine merchants in 1276 received 11¼ marks per sack of *collecta*. In 1294 and in Pegolotti, the abbey's middle-grade wool was valued at only 10 marks and 12 marks respectively.[174] This certainly implies that lay producers could deliver a reasonably high-quality product and that merchants trusted monks to prepare it to a high standard.

Indeed, both in the case of this Fountains contract for 62 sacks and that of Meaux for 53 sacks, the merchants proved themselves to have considerable confidence in the monks' capacity to deliver huge amounts of wool. In 1280, the monks of Meaux made two sizeable contracts, one with the Cerchi for 90 sacks of good wool and the other with the Riccardi for 53 sacks of *collecta*. This does not, however, imply that the Cerchi had muscled their Lucchese rivals out of the market for the highest-quality product, for the Riccardi valued the *collecta* at 12½ marks per sack, while the Cerchi valued good wool at 10 marks each.[175] This potentially stemmed from the fact that the good wool of the abbey came from the marshlands nearer the Humber estuary, while the *collecta* was to be drawn from upland areas further north up the Yorkshire coast, where pastures may have been more abundant and richer. Enormous contracts, such as that made with Rievaulx abbey by the Mozzi in 1286 for 168 sacks, moreover, could at times of distress and disease hardly have been made up from the depleted flocks of the monastic estate.[176] Merchants were willing to take lesser-grade wool, but appeared to have wanted still to secure the best quality available and have it treated in a professional manner. This attitude may explain the clause in John Wermond's contract with Darnhall, which induced the monks to dress the 12 sacks of *collecta* that they had promised to deliver in the manner of Abbey Dore, another Cistercian foundation in nearby Herefordshire.[177]

The high value given to *collecta* of Yorkshire and the East Midlands, however, may not have been a purely northern phenomenon. Although the monks of Lewes priory in Sussex never received more than 6 marks per sack

[173] E 159/72, rot. 45d. *Advance Contracts*, no. 157.
[174] C 54/93, m. 3d. *Advance Contracts*, no. 19. There is some controversy surrounding the date of the treatise of Pegolotti. Lloyd suggests that the compilation was produced from documents dated 1318–1321, whilst Munro argues that it is more likely to have been compiled from documents of 1280s–1290s. See Munro, 'Wool Price Schedules and the Qualities of English Wools'.
[175] E 159/53, rot. 12d., E 368/53, rot. 14. *Advance Contracts*, nos. 42, 43.
[176] E 159/59, rot. 9d., E 368/59, rot. 19d. *Advance Contracts*, no. 86.
[177] C 54/92, m. 2d. *Advance Contracts*, no. 13.

for their wool, which was clearly of a lesser-grade Downland variety,[178] across Buckinghamshire, Bedfordshire and Oxfordshire, one of the hot-beds for the purchase of *collecta*, prices were generally similar to those in the North.[179] The 12 marks per sack rate that Reginald de Molin and his fellows were willing to pay for 21 sacks of Biddlesden *collecta* in 1276 was not exceptional.[180] In 1290, Biddlesden again contracted to deliver 4 sacks of *collecta* valued likewise at 12 marks per sack.[181] Four years earlier, John de Columbariis had agreed to deliver 10 sacks from the good *collecta* of Newbury in Berkshire to the Riccardi at 10 marks per sack.[182]

One consideration which, however, it might pay to bear in mind is that the merchants might have factored greater transport costs into payment for *collecta* wool, as on occasions, the geographical extent of the area from which it might be drawn was truly enormous. The 1280 contract of the Riccardi with Meaux precisely sets out that the wool is to be gathered from 'the *collecta* of Holderness in the areas between Bridlington and Kirkham and York',[183] an area of several hundred square miles. Moreover, several con-tracts, though by no means a majority, explicitly factor in the costs of transport from producer to port or a pre-arranged place of delivery, which are to be laid squarely upon the monks. As part of the deals brokered with Flaxley abbey, Thomas de Basinges arranged for the carriage of the con-tracted wool from the abbey at the monks' costs to his chambers in London.[184] This cannot have been an inexpensive undertaking. At times of more general local, regional or even national disturbance, this must have been an especially dangerous charge upon the monks. John Wermond of Cambrai contracted with the monks of Darnhall that the wool they had been able to gather should first be taken to Hereford for dressing and then 'at their own perils' to the chambers of his attorney, Giles de Ayre, in London, 'which shall include perils of war or of other similar disturbance of the peace'.[185] Carriage charges might also include extraneous local increments, such as the wharvage which the monks of St Swithun's, Winchester were forced to pay

[178] E 159/61, rot. 14. *Advance Contracts*, no. 104.
[179] E 13/8, m. 3d.; E 159/53, m. 12d., E 368/53, rot. 14 (Banbury); E 13/14, m. 16d. (Biddlesden); E 159/60, rot. 15, E368/60, rot. 13d. (Dunstable); E 159/81, rot. 60d. (Lambourn and Aldbourne); E 159/59, rot. 8d. (Newbury). *Advance Contracts*, nos. 33, 41, 85, 91, 126, 181.
[180] E 13/4, m. 8–8d. *Advance Contracts*, no. 17.   [181] E 13/14, m. 16d. *Advance Contracts*, no. 126.
[182] E 159/59, rot. 8d. *Advance Contracts*, no. 85.
[183] '*de collecta de Holderness' versus Bridelington' et versus Kirkham usque ad Eboracum*'. E 159/53, rot. 12d., E 368/53, rot. 14. *Advance Contracts*, no. 14.
[184] E 159/51, rot. 20d., E 368/51, rot. 13d. and schedule; E 159/55, rot. 6. *Advance Contracts*, nos. 23, 64.
[185] C 54/92, m. 2d.: '*les avantdiz abbe e convent serront carier lavantdite leine en la cite de Londres sor lor custages propres e a lour perils e a lor aventures, quele aventure ke seit de guerre ou dautre disturbance*'. *Advance Contracts*, no. 13.

when delivering wool to the king in 1294.[186] Overall, though, merchants were keen to put the charges of carriage, which appear to have been set in the contracts at around 10 shillings, upon monastic producers, for they enjoyed freedom from a myriad of tolls across the country.[187] Indeed, William Servat of Cahors was disturbed to find he was being charged toll to pass with a shipload of wool through the lands of the abbot of Selby in Yorkshire, for he should have been exempt as a citizen of London.[188]

Delivery and distribution

Whoever paid the costs of carriage, ultimately the finished, packaged sacks and sarplers of wool had to be delivered, from the merchants' point of view, to the most convenient location either for shipping direct to continental markets, or for onward journey from a local collection point to the nearest port. Of the identified contracts, seventy-two specify a place for delivery. Of these, only seven require delivery within the monastic or lay estate.[189] This stands in stark contrast to the details provided by the submissions of the Italian merchants in 1294, where the overwhelming majority of producers are to deliver their product within the monastic precinct, presumably for inspection prior to collection by the merchants' agents on their tour round the country.[190]

Wool gathered in this way almost certainly found its way to one of several leading regional wool distribution centres throughout England, and it is evidence of these which the majority of these 72 contracts most readily provide. The North of England appears to have been served by two centres at York and Clifton, a suburb of York lying on the Ouse, making for easy

---

[186] E 159/69, rot. 62. *Advance Contracts*, no. 153.

[187] E 13/4, m. 8 (Biddlesden); E 159/66, rot. 44, E 368/64, rot. 36 (Vaudey). *Advance Contracts*, nos. 17, 145.

[188] E 159/87, rot. 70. *Advance Contracts*, no. 192.

[189] E 159/53, rot. 9, E 368/53, rot. 10 (Swineshead); E 368/53, rot. 14d. (Pontefract); E 159/59, rot. 8d. (Newbury); E 159/61, rot. 12d., 62, rot. 14. (Thorpe Arnold); E 159/60, rot. 20 (Wells, Norfolk); E 159/87, rot. 70 (Pipewell). *Advance Contracts*, nos. 36, 46, 85, 97, 101, 108, 192.

[190] E101/126/7, mm. 13–28. *Advance Contracts*, nos. 204–216. Those houses concerned are: Beaulieu (Hants.); Bolton in Craven (Yorks.); Bullington (Lincs.); Burton (Staffs.); Clattercote (Oxon.); Drax (Yorks.); Ellerton (Yorks.); Eynsham (Oxon.); Grimsby (Lincs.); Halton (Lincs.); Hampole (Yorks.); Haverholme (Lincs.); Holy Sepulchre, Lincoln (Lincs.); Humberstone (Lincs.); Kingswood (Wilts.); Kirkstead (Lincs.); Marrick (Yorks.); Marton (Lincs.); Merevale (Warks.); Newburgh (Yorks.); Newnham (Herefords); Newstead-on-Ancholme (Lincs.); North Ferriby (Yorks.); North Ormsby (Lincs.); Nostell (Yorks.); Quarr (IOW); Repton (Derbys.); Revesby (Lincs.); Sempringham (Lincs.); Sixhills (Lincs.); St Leonard's Hospital, York (Yorks.); St Osith (Essex); Stixwould (Lincs.); Stratford (Essex); Sulby (Northants.); Swineshead (Lincs.); Thame (Oxon.); Thetford (Norfolk); Tintern (Wales); Tupholme (Lincs.); Wykeham (Yorks.).

river transport to the Humber estuary. Wool from both the North and West Ridings of Yorkshire was to be dispatched there, but also, as the 1294 schedules demonstrate, wool from across northwest England. The monks of Rievaulx made particular use of York, where, indeed, the abbot had lodgings and could perhaps supervise delivery.[191] John de Bulmere was also to deliver his contracted 7 sacks to the Riccardi there in July 1290, as was Robert Ughtred with his 6 sacks to the Frescobaldi in 1301.[192] In 1294, the brethren of York's own St Leonard's Hospital, nearby Jervaulx, Easby, Marrick and Ryland, were to make deliveries at York, along with the more distant Cumberland house of Calder in Coupland and from Lancashire, Cartmel and Furness.[193] Clifton may have been employed by some merchants to escape municipal tolls, although it was probably a more convenient place for delivery as in three of the four contracts in which it is named as the place for delivery the monks of Fountains are the producers.[194] The only other occasion comes in 1299, when the monks of Byland contract to deliver their produce there.[195] A handful of contracts dealing exclusively with the nearby Cistercian abbey of Meaux stipulate delivery in the town of Hull itself.[196] In 1294, only the Yorkshire nunnery of Swine contracted to deliver wool directly in Hull itself, although the nearby houses of Coverham and the Augustinian priory at Bridlington were to carry their produce to Hull Bridge, a point crossing the River Hull a few miles north of Hull between the town and Beverley, a convenient place for loading wool onto barges for transport to port.[197] In the same year, the monks of Coverham contracted with the Frescobaldi to deliver wool at Boroughbridge east of York.[198] Further north, travel even to York might have overstretched the resources of the Cumberland abbey of Holmcultram and the Northumberland Cistercian abbey of Newminster and they were consequently to deliver their wool at Newcastle.[199]

Elsewhere, other regional centres equally flourished. In East Anglia, King's Lynn, lying in the mouth of the Wash opposite Boston, was the

[191] E 159/59, rot. 9d., E 368/59, rot. 19d.; E 159/60, rot. 16d., E 368/60, 14d.; E 159/61, rot. 11d. *Advance Contracts*, nos. 86, 92, 99.

[192] E 159/63, rot. 21, E 368/61, rot. 26; E 159/74, rot. 41d. *Advance Contracts*, nos. 117, 165.

[193] E 101/126/7, mm. 14, 16, 18, 20, 23, 24, 25. *Advance Contracts*, nos. 206, 207, 209, 210, 214, 215, 216.

[194] C 54/93, m. 3d.; E 159/52, rot. 13, E 368/52, rot. 12d; E 159/60, rot. 16d., E 368/60, rot. 14d. *Advance Contracts*, nos. 19, 26, 93.

[195] E 159/72, rot. 45d. *Advance Contracts*, no. 157.

[196] E 159/53, rot. 12d. E 368/53, rot. 12; E 159/60, rot. 18; 61, rot. 14; 62, rot. 15. *Advance Contracts*, nos. 42, 43, 95, 103, 109.

[197] E 101/126/7, mm. 12, 17, 25. *Advance Contracts*, nos. 205, 208, 216.

[198] E 101/126/7, m. 16. *Advance Contracts*, no. 207.

[199] E101/126/7, mm. 14, 16. *Advance Contracts*, nos. 206, 207.

obvious location to send wool. The priors of Westacre, Coxford and Shouldham in Norfolk all agreed to send their wool there.[200] To the south of the region, however, Stratford in Essex, lying close to the Thames estuary, not only attracted the wool of the local abbey, but also that of Coggeshall and Tilty in Essex.[201] Principally though, the south of England appears to have been mainly geared around the port of London, while for the abbots of Ford in Dorset and of Hyde and Netley in Hampshire, it must have seemed eminently more sensible to deliver their contracts with the Riccardi respectively in 1293/4 at Southampton,[202] or for the Surrey Cistercian abbey of Waverley to carry their wool the short distance to Kingston-upon-Thames.[203] Many religious houses in the south and east of England, including the Home Counties, delivered to the merchants in London.[204] Nine contracts surviving on the Memoranda Rolls, relating to the Cistercian abbeys of Biddlesden, Darnhall (Cheshire), Flaxley (Gloucs.) and Tilty, the Benedictine house of Tickford (Bucks.), Roger le Bret of Sopwere and Robert le Blund of Lacock in Wiltshire, Reginald Maniword of Hereford, Jordan de Kendal of the Chilterns and William Wantyng of Berkshire, require delivery in the capital.[205] The Upper Thames also appears to have been employed as a direct conduit to London. In 1294, Bruern abbey in the Cotswolds was to send its wool to Henley, possibly for further river carriage onwards to London.[206]

Most prominent of all, however, is the port of Boston in Lincolnshire, which is set out as the place for delivery in no less than 24 surviving contracts.[207] Not only did merchants gather wool from the surrounding

---

[200] E 368/53, rot. 12d.; E 159/60, rot. 17d.; E101/126/7, m. 17. *Advance Contracts*, nos. 38, 94, 208.

[201] E 368/53, rot. 13 (Tilty); E101/126/7, m. 16 (Coggeshall). *Advance Contracts*, nos. 45, 207.

[202] E 159/66, rot. 43, E 368/64, rot. 35 (Ford); E 101/126/7, m. 15 (Netley), 25 (Hyde). *Advance Contracts*, nos. 143, 207, 216.

[203] E 101/126/7, m. 21. *Advance Contracts*, no. 212.

[204] In 1294, for example, the Sussex abbeys of Bayham and Robertsbridge, the Bedfordshire abbey of Wardon, the Essex abbeys of Waltham and Tilty and the Buckinghamshire abbey of Tickford were to deliver wool to London: E 101/126/7, mm. 13, 17 (Waltham), 18 (Warden), 25 (Bayham, Robertsbridge). *Advance Contracts*, nos. 205, 208, 209, 216.

[205] C 54/92, m. 2d. (Darnhall); E 159/51, rot. 20d., E 368/51, rot. 13d. and schedule (Flaxley); E 159/52, rot. 12, E 368/52, rot. 11d. (Lacock); E 368/53, rot. 13 (Tilty); E 159/55, rot. 6 (Flaxley); E 159/57, rot. 13, E 368/57, rot. 12d.; E 159/60, rot. 20d. (Maniward); E 159/58, rot. 13 (Biddlesden); E 159/60, rot. 15, E 368/60, rot. 13d. (Kendal); E 159/66, rot. 48, E 368/64, rot. 41 (Newport Pagnell); E 159/81, rot. 60d (Wantyng). *Advance Contracts*, nos. 13, 23, 25, 45, 64, 74, 75, 91, 98, 146, 181.

[206] E 101/126/7, m. 16. *Advance Contracts*, 207.

[207] E 159/32, rot. 17; E 159/60, rot. 20 (Robert de Tateshale, Lincolnshire); E 159/33, rot. 2d. (Stephen de Chaendut, Northamptonshire); E 159/33, rot. 5; 34, rots. 1d., 2 (John de Burgh and William Blunt, Derbyshire); E 159/52, rot. 15, E 368/52, rot. 15 (Combermere, Cheshire); E 13/8, m. 9d. (Juliana le Bretun, Chipping Norton); E 159/54, rot. 11d., E 368/54, rot. 11 (Stone, Staffordshire); E 159/55, rot. 9, E 368/55, rot. 8 (Roger de Toftes, Norfolk); E 13/10, m. 2 (Humberston,

area, they induced producers to deliver at Boston across vast distances. The bulk of deliveries in 1294 came from the East Midlands and it might be considered probable that most of the wool stipulated for collection within the monastic precincts of this area in this year would also have found its way by means of the rivers Welland and Witham, which flow into the Wash at Boston. Certainly for the monks of Garendon and Our Lady of Leicester, carriage perhaps as far as Spalding, where the Welland was navigable, might have saved a rather longer journey than the relatively short distance they would actually have had to cover. The same would be true for the monks of Pipewell in Northamptonshire; all of the four contracts arranged by the Cahorsin merchants stipulated delivery at Boston. The lengths to which some monks would have to go to make delivery really make Boston's pre-eminence very clear. Most of the Welsh or marcher abbeys with whom contracts had been arranged in 1294 were to deliver their wool to Boston.[208] The surviving contracts with Combermere all stipulate delivery at Boston. This is not surprising, for Boston, as T. H. Lloyd has demonstrated, led the way in exporting wool from England in the late-thirteenth and early fourteenth centuries and was *the* magnet for wool throughout the period.[209]

One of the principal reasons for this must undoubtedly have been the fair of St Botulph held each year between the feasts of St Botulph (11 June) and St Bartholomew (24 August). Although only one contract specifically dictates delivery at the Boston fair, the dates at which other deliveries were due strongly suggests that merchants made extensive use of the means of exchange which the fair provided.[210] The overwhelming majority of all contracts ask for delivery within the period between the feast of St Botulph and the gule of August, the first day of that month. More specifically, the wool-trading year, dictated as it was by the early-summer shearing season,

---

Lincolnshire); E 159/59, rot. 12d. (Lewes, Sussex); E 159/61, rot. 19 (Roger de Huntingefeld, Lincolnshire); E 327/541; E 159/62, rot. 4; C 54/108, mm. 8d–9d, E 159/64, rot. 10, E 368/62, rot. 14; E 159/87, rot. 70 (Pipewell, Northamptonshire); E 159/62, rot. 17d. (Roger de Genny, Lincolnshire); E 159/64, rot. 25d., E 368/62, rot. 29 (Roger Bozon of High Peak); E 159/66, rot. 44, E 368/64, rot. 36 (Vaudey, Lincolnshire); E 13/27, m. 69 (Sawtry, Cambridgeshire and Huntingdonshire); E 210/7015 (Thomas of Langar and Henry of Pluckley). *Advance Contracts*, nos. 2, 3, 4, 5, 6, 7, 28, 35, 51, 61, 67, 87, 97, 106, 110, 114, 133, 134, 145, 156, 174, 192, 221, 222.

[208] The English houses who are to deliver to Boston in 1294 are: Dale (Derbyshire); Sawtry (Huntingdonshire); Alvingham; Bardney; Barlings; Crowland; Revesby; South Kyme; Spalding (Lincolnshire); Kenilworth (Warwickshire); Guisborough (Yorkshire). The Welsh houses include Basingwerk in Flintshire, Combermere, Dieulacres, Hulton and Stanlaw in Cheshire, St Werburgh's in Chester itself, Rocester and Darley in the High Peak and Croxden in Staffordshire: E 101/126/7, mm. 14–24. *Advance Contracts*, nos. 206–215.

[209] Lloyd, *English Wool Trade*, p. 64.

[210] E 159/72, rot. 45. *Advance Contracts*, no. 156.

appears to have been geared to midsummer and its aftermath, for by far the most common date for delivery is the quindene of the Nativity of St John the Baptist on 8–9 July each year. Merchants almost certainly used the opportunities provided by the summer fairs to receive delivery of wools and bargain for the next year's crop. This is further evidenced in that another four contracts stipulate delivery at or during fairs. Godfrey, prior of Pontefract, contracted to deliver 80 sacks over eight years to Giacomo Fronte and his fellows of Florence at the Stamford fair each year. Whether the wool would then be taken to Boston for export can only be speculated upon.[211] Thomas Luard, vicar of Wellington in Shropshire, sold his wool to Richard Borrey of Shrewsbury at the most convenient local exchange for both parties, the Shrewsbury fair.[212] Four Northampton burgesses contracted to deliver 6 sacks to Baroncino Gualteri in 1279 at the next upcoming fairs of Stamford and St Ives (Hunts).[213] In the Hilary term of 1280, moreover, four Banbury burgesses arranged to deliver 4¼ sacks to Baroncino at the Northampton fair.[214]

The English wool trade at a local level

There can be little doubt that the English wool trade was highly localized. In their search for the best quality wool available in the largest quantity, continental merchants scoured almost every county of England, penetrating deep into wool-producing societies. They certainly knew who to deal with and who had the best produce, as the treatise of Francesco Balducci Pegolotti shows in abundance. Of contracts which can positively be identified by county, clear areas of intense regional and local activity emerge. The East Midlands, represented in the contracts by Leicestershire (including Rutland), Warwickshire and Northamptonshire, with fourteen, twelve and nine respectively, was a region of some importance. Evidence for sales to the Riccardi in the towns of Leicester, Coventry, Hinckley, Warwick and Northampton stands side by side with contracts sealed with parties from more rural areas, notably Skeffington, Thorpe Arnold and Pipewell abbey.[215] The area itself, being in the heart of England close to the urban manufacturing centres of Nottingham and Lincoln and within easy reach

---

[211] E 368/53, rot. 14d. *Advance Contracts*, no. 46.
[212] E 159/56, rot. 4; E 368/56, rot. 4. *Advance Contracts*, no. 69.
[213] E 13/8, m. 9d. *Advance Contracts*, no. 34.
[214] E 159/53, rot. 12d.; E 368/53, rot. 14. *Advance Contracts*, no. 41.
[215] E 13/8, mm. 1d., 28 (Coventry); E 13/8, mm. 1d., 21 (Leicester); E 159/54, rot. 12d, E 368/54, rot. 12 (Hinckley); E 159/54, rot. 18, E 368/54, rot. 16 (Warwick); E 13/8, m. 9d., 9, m. 7 (Northampton);

of Boston, lent itself to the merchants' purposes. When it is combined with the seventeen contracts emanating from Nottinghamshire and Derbyshire, it is clear that the area must have made a real contribution to merchants' profits.

Slightly further south in a corridor fringed by the Trent and Thames to the West and Ermine Street to the East, the wools of the Chilterns and uplands of Buckinghamshire, Bedfordshire, Oxfordshire and Berkshire were equally sought after. Oxfordshire itself appears in thirteen contracts. Banbury, Dunstable and Baldock can be shown to have been centres of considerable importance for merchants radiating out from London, while the Cistercian abbeys of Biddlesden, Thame and Wardon and the priory of Wroxton make a striking number of appearances, perhaps suggesting that the supply of wool from this region was not the most forthcoming.[216] Further south, both Hampshire towns of Winchester and Andover occur on a handful of occasions, perhaps implying the area's wool was of a lesser grade, or that perhaps it was a touch more insular. This is doubtful as quite a number of Andover merchants had goods arrested in Flanders in 1274.[217] As with York, it may have been a local collection centre for wools coming in from further afield. One striking contract sealed in 1287–8 by Reginald Maniward with the Riccardi for 5 sacks of Marcher lambswool stipulates delivery in the city.[218] In the first of their surviving contracts with the Riccardi, moreover, the cathedral priory of St Swithun's, Winchester commits to delivering 240 sacks over six years at the Barton outside the city. Perhaps as with Clifton, this was to circumvent municipal taxes.[219]

Yorkshire vs. Lincolnshire

Without doubt, however, the two main regions of England which are dealt with predominantly in the surviving body of contract material are the three ridings of Yorkshire with a total of forty-three contracts – four cannot be

---

E 159/54, rot. 19, E 368/54, rot. 17d.; E 159/54 rot. 20 (Skeffington); E 159/62, rot. 14 (Thorpe Arnold); C 54/108, mm. 8d.–9d.; E 327/541, E 159/62, rot. 4, 64, rot. 10, 87, rot. 70, E 368/62, rot. 14 (Pipewell). *Advance Contracts*, nos. 31, 34, 49, 50, 55, 57, 58, 62, 108, 110, 133, 192, 221.

[216] See, for example: E 13/8, m. 3d. (Banbury); E 13/4, m. 8d., 14, m. 8d. (Baldock, Dunstable, Warden); E 159/58, rot. 13 (Biddlesden); E 13/5, m. 2 (Thame); E 13/8, mm. 11, 15d., E 159/45, rot. 18, E 368/44, rot. 11d; E 159/60, rot. 13d. E 368/60, rot. 11d. (Wroxton). *Advance Contracts*, nos. 12, 17, 18, 33, 39, 44, 75, 90, 123.

[217] E 163/5/17. For Winchester, see E 159/58, rot. 16, E 368/58, rot. 19; E 159/59, rot. 4 and schedule; E 159/64, rot. 22d., E 368/62, rot. 27. *Advance Contracts*, nos. 78, 82, 122.

[218] E 159/61, rot. 13. *Advance Contracts*, no. 102.

[219] E159/58, m. 16. *Advance Contracts*, no. 78.

ascribed to a particular riding, eleven to the East Riding, seventeen to the North and eleven to the East – and Lincolnshire with a total of 42 contracts – the county itself, with no specification of area, accounts for six contracts, Lindsey for seventeen, Holland for six and Kesteven for thirteen. Yorkshire has long been the principal focus of scholarly research historically and archaeologically. Half a century ago, Denholm-Young examined the Holderness wool trade in connection with the seigneurial activities of the counts of Aumale in the East Riding.[220] More recently, B. Waites and E. Jamroziak have assessed the interplay of monk and merchant in the wool trade of North and East Yorkshire.[221] C. Platt also focused on the county in his examination of the grange in medieval England.[222] Lincolnshire, whose produce was among the most highly prized and priced of medieval wools,[223] has, somewhat perversely, been largely neglected by scholars despite the relative wealth of information available.[224]

Boston in Holland has long been recognised as England's chief wool-exporting port and the county itself one of the most important medieval wool-producing areas. From 1275 onwards, Boston handled over 9,500 sacks a year compared to London's 7,000, Hull's 3,400 and Lynn's 1,350.[225] Much of the Italian export flowed through the port, which ultimately served as the hub for much of the county's wool traffic. Cargoes could flow to Boston along the River Welland from Spalding, bringing the wool-producing religious houses of Crowland and Vaudey, Spalding and Sempringham into its immediate catchment area. Navigable from Spalding to the Wash, the Welland probably also dealt with traffic from the hinterland of Kesteven and the towns of Grantham and Stamford, as well as from Melton, Rutland and further inland. Three contracts survive concerning Grantham's participation in the trade, while Stamford fair presumably proved a draw to much of the wool traffic of the East Midlands, as it lies close to Ermine Street from Lincoln to London. Indeed, the Castreton family from Casterton just north of Grantham loom large in the local industry.[226]

[220] Denholm-Young, *Seigneurial Administration*, pp. 53–63.
[221] Waites, 'Monasteries and the Wool Trade in North and East Yorkshire During the 13th and 14th Centuries'; Jamroziak, 'Rievaulx Abbey'.
[222] C. Platt, *The Monastic Grange in Medieval England: A Reassessment.*
[223] See, for example, Lloyd, 'Movement of Wool Prices', pp. 70–71.
[224] J. P. Bischoff did, however, focus on Lincolnshire religious houses, in his assessment of the reliability of Pegolotti's list: Bischoff, 'An Honest Merchant?'
[225] Lloyd, *English Wool Trade*, p. 64.
[226] E 13/8, m. 1d, 12, m. 6; E 210/7015. *Advance Contracts*, nos. 30, 81, 222.

While Boston itself appears to have taken its share of the local wool trade,[227] other towns within the county probably played a larger role in gathering raw materials. Lincoln, the county town, of course, was a major centre for cloth and wool manufacture, although only one contract calling for delivery of wool there has survived.[228] Nevertheless, in 1294, the heads of Beauchief in Derbyshire and Newstead and Mattersey in Nottinghamshire were to deliver their wool to Lincoln.[229] Moreover, the abbot of Rufford in Nottinghamshire was specifically ordered to deliver his wool to Sheepwash, which can perhaps be identified as a hamlet lying between the villages of Washingborough and Heighington, three miles southeast of Lincoln.[230] Whether this too was a tiny wool-processing centre is not easy to say. Both Lincoln and Sheepwash, though, lie on or close to the River Witham, the main arterial river running through the heart of the county, which flows into the Wash at Boston. Along its banks in close proximity lie the houses of Bardney, Barlings, Bullington, Kirkstead, Revesby, South Kyme and Tupholme and it is easy to imagine wool produced by their brethren being shipped by barge to Boston for export.

It is in the north of the county, though, where the bulk of the trade, as attested by the contracts, appears to have taken place. Throughout the Middle Ages, Lindsey wool ranked among the top three grades in terms of quality and price and clearly the Italian merchants were keen to access a reasonable share.[231] The vast majority of Lindsey's religious houses from Alvingham in the far northwest on the Humber estuary to the tiny foundations of North Ormsby and Marton close to the east coast at Skegness appear among the lists compiled by the Italian merchants in 1294. The information provided for the king also throws up a highly significant, very localised example of the wool trade in action. In the northeast of Lindsey, a trio of closely connected religious houses – the Augustinian abbey of Thornton, the Cistercian nunnery of Nun Cotham and the Premonstratensian priory of Newsham – lie within a three-mile radius of each other. All were to deliver their wool, which they owed respectively to the Cerchi Bianchi, the Frescobaldi, the Spini and the

---

[227] In November 1290, for example, a conglomerate of Boston merchants was attached to answer Enrico da Poggio of the Riccardi before the Exchequer Court for 12 sacks of wool and £13 4s 10d: E 13/14, m. 13d. *Advance Contracts*, no. 125.

[228] That of Adam Kokerel and Robert le Venur for six sacks of wool to the Riccardi: E 159/65, rot. 27, E 368/63, rot. 20. *Advance Contracts*, no. 138. For Lincoln's position in the trade see J. F. Hill, *Medieval Lincoln* (Cambridge, 1948).

[229] E 101/126/7, mm. 14, 15, 20. *Advance Contracts*, nos. 206, 207, 211.

[230] E 101/126/7, m. 17. *Advance Contracts*, no. 208.

[231] Lloyd, 'Movement of Wool Prices', pp. 70–1.

Mozzi – no one order appears to have gained, or attempted to gain the upper hand in the Lincolnshire wool trade – at a place described as *Skitermelne* in the waters of the Humber.[232] On closer inspection, this is almost certainly the modern-day Ulceby Skitter, which lies on the Skitter Beck flowing into the Humber north of Grimsby, a village lying exactly in the middle of the triangle made by these three houses. It may well be that the mill had developed into a renowned and trusted wool-processing centre owned by the monks of Thornton, whose skills and storage facilities they were willing to share with other local wool-producing houses.[233]

Further west, the River Ancholme perhaps acted as a conduit for the producers of northwest Lindsey, such as Norman Darcy or John de Reddemere of Appleby, a village lying in close proximity to the river.[234] John, however, in the contract made with his Riccardi patrons in 1280, agreed to deliver 30 sacks of wool produced on his manors to the Riccardi at Kelsey. Regardless of whether this is North or South Kelsey, both villages are a considerable journey from the coast and lie closer to equidistant between Appleby and Lincoln. It is difficult to decipher exactly what interpretation could or should be put on such deals. John may have held land in the area, but perhaps Kelsey was another local centre for the gathering of *collecta*, at least three contracts for which still survive.[235]

An important question which ought to be posed is to what degree qualitative differences in wool are represented in valuations of wool. Unfortunately, very little material survives relating to the price of Lincolnshire wools. What there is tends to demonstrate agreement with the established principle that the county's wool was of superior grade and that every Italian merchant house wished to access as much as possible. In 1279, Elias, abbot of Swineshead near Boston in Holland, garnered 14 marks per sack on a contract to deliver 12 sacks of the abbey's good wool to the Falconieri of Florence.[236] Thirteen years later Adam, abbot of the nearby Cistercian abbey of Vaudey, likewise received 14 marks per sack on a delivery of 10 sacks to the Riccardi.[237] The remaining evidence must,

[232] E 101/126/7, mm. 17, 18, 20, 22, 25. *Advance Contracts*, nos. 208, 209, 211, 213, 216.
[233] If so, this is reminiscent of the contract made between the prioress of the Benedictine nunnery of Arden in the North Riding and the Frescobaldi in 1284, whereby the nuns promised to deliver their wool to Thorpe, a grange of the Cistercian abbey of Byland in the Coxwold-Gilling gap: E 13/26, m. 23. *Advance Contracts*, no. 71.
[234] E 159/55, rot. 10 (Darcy); E 159/53, rot. 13, E 368/53, rot. 15 (Reddemere). *Advanced Contracts*, nos. 63, 48.
[235] E 159/65, rot. 27, E 368/63, rot 20; E159/65, rot. 33d, E 368/63, rot. 26d.; E 159/66, rot. 43d., E 368/64, rot. 35d. *Advance Contracts* nos. 138, 141, 144.
[236] E 159/53, rot. 9, E 368/53, rot. 10. *Advance Contracts*, no. 36.
[237] E 159/66, rot. 44, E 368/64, rot. 36. *Advance Contracts*, no. 145.

however, be taken from the 1294 Exchequer Schedules and the list of English abbeys compiled by Francesco Balducci Pegolotti. Across the county, high prices are laid out for good wool and it does not appear to be a trend that relates solely to one Order or one merchant company. The wools of the low-lying river valleys of mid-Lincolnshire, rather than those of the gently rolling uplands of the Wolds and northwest Lindsey or of the low-lying marshlands of the southeast of the county in Holland and South Kesteven, appear to command the highest values. The Benedictine nunnery of Stainfield in Lindsey leads the way through a contract with the Mozzi where sacks of good wool are worth 21½ marks, a value which rises inexorably to 28 marks – the third-highest amount recorded – in Pegolotti's list.[238]

The Cistercians at Kirkstead, a short distance from Stainfield, received 20½ marks per sack from the Cerchi Bianchi and were valued at 24 marks by Pegolotti.[239] The Premonstratensians at Barlings, moreover, received 20 marks per sack in 1294 from the Cerchi Neri and 24 marks in the 1320s.[240] While not so highly prized, the wools of Kesteven also show high values. The Augustinian priory at South Kyme received 18 marks for its wool from the Bardi in 1294, while the Templar house at Temple Bruer obtained 20 marks.[241] By some way the least valuable wool comes from the northeast of the county on the fringes between the rolling slopes of the northern Wolds and the marshy coastal plain. The Augustinians at Thornton, for example, could only obtain 12½ marks for their good wool in 1294 from the Frescobaldi Bianchi and the Cerchi Bianchi. A few miles to the east, their fellow canons in Grimsby only managed 10 marks per sack from the Mozzi. Perhaps the fact that they had contracted for only 2 sacks made them a less profitable marketer of their produce, a problem that most of their county contemporaries do not appear to have suffered.[242]

Overseas trade

In similar vein to the requirements for a more in-depth examination of the breadth and depth of the local trading links of foreign merchants, the methods by which wool reached its destination overseas are also not greatly elucidated in the surviving body of contract evidence. A document drawn

[238] E 101/126/7, m. 17; *Advance Contracts*, no. 208. *La Pratica Della Mercatura*, p. 265.
[239] E 101/126/7, mm. 20, 22. *Advance Contracts*, nos. 211, 213. *La Pratica Della Mercatura*, p. 260.
[240] E 101/126/7, m. 23. *Advance Contracts*, no. 214. *La Pratica Della Mercatura*, p. 263.
[241] E 101/126/7, m. 24. *Advance Contracts*, no. 215.
[242] E 101/126/7, mm. 17, 22, 25. *Advance Contracts*, nos. 208, 213, 216.

up for Edward I in *c.* 1274 highlights the activities of English and Irish merchants in Bruges, Douai and Tourhout.[243] Merchants of Andover, Dunstable and St Albans, to name but a few, had wool and other goods which they had purchased from the religious houses of Netley, Winchester cathedral priory, Flaxley abbey, Beaulieu abbey and the knights of the Hospital of St John of Jerusalem. Very little else of note has so far been identified, save for an agreement made by Arnold de Soliz of Cahors, whereby he bound himself in the wool he expected to receive from Pipewell abbey to cover debts he had accrued at the fair of Bar.[244] Evidence too survives of the fraudulent concealment and traffic in wool possessed by foreign merchants hoping to escape the king's seizures of 1306–7 caused by the ban on exports during the Anglo-French conflict. Many English customs officials, Edward I had heard, had taken bribes from foreign merchants to release wool belonging to them from impound. Needless to say, this abhorrent practice was to be nipped in the bud before it proliferated too widely.

In October 1276, Giles de Ayre, attorney of Herbert Wermond of Cambrai, appeared before the Chancery Court to press his claim for 14 sacks and 20 stones of wool which he claimed the abbot of Louth Park in Lincolnshire had withheld from him unjustly over the last few years. Although a deal was brokered whereby Giles would pay a further advance for the same amount of wool over renegotiated terms, the difficulty remained that the entire wool crop of the abbey had been sold by the abbot's predecessor for the next four years to Hugelinus Sampy and his fellows of Florence and by the present abbot for the six years after that. The king intervened and ordered the defaulting abbey to ensure that Giles received delivery before any of the others.[245] This may have resulted in further litigation, although none has been found. Six years earlier, the prior of Thornholme in Lincolnshire had agreed to sell 75 sacks of wool to Master William of Louth, who had therefore paid an advance of 950 marks. During the next five years, however, no delivery had been made and, instead, the prior had contracted to sell his produce to other parties presumably at a higher price.[246] In combination with the Exchequer Schedules of 1294, which themselves on occasion highlight the multiplicity of contacts individual religious houses enjoyed with various merchants' companies simultaneously, it is clear that competition for wool was rife and fairly cut-throat in England in the late thirteenth century.

[243] E 163/5/17.   [244] E 159/62, rot. 9d. *Advance Contracts*, no. 112.
[245] C 54/93, m. 18d. *Advance Contracts*, no. 14.   [246] E 13/1E, m. 14d. *Advance Contracts*, no. 11.

Indeed, it is comparatively rare for an institution to enjoy contacts with only one merchant house throughout the entire period of the survey. The Premonstratensian house of Tupholme in Lindsey enjoyed continuity in contacts with the Mozzi, who purchased two contracts in 1284 to endure up to 1290 and 1296 respectively. They are also found receiving the abbey's wool in 1294. The monks of Rocester in the High Peak in Staffordshire similarly sold their wool to the Mozzi from 1288 to 1296.[247] All four surviving contracts concerning the cathedral priory of St Swithun's, Winchester are conducted with the Riccardi of Lucca.[248] Nevertheless, in 1288, a time at which the prior had contracts in operation with the Riccardi, he acknowledged a debt of £163 6s 8d to Ristorio Bonaventure, Simone Gerardi, Chino Bosii and their fellows of the Mozzi of Florence.[249] Unfortunately, there is no wider context provided for this debt and it may have been purely a loan to the monks in a time of hardship rather than one repayable in wool. Both the Cistercian abbey of Tilty in Essex and the Cluniac priory of Pontefract had similarly entered into pecuniary debts with Italian merchants well before any evidence of deals in wool surface.[250] On the other hand, all may have been an attempt to tap a lucrative source of relatively cheap wool and move into a vacuum left by the departure, enforced or otherwise, of other parties.

Several religious houses were clearly courted by a number of factions and probably did their best to encourage greater competition. The Cistercians at Fountains contracted with two or perhaps three factions of Florentine merchants between 1279 and 1296, the Cerchi taking 192 sacks, the Bardi 27 sacks and the Mozzi 79 sacks. By 1291, however, the Riccardi were receiving delivery of 19½ sacks at a reduced rate and by 1294 they were deeply involved in the abbey's wool business.[251] At Newsham in Lindsey, the Premonstratensian canons had contracted to deliver all of their wool to the Mozzi from 1285 to 1296, but in 1294 they are recorded as dealing with the Spini, the Cerchi Bianchi and the Frescobaldi Bianchi.[252] All parties, it would seem, had an eye for the best advantage and were unscrupulous in committing their stocks to several potential buyers to garner as much profit as possible.

---

[247] *Della Decima*, pp. 324–325; E 101/126/7, m. 17. *Advance Contracts*, no. 208.
[248] E 159/58, rot. 16, E 368/58, rot. 19; E 159/59, rot. 4 and schedule; E 159/64, rot. 22d., E 368/62, rot. 27. *Advance Contracts*, nos. 78, 82, 122.
[249] E 13/13, m. 14.   [250] E 13/4, m. 6.
[251] C 54/93, m. 3d.; E 159/52, rot. 13, E 368/52, rot. 12d.; E 159/60, rot. 16d.; E 368/60, 14d.; *Della Decima*, p. 325; E 101/126/7, m. 12. *Advance Contracts*, nos. 19, 26, 93, 205.
[252] *Della Decima*, p. 324; E 101/126/7, mm. 18, 20, 22, 25. *Advance Contracts*, nos. 209, 211, 213, 216.

In three interesting cases, moreover, the Benedictine nunnery of Arden and the Cistercian abbeys of Biddlesden and Combermere appear to have made carefully calculated decisions about the sale of their wool crop, ensuring that there would not be any hiatus in sales. On 24 August 1284, Margaret, prioress of Arden, agreed to provide Coppus Cotteny and the merchants of the Frescobaldi with the entire annual crop of her house, some ten sacks a year. The first date of delivery specified in the contract, however, was the feast of the Nativity of St John the Baptist [24 June] 1291 and further deliveries were to be made each year on the same day up to 1303.[253] The postponement of immediate delivery had likely been due to her agreement to sell her crop to the Mozzi from 1285 to 1290, a contract which had already been arranged by the time Simone Gerardi received it in 1284.[254] Such deals ensured the prioress and her successors would have purchasers for their wool over an extended period. Biddlesden abbey enjoyed similar success in attracting custom. Contracts have survived for the periods 1276–8, 1280, 1284–5, 1285–9 and 1290, meaning a possible hiatus of just five years in this period, although that is rather unlikely.[255] The greatest apparent success in attracting repeated custom, though, should be attributed to the monks at Combermere, who managed to agree contracts covering the entire period from 1279 to 1328.[256] It should, of course, be remembered that they reneged, at least in part, on all of these deals and the persistence and good faith of the Frescobaldi, with whom they dealt, is remarkable. If evidence from the advance contracts for the purchase of wool is concerned, they were not alone.

In summary, this chapter has demonstrated the rich variety of source material available for the study of the English wool market during this period and we have also been able to show that these materials exist in a much larger volume than has previously been appreciated. Both monastic and lay producers represent the growers contracting to sell their wool in advance, but it is clear from the sources that the monastic share of the market eclipsed that of lay farmers. The religious orders contracted to sell just over 4,432 sacks of wool by advance contract, whilst laymen only contracted for 843 sacks, representing just 16 per cent of the total market. The purchasers of the wool are clearly dominated by Italian merchant societies who contract for over 66 per cent of the advance commodity, split

---

[253] E 13/26, m. 23. *Advance Contracts*, no. 171.   [254] *Della Decima*, p. 325.

[255] E 13/4, m. 8–8d., 14, m. 8d.; E159/58, rot. 13; *Della Decima*, p. 324. *Advance Contracts*, nos. 17, 123, 75.

[256] E 159/52, rot. 15, E 368/52, rot. 15; E 159/72, rot. 45; E 159/82, rot. 81. *Advance Contracts*, nos. 28, 156, 182.

mainly between the cities of Florence and Lucca. However, the Italians are not alone in this market and are joined by a cosmopolitan sample of Europe-wide buyers from Spain, France, Flanders and Germany. The advance nature of the contracts benefited both buyer and seller, principally by guaranteeing a regular supply of high-quality wool to the buyer and by bringing liquidity to cash-strapped monasteries. However, it is also the advance nature of the contracts that inevitably led to legal dispute as the contracts ran their course. It follows that these legal disputes provide the basis for the source material that has survived for this innovative market in forward selling. We now turn our attention to one particular abbey to learn how an appetite for continual exposure to this market led to eventual ruin.

CHAPTER 3

Case study – Pipewell Abbey, Northamptonshire

This chapter will focus upon one particular abbey, the Cistercian monastery of Pipewell in Northamptonshire. The period under discussion, the late thirteenth and early fourteenth centuries, appears to be one when monasteries had to deal with systemic indebtedness and murrain which affected the productivity of their flocks. How does the series of forward contracts negotiated and renegotiated between Pipewell and Cahorsin merchants help us understand this troubled period in monastic history? In order to appreciate the importance of the contracts to monastic finance and wider credit relationships, we now focus on an individual, if perhaps extreme, case study.

CRISES OF MONASTIC FINANCE?

'Remember dearest brethren and reverend fathers that by the said recognisances and due to seven years of dearth and common murrain of beasts, the goods of the house of Pipewell had been so exhausted that nothing remained for the meagre sustenance of the monks; sometimes they sat in the refectory for three or four days with only black bread and potage, at other times they wandered from market to market to buy bread, and this they patiently endured. I, the wretch and sinner who have occupied the place of abbot, therefore counsel, ask, implore, and warn in as much as I am able, lest another abbot fall so deeply into the hands of Lombards, that they heed the French maxim *'leger est aprendre mes fort est a rendre'*.[1]

---

[1] 'It is easy to take but hard to give': London, British Library, Stowe MS 937, f. 143v., 'Memorandum fratres carissimi patresque reverendi quod per predictas recogniciones et propter vij annorum sterilitates et per communem morinam bestiarum, bona domus de Pipewell' adeo fuerunt consumpta, que eorum residuum non sufficiebat ad exilem dicte domus monachorum sustentacionem, set aliquando sedebant in refectorio per iii vel iiij dies cum nigro pane et potagio tantum et aliquando emebant panem suum de foro ad forum, et hoc omnia pacienter sustinuerunt. Hinc est quod ego miser et precator qui aliquando occupavi locum abbatis consulo, rogo, supplico, et quatenus possum moneo ne aliquis abbas de cetero ita profunde concidat in manus Lumbaudorum, quia gallice dicitur leger est aprendre mes fort est arendre'.

The words of William of Lawford, the recently deposed abbot of the Cistercian monastery of Pipewell in Northamptonshire,[2] provide us with one of the most distressing English testimonies to the agrarian calamity sweeping Europe in the early fourteenth century.[3] This candid mixture of apology and exhortation resonates, moreover, in the crises of monastic finance prevalent over the past fifty years and emphasises human frailty over environmental factors in the accumulation of the debts responsible for the three-year dispersal of the convent *pretextu paupertatis* in September 1323.[4] How did such frailty manifest itself?

Crammed onto a blank folio of a late-thirteenth-century cartulary, Lawford's *cri de coeur*[5] is conspicuously tacked onto a list of fifteen recognisances for debt, totalling around £2,400, amassed since 1314. Most relate to wool that his predecessors had sold but struggled to deliver. As we have discussed in the previous chapter, Cistercian wool, which was prepared to the highest standard, encouraged merchants from across Europe to invest huge capital to fuel the burgeoning luxury cloth trade in the Low Countries. Business partners exchanged vast numbers of sacks for delivery within a few months or even up to twenty years with large cash advances, which are generally viewed as loans against the security of wool. We discuss our own findings regarding the nature of the contracts in Chapter 4. Historians of both the English and the monastic economy have long suggested that, in exploiting their most lucrative asset on local and international markets, Cistercian abbots dynamised English export trade and credit networks particularly in the half-century on either side of 1300, but entered a vicious circle where such 'loans', initially sunk into building and maintenance expenses and meeting royal and papal tax demands, increasingly serviced debts accumulated by previous advances left unpaid.[6] Virulent sheep disease struck four times between 1258 and 1317, ravaging flocks, reducing supplies of wool available for the market, and so threatening to sever the credit links which had become the lifeblood of the monastic economy in Britain.[7]

For some monastic historians, such transactions epitomised the alienation of the Cistercian Order from the original 'ideals' of seclusion and

---

[2] William was deposed on 24 April 1323: BL Cotton MS Otho B xiv, f. 161r.
[3] Kershaw, 'The Great European Famine'.   [4] BL Cotton MS Otho B xiv, f. 150r.
[5] Power, *The Wool Trade in English Medieval History*, p. 43.
[6] Whitwell, 'English Monasteries and the Wool Trade'; R. A. Donkin, *The Cistercians: Studies in the Geography of Medieval England and Wales* (Toronto, 1978), p. 17; Lloyd, *English Wool Trade*, pp. 288–312.
[7] Kershaw, 'The Great European Famine,' p. 27.

self-sufficiency established in the twelfth century.[8] Extensive credit relationships potentially embroiled abbots in usury, as wool contracts often disguised hidden interest charges,[9] while recurrent reliance upon foreign credit has strengthened suspicions of abbots' motives and promoted accusations of greed and financial mismanagement. Certainly, Abbot Nicholas, who was charged with righting Pipewell's finances after Lawford's deposition, bitterly insists that William's greedy, dishonourable rule led directly to dispersal, a fate common to several English Cistercian monasteries in the late thirteenth and early fourteenth centuries.[10] Kirkstall and Rievaulx (Yorks.) dispersed in 1281 and 1292 respectively, while the General Chapter received petitions to that end from Vaudey (Lincs.) in 1280, Flaxley (Gloucs.) in 1281, Fountains (Yorks.) in 1291, and Bruern (Oxon.) in 1293.[11] C. Graves, however, argues that dispersal induced in this manner was far from the severe penalty it might appear and represented 'a normal event, even if an unhappy one' in Cistercian history.[12] Sanctioned by the Cistercian General Chapter, dispersal reduced ordinary expenditure and released resources for debt resettlement by sending the brethren to seek sustenance in other houses of the Order.[13] Whilst essentially therefore a temporary resort, rarely have the often tortuous processes and myriad combination of factors creating penury, or the undulations between indebtedness, recovery, and disaster, been charted in detail.

In a recent examination of the wool sales which crippled Rievaulx abbey in the late thirteenth century, E. Jamroziak, however, concludes that the abbey's economy and future financial well-being were bound inextricably to raising credit through wool regardless of the damage this wrought in the short term.[14] Rievaulx, of course, one of the great Yorkshire houses

[8] D. Knowles, *The Religious Orders in England*, II (Cambridge, 1948), p. 68; J. E. Madden, 'Business Monks, Banker Monks, Bankrupt Monks: The English Cistercians in the Thirteenth Century', *Catholic Historical Review* 49 (3) (1963), pp. 341–364.

[9] See the case of Bordesley abbey: *Rotuli Parlamentorum*, I, p. 1; Lloyd, *English Wool Trade*, p. 291.

[10] BL Cotton MS Otho B xiv, f. 159r. It has been shown that as a reaction to the agrarian crisis, dispersal was a continental-wide issue for monasteries in the early fourteenth century. For instance, the Cistercian Abbeys of Villers at Tilly in Brabant and Val Saint-Lambert in Liégeois were dispersed between 1315 and 1316: W. Jordan, *The Great Famine: Northern Europe in the Early Fourteenth Century* (Princeton, 1996), 70–71.

[11] G. Barnes, *Kirkstall Abbey, 1147–1539: An Historical Study* (Leeds: Publications of the Thoresby Society, LVIII, no. 128, 1984), pp. 43–45; *Statuta Capitulorum Generalium Ordinis Cisterciensis ab anno 1116 ad annum 1786*, ed. J. Canivez (Louvain, 1934), III, 202 (1280: 44), 215 (1281: 63), 258 (1291: 61 (Rievaulx), 62 (Fountains), 266 (1293: 31).

[12] C. V. Graves, 'The Economic Activities of the Cistercians in Medieval England (1128–1307)', *Analecta Sacri Ordinis Cisterciensis* 13 (1957), p. 37.

[13] L. J. Lekai, *The Cistercians: Ideals and Reality* (Dallas, 1977), pp. 304–305. In 1189 the General Chapter stipulated that convents could only be dispersed by 'due investigation and authorization', an order reiterated in 1269: *Statuta*, I: 114 (1189: 18), III: 71 (1269: 15).

[14] Jamroziak, 'Rievaulx Abbey'.

of international renown, enjoyed sprawling pastures suitable for grazing thousands of sheep and forged business contacts with the leading Florentine and Lucchese merchants at Edward I's court. Not all Cistercian houses were as suited to large-scale wool production or to consistently luring Italian silver. Pipewell, a house of lesser means, was one such place.[15] Nevertheless, successive abbots forged a now infamous business partnership with a group of southern French merchants, which became ingrained in the abbey's economic fabric for over five decades, encompassing the peaks and troughs of the English economy from 1280 to 1330. Oscillating between profitability and financial paralysis, and threatening dispersal in 1296 and 1328, its ramifications dictated abbatial policy and possibly transcended the ephemeral, profit-driven motives of many such deals. This chapter examines the creation, development, and consequences of this partnership from a wider variety of sources than is available for Rievaulx, investigating mechanisms of trade, indebtedness, and debt resolution. It also assesses whether an unwillingness to forsake the partnerships with the Cahorsins plunged Pipewell into the financial morass.

THE WOOL CONTRACT

Last-listed of the 15 Recognisances is a bond for £213 and 22 sacks of wool owed to William Servat of Quercy. This represented the arrears of perhaps the most famous advance wool contract from a surviving corpus of well over 300 documents.[16] On 28 February 1291, the verdict of a panel of arbitration convened by Edward I to settle a dispute between John de Hillun, abbot of Pipewell, and a partnership of the Cahorsin merchants (Arnaud de Soliz, Jean de Redole, Gerard de Briole and Servat), concerning a breach of a wool contract was enrolled onto the Close Rolls of the English chancery.[17] Subsequently published in calendar form,[18] this has regularly

---

[15] Its annual wealth in 1291 is estimated at £154 compared with £241 at Rievaulx, while sheep numbers, as will be seen below, rarely can have reached 2,000 at Pipewell, but exceeded 5,000 at Rievaulx: *Taxatio Ecclesiastica Angliae et Walliae Auctoritate P. Nicholai IV circa A.D. 1291*, ed. J. Caley (London: Record Commission, 1802), pp. 48–49, 53–55, 67, 72, 92, 109, 241, 257: Jamroziak, 'Rievaulx Abbey', p. 208.

[16] While such agreements have been common currency for over a century, the extent of the surviving corpus – over one third of which concerns Cistercian abbeys – has now been fully collated in *Advance Contracts*. In addition, Dr Pamela Nightingale of the Ashmolean Museum, Oxford is finalising a database for TNA of Certificates of Statute Merchant and Statute Staple (C 131, C 241). From 1284 to 1311 eighty-seven certificates were registered involving laymen as debtors for wool: Nightingale, 'Knights and Merchants'.

[17] C 54/108, mm. 8d.–9d; E 159/64, rot. 10, E 368/62, rot. 14. *Advance Contracts*, no. 133.

[18] *CCR, 1288–96*, pp. 192–195.

attracted the attention of historians because the settlement that restructured the contract, whilst sharing basic elements with contemporary agreements, has unique features which provide a window into the medieval woollen industry and monastic credit.[19] Only T. H. Lloyd, however, traced the original contract drafted twenty-six months earlier, and it is *these* details that must guide the discussion.

On 12 November 1288, John de Hillun bound himself in the Exchequer to deliver 360 sacks of wool to the Cahorsins over the next fifteen years. Nine sacks of good wool, three sacks of middle-grade, seven of locks,[20] and five of *tayller*[21] wool made up each annual delivery, and every sack was to be free from matted wool ('cot'), black or grey impurities, and all cheap fleece wool. Priced at 18 marks in the first five years and at 21 marks for the remainder, good wool would be delivered to the merchants each year on 22 July at the Boston fair, along with middling wool priced at 12½ marks for the first five years and 14 thereafter, locks priced initially at 10 marks and then at 13, and *tayller* priced at 12 marks per sack only in the final ten years. In return, the merchants agreed to pay a series of complex advances to be offset against the delivery of wool and to provide a tun of wine each year. Two initial advances of £120 and £160 had been forwarded before the enrolment, which were to be allowed to the merchants annually. Additional advances of £63 6s 8d and £73 6s 8d were to be made on Sunday after Martinmas and Sunday after Easter each year. The monks were to accommodate the merchants' dresser, to whom was delegated the task of supervising the clip and preparing it for delivery. Moreover, they were to receive and husband 733 sheep provided by the merchants, who would contribute half of their maintenance costs with the intention that both the wool and any issue would be split between the two parties annually. At the end of the contract, all surviving sheep and the profits of their sale were to be divided equally.

Second in quantity only to the 400 sacks sold by the Cluniac prior of Lewes to the Riccardi of Lucca, this contract was potentially the most lucrative of all surviving agreements.[22] For wool valued at £3,445, the Cahorsins paid £280 upfront and promised a further £2,050 in advance over the course of the contract, leaving them a final £1,115 to settle at £74 6s 8d a year. Why, though, did the monks incur such an enormous

---

[19] Power, *The Wool Trade in English Medieval History*, pp. 43–44; Graves, 'Economic Activities', pp. 31–33; Lloyd, *English Wool Trade*, pp. 295–296.

[20] '*que cadent de ovibus in locacione et ante tonsionem*': E 159/62, rot. 4. *Advance Contracts*, no. 110.

[21] This is specified as being pressed into the common wool: '*brusetur inter communem lanam*'.

[22] E 159/61, rot. 14. *Advance Contracts*, no. 104.

debt if only two years later they were unable to deliver? Why, indeed, did the merchants invest so much capital when problems must already have been evident? Both the contract itself and the factors promoting it provide the key.

Before moving on, though, it is important to place these contracts within the corpus of evidence for the history of the abbey's involvement with wool. Governmental sources allow the processes of trade and credit to be followed closely. As we have discussed, the Exchequer Court, in particular, seems to have been the primary mechanism employed by foreign merchants in registering contracts and prosecuting defaulters, and its Plea (E 13) and dual series of Memoranda Rolls (E 159, 368) supply a rich and varied paper trail. Pipewell abbey itself, more importantly, had a productive scriptorium. Three cartularies survive from the mid–late thirteenth century.[23] A further register, probably in the process of compilation through the last quarter of the thirteenth century appears, from Lawford's scrawl at least, to have been in use in the fourteenth century.[24] Perhaps the most important is a chronicle and register of documents compiled towards the middle of the fourteenth century.[25] Internal evidence suggests it was written either by, or for, Abbot Nicholas (1323–50), as a list of abbots concludes with Lawford, his immediate successor. It is a source to be treated with caution, for its purpose seems to be to exonerate Nicholas from blame for the dispersal, an event unparalleled in the abbey's history which he had overseen.[26] It is therefore coloured by the compiler's experiences of the harshness of existence brought on by debt and famine and by an attempt to counter dissent in the convent in the mid-1330s[27] by pinning the blame principally on William Lawford.[28] It is, however, our sole surviving narrative. Moreover, the compiler had access to, and employed, previous abbots' annual account rolls, cellarers' stock accounts and bursars' rolls, which have now been lost.[29] His distillation of information mined from the abbey's cartularies and surviving muniments is dextrous and a great deal of his evidence concerning recognisances and land transfers can be corroborated from other sources. Its survival makes

---

[23] BL Cotton MS Caligula A XII, ff. 2–159v.; A XIII; Additional MS 37022 – this is now badly damaged and ripped twice horizontally; it is the work of several scribes probably in mid-century.

[24] BL Stowe MS 937.

[25] BL Cotton MS Otho B xiv, ff. 150r–205r. It must have been completed by 1343, as a different hand inserts evidence concerning a plea not resolved until that year: f. 196v.

[26] BL Cotton MS Otho B xiv, ff. 150r.–151v., 197r.

[27] A reference survives, for example, to complaints about a lack of firewood in winter: f. 159r.

[28] *'qui non bene se habuit in regimine domus'*: f. 197r.

[29] BL Cotton MS Otho B xiv, ff. 151v., 158v., 161r., 161v.

Pipewell's experiences with debt and the wool trade arguably the best documented house in England.

SHEEP FARMING

Like many other houses of the Order, sheep farming was naturally concomitant with the abbey's foundation and development.[30] Sited in oak woodland on the fringes of Rockingham forest in northern Northamptonshire, Pipewell, with its heavy clay soils, was not wholly conducive to arable cultivation and fostered a mixed economy.[31] While Pipewell's founders in 1143 sought seclusion and the self-sufficient existence dictated by the early *capitula* of the Order, which condoned solely manual labour, animal husbandry and the tilling of the soil, its estates could not always meet the subsistence needs of the community.[32] Though the late-twelfth and thirteenth centuries witnessed considerable forest clearance and assarting of land to extend the area under cultivation,[33] frequently in the late-thirteenth and early fourteenth centuries abbots had to buy grain to sustain the convent. During the Barons' War, for example, the abbot of Croxden (Staffs.) sold Abbot Gerard (1256–9) all of his grain at Tugby (Leics.) for one year. From 1308 to 1311, the monks regularly purchased poor-grade grain at high prices.[34] Moreover, although successive abbots contravened Cistercian legislation forbidding the purchase of churches, tithes, villages and seigneurial dues from mills,[35] such assets could not match the accumulation of estates better suited to sheep husbandry, which could be applied to meeting the rising costs of the convent.

The monastic precinct at Pipewell stands 107–114 metres above sea-level. The main bulk of its estates straddles the border between Northamptonshire and Warwickshire southwest of the abbey and covers the heathland, which rises to 200 metres near Cold Ashby before sloping down to the banks of the Avon north of Rugby. The majority of its granges were situated in this area and enjoyed sizeable pastures and sheepfolds, though nothing to the

---

[30] Donkin, *Cistercians*, pp. 68–73.
[31] G. Foard, 'Medieval Woodland, Agriculture and Industry in Rockingham Forest, Northamptonshire', *Medieval Archaeology* 45 (2001), pp. 41–97.
[32] Lekai, *The Cistercians*, p. 26.   [33] BL Cotton MS Otho B xiv, ff. 150r.–152v.
[34] BL Cotton MS Otho B xiv, ff. 154v., 157r. For other examples see ff. 150v., 160v., 188v.
[35] Outlawed as early as 1134: *Statuta*, I, 14–15. For Pipewell's seigneurial instruments: E 326/2655, 2706, 2712 (vills of Newbold, Little Lawford, Harborough); E 326/8825, E 329/188 (tithes in Cold Ashby); E 327/55 (Cold Ashby, Elkington and Thornby); BL Cotton MS Otho B xiv, ff. 157r. (mill at Oakley), 158v. (Rugby), 159v. (Roxton, Barford, Desborough, Little Lawford), 160r. (Church Lawford), 163r. (Rothwell), 183v. (Winwick).

extent of those in Yorkshire.[36] Alongside the home granges of East Grange and West Grange, two main groups stand out: a Northamptonshire upland cluster containing Braybrooke, Cold Ashby, Elkington, and Winwick; and a Warwickshire riverside cluster of Rugby, Newbold-on-Avon, Dunchurch, Cawston and Church, Little and Long Lawford. In Northamptonshire, sheepfolds existed at Yelvertoft and Winwick. In the former, the monks pastured 180 of Richard de Hensa's ewes with their own sheep early in the thirteenth century, while in the latter Randolph de Blockeville granted them pasture for 720 sheep.[37] Nearer the abbey, 120 sheep were pastured at Oakley and a further 250 of the abbey's beasts at Benefield in a clearing in Rockingham forest.[38] In Warwickshire, 300 ewes grazed at Bilton and another 300 on Cawston Heath, both west of Rugby, while at Long Lawford there was pasture for 1,000 sheep. In the first half of the thirteenth century, 200 sheep from their sheepfolds at Marham were held with sheep of the lord of Rugby.[39] In addition, Pipewell owned a low-lying grange and 180 acres of marshland pasture concentrated on Whaplode in the Lincolnshire fens.[40]

In total, evidence survives of pasture for over 3,000 sheep. Translating this into production capacity is difficult, however, and should not be taken as an upper or lower limit. Cartulary figures of grants of pasture do not translate incontrovertibly into flock size, as fluctuations in climate and disease shaped flocks, which often appear to have dipped considerably below this number. No evidence survives, moreover, of the weights and measures used at Pipewell, and even locally there were variations from the accepted sack weight of 26 stones, at 14 lb per stone. In 1290, two Londoners sold six sacks to the Riccardi from the pastures of Rothwell, in which hundred Pipewell lies, and each sack was to contain 30 stones at 13 lb per stone.[41] While Lloyd has calculated average fleece size as something just under 2 lb, variations in breed, climate, pasture, and nutrition created a lack of uniformity.[42] But, even with these qualifications, possible flock size and capacity can be assessed. An average sack of standard weight probably

[36] Waites, 'Monasteries and the Wool Trade in North and East Yorkshire during the 13th and 14th Centuries'.
[37] BL Cotton MS Caligula A XIII, f. 43r.; Otho B xiv, f. 183v.
[38] BL Cotton MS Otho B xiv, f. 164r.; *Rotuli Parliamentorum.*, II, ii, pp. 22–23.
[39] BL Cotton MS Caligula A XIII, f. 80r. (Bilton); Otho B xiv, ff. 157v. (Cawston Heath), 191r. (Marham, Long Lawford).
[40] BL Cotton MS Otho B xiv, f. 177v.
[41] E 159/63, rot. 25d; E 368/61, rot. 29. *Advance Contracts*, no. 119.
[42] Lloyd, 'Movement of Wool Prices', p. 2.

contained 200–260 fleeces.[43] For Pipewell to have filled the 24 sacks they promised to the Cahorsins from their own sheep would require around 5,500 sheep. But a contemporary estimate by a Florentine merchant, Francisco Balducci Pegolotti, puts annual output at 14 sacks, commensurate with a flock of just over 3,000 sheep.[44] To put this into context, Meaux (Yorks.) kept a flock touching 11,000 in 1280, Rievaulx had amassed well over 5,000 by the same year, Kirkstall around 6,500 by 1320, while the Benedictine fenland behemoth, Crowland, boasted 16,000 sheep before scab hit in the 1270s.[45] Converting these into annual output, Pegolotti gives respective totals of 25, 60, 25, and 30 sacks.[46]

It was crucial, therefore, that both locally and nationally, abbots of Pipewell possessed a marketable commodity of high quality. Medieval wool-pricing evidence, the main arbiter of quality, is sparse though.[47] Fortunately, two price schedules for wool marketed by British monastic producers survive and both, when taken with the contract, suggest that while Pipewell never attained the front rank in production, its wool was among the most revered.

As we have discussed earlier, sometime in the late 1330s, Pegolotti, a leading light in the Bardi company of Florence, prepared a handbook for merchants trading across Europe. Drawing on his experience as a Bardi agent in London from 1317 to 1321, which included the agreement of at least one contract with Pipewell in 1318,[48] and on information possibly dating to the 1280s,[49] he inserted a list of 200 British monastic wool producers with prices for 194 of them.[50] They include seventy-seven Cistercian monasteries and nunneries. Its good wool being valued at 22 marks, Pipewell ranks ninth among Cistercians. Only two other houses nationwide surpassed this value, confirming Pipewell's position within the top 6 per cent of monastic wool producers. Caution, though, should be exercised, as Pegolotti explicitly states that his prices are those on the Flemish market and that the costs of

---

[43] The Augustinian prior of Wroxton (Oxon.) sold 1,820 fleeces to the Spaniard, Peter de Mundenard, in 1280, laden into six sacks of 260 fleeces each: E 13/8, m. 15d. *Advance Contracts*, no. 44.

[44] *La Pratica Della Mercatura*, p. 262.

[45] Waites, 'Monasteries and the Wool Trade in North and East Yorkshire during the 13th and 14th Centuries', p. 112; Jamroziak, 'Rievaulx Abbey', p. 208; Barnes, *Kirkstall Abbey*, p. 40; Power, *The Wool Trade in English Medieval History*, p. 35.

[46] *La Practica Della Mercatura*, pp. 260, 268.

[47] Lloyd, 'Movement of Wool Prices'; Munro, 'Wool-Price Schedules and the Qualities of English Wools'.

[48] *Calendar of the Charter Rolls preserved in the Public Record Office, 1318–23* (London, 1903), p. 94. Subsequent references are to *CCR*.

[49] Munro, 'Wool-Price Schedules and the Qualities of English Wools', pp. 134–135.

[50] *La Pratica Della Mercatura*, pp. 258–269: 173 are English, 15 Scottish, and 12 Welsh. Prices are omitted for two English houses and four Welsh houses.

carriage and a good profit should be factored in.[51] His prices may therefore be commensurately inflated. But, even if, as Munro suggests, shipping, marketing and taxation charges account for around 20 per cent of the value of each sack sold in Flanders, the domestic price of Pipewell wool at around 17 marks, which tallies with the initial lower sale price agreed with the Cahorsins in 1288, would still have competed, as the Exchequer Schedule of 1294 demonstrates.[52]

We have described how, in June 1294, Edward I stockpiled assets to finance war with Philip IV in Gascony by seizing the wool of foreign merchants then in England and forcing representatives of ten Italian companies to submit details of their current wool contracts to inform him of the finances he could muster.[53] Their submissions list 133 monastic producers, 57 of which are Cistercian.[54] Pipewell's absence, however, suggests that Cahorsin cash had firmly secured its wool. Nevertheless, if we were to take 17 marks as representing the value of each Pipewell sack, it would slot in eleventh among Cistercians and seventeenth across all Orders. Taking the stated contract value of 21 marks raises the abbey to second among Cistercians and third nationwide.

Purely in terms of quality, then, Pipewell outstripped the wealthy Benedictine abbeys of the Fens and the large Cistercian producers of Yorkshire. Crowland, Peterborough, and Ramsey had the combined potential to deliver upwards of 100 sacks a year, but the wool of their hardy Fenland sheep only commanded 12 marks per sack.[55] Rievaulx could produce an estimated 40–50 sacks a year, but fetch a maximum of 18 marks per sack.[56] Even comparison with Fountains, which could deliver 76 sacks a year, is favourable. In 1294, the Riccardi purchased the entire clip and paid only 15 marks for good wool. Pegolotti advised that Fountains wool could sell at 20 marks.[57] Pipewell clearly belonged to a group of specialist smaller-scale producers who marketed 'an intrinsically better product' than their competitors.[58] The houses whose wool exceeded Pipewell in value correlate well across both schedules and cluster in three main areas – the Welsh march, Lindsey in Lincolnshire and the Cotswolds – whose wool consistently dominated the export market throughout the later Middle Ages.[59] Both Bruern on the Oxfordshire edge

[51] *La Pratica Della Mercatura*, p. 269.
[52] Munro, 'Wool-Price Schedules and the Qualities and English Wools', p. 125.
[53] E 159/68, rot. 82; M. C. Prestwich, *Edward I*, pp. 377–381.
[54] E 101/126/7, mm. 11–25. *Advance Contracts*, Appendix I.   [55] *La Pratica Della Mercatura*, p. 268.
[56] Jamroziak, 'Rievaulx Abbey', p. 208; E 159/61, rot. 11d. *Advance Contracts*, no. 99.
[57] E 101/126/7, m. 13; *Advance Contracts*, no. 205. *La Pratica Della Mercatura*, p. 260.
[58] Donkin, 'Cistercian Sheep Farming and Wool Sales', p. 2.
[59] Lloyd, *Movement of Wool Prices*, p. 70.

of the Cotswolds and Thame on the chalk downs further east cornered the market in quality. The former sold around 12–14 sacks of good wool a year but received 17 marks in 1294 and 25 in Pegolotti's list, while Thame marketed as few as four sacks a year, but garnered 22 and 28 marks respectively.[60] The marshy perimeter of the River Witham in mid Lincolnshire also nurtured Lindsey sheep of rare quality. The Benedictine nunnery of Stainfield, the Premonstratensian abbey of Barlings, and the Gilbertine priory of Bullington, separated by no more than four miles, contracted for 40–55 sacks combined and attracted sack prices averaging 19 marks in 1294 and 25 marks in Pegolotti's schedule.[61] Finally, the wool of the Cistercian abbeys of Tintern and Abbey Dore on the Welsh Marches proved especially lucrative, both commanding 28 marks per sack according to Pegolotti.[62] Abbey Dore, at least, appears to have perfected preparation techniques. In 1275, Herbert Wermond of Cambrai purchased 12 sacks of *collecta* from Darnhall, insisting that it be of the same standard as that of Dore.[63]

For Pipewell, too, it is conceivable that dextrous wool preparation marked it out. The monks consistently sorted and graded their wool, but the high price it fetched is suggestive of greater care than even its local Cistercian rivals, many of whom adopted similarly innovative methods.[64] Perhaps as importantly with a medium-sized flock, successive abbots had to cajole local lay producers into selling their wool through the abbey, a product marketed as *collecta*. Greater bulk attracted more investment and the neighbouring districts around Leicester, Northampton, Warwick, and Coventry were rich in small gentry producers looking for, and often finding, an outlet for their demesne produce.[65] Though some merchants frowned upon *collecta* and demanded wool *de stauro suo* (from his stock),[66] proper dressing could still make it a lucrative product. As we discuss in Chapter 4, *collecta* fetched over 80 per cent of the value of good wool, while middle-grade managed only 68 per cent. Could it be that Pipewell

---

[60] E 101/126/7, mm. 16, 18 (Bruern), 17 (Thame); *Advance* Contracts, nos. 207–209. *La Pratica Della Mercatura*, p. 262.

[61] E 101/126/7, mm. 17 (Stainfield, Bullington), 23 (Barlings); *Advance* Contracts, nos. 208, 214. *La Pratica Della Mercatura*, p. 263 (Barlings), p. 265 (Bullington, Stainfield).

[62] *La Pratica Della Mercatura*, p. 261.

[63] C 54/92, m. 2d.: '*e ausi bone cume la meilleure coilliette de Dore*'. *Advance Contracts*, no. 13.

[64] Sixty surviving contracts, overwhelmingly with Cistercian houses, explicitly stipulate that the wool is to be dressed and packaged before delivery.

[65] E 13/8, mm. 1d., 21, 28; 9, m. 7; E 159/54, rots. 18, E 368/54, rot. 16; E 159/54, rot. 19, E 368/54, rot. 17d.; E 159/54, rot. 20; E 159/61, rot. 12d.; 62, rot. 14; 63, rot. 25d, E 368/61, rot. 29. *Advance Contracts*, nos. 29–32, 49, 50, 62, 56–58, 101, 108, 119.

[66] E 159/55, rot. 9, E 368/55, rot. 8; E 159/59, rot. 4; 64, rot. 22d., E 368/62, rot. 27; E 159/66, rot. 48, E 368/64, rot. 41. *Advance Contracts*, nos. 61, 82, 122, 146.

had been able to take a firmer grasp on local, non-monastic produce than its Cistercian neighbours? None of Combe and Merevale (Warks.), Biddlesden (Bucks.), and Garendon (Leics.) got within 2 marks per sack of the value of its wool in Pegolotti's schedule.

A quality product, however, was no guarantee of financial success. Accessibility, proximity to local markets, and an aggressive marketing strategy played pivotal roles. Though sited within Rockingham forest, Pipewell lay near arterial routes south to Oxford and north to Stamford and Leicester, as well as east–west to Peterborough, Warwick, and Coventry. Richard Hensa of Yelvertoft had also granted the convent a path through his lands leading onto Watling Street.[67] West Haddon and Naseby, villages in which the abbey had land, were marketplaces on routes through which travellers seeking river crossings at Wellingborough and Banbury passed.[68] More pertinent to the wool business was Pipewell's accessibility to Northampton, St Ives, and Boston, where three of the four main international fairs of England were held.[69] The former could be reached by road, while Boston, the principal hub of the wool export trade towards the end of the thirteenth century, sits at the mouth of the Nene and the Welland, navigable from Peterborough and Stamford respectively. This not only eased the transportation of wool to port, but opened Pipewell to the streams of merchants flooding the East Midlands in search of wool. Pipewell, though, would not have been unknown to them.

PIPEWELL AND THE WOOL TRADE

June 1272 marked the height of the long-running crisis in Anglo-Flemish relations. This provoked an embargo on exports to Flanders, and thus Thomas de Grafton, the abbey's proctor, acquired permission to export wool to the Continent.[70] His licence was one among hundreds issued to English and European merchants who were thus ensured other outlets for the most profitable of many saleable commodities, having been deprived of the principal market.[71] For monastic producers, the embargo threatened to cut off their very lifeblood. As early as 1225, the abbot of Garendon had

---

[67] BL Cotton MS Caligula A XIII, f. 43r.
[68] P. Goodfellow, 'Medieval Markets in Northamptonshire', *Northamptonshire Past and Present* 7 (1989), p. 307.
[69] E. W. Moore, *The Fairs of Medieval England* (Toronto, 1985).
[70] *CPR, 1266–72*, p. 689; Lloyd, *English Wool Trade*, pp. 28–39; Roon-Basserman, 'Die Handelssperre Englands gegen Flandern'.
[71] *CPR, 1266–72*, pp. 553–567, 688–693, 702–704.

received licence to take wool to Flanders.[72] English monastic wool producers, moreover, had long attracted Flemish silver. On 8 January 1265, the abbot of Pipewell, seven other Cistercian abbots, and three Gilbertine priors, were ordered to indemnify Flemish merchants from damages potentially incurred by their failure to collect wool they had paid for in advance due to their fear of entering the kingdom during the Barons' War.[73] An apparently contemporary schedule, possibly drawn up as an *aide-memoire* in the Anglo-Flemish crisis, lists ninety-five British wool-producing monasteries, sixty-four of which, including Pipewell, are Cistercian.[74] It seems clear, therefore, that at Pipewell and elsewhere, abbots adopted an innovative, aggressive approach to exploiting their best asset, which helped British Cistercian abbots engineer the thirteenth-century revolution in the Order's economy away from self-sufficiency towards supranational business, cash and credit networks.[75]

Possibly the earliest surviving indenture for an advance sale of wool, indeed, concerns Pipewell abbey. At Candlemas 1242, Abbot William sold the coming year's clip to two prominent Londoners, Adam of Shoreditch, goldsmith, and John of Toulouse, a future mayor, for an advance of £80.[76] In so doing, he flouted long-standing Cistercian legislation against the taking of money in advance of delivery of wool. This practice had been outlawed in 1189 for deals stretching over a year as it threatened to immerse abbeys in debt and embroil them in potentially usurious transactions. As the thirteenth century progressed, though, fewer abbots took heed of this prohibition, bringing a restatement in 1277. A year later, sales were licensed for longer periods, although payments were only to be accepted for one year. Pressure from abbeys whose flocks were suffering from scab ultimately forced the General Chapter into allowing receipt of larger sums on condition they were applied to reducing debt.[77] Such flexibility tacitly acknowledged the importance that credit had come to have in monastic finances because abbots had long been accessing privileges to secure their place as producers in the wool market.

---

[72] *CPR, 1216–25*, p. 522.
[73] *CCR, 1264–8*, p. 84.
[74] E. Varenbergh, *Relations Diplomatiques entre le Comte de Flandre et l'Angleterre* (Brussels, 1874), pp. 214–217; Munro, 'Wool-Price Schedules and the Qualities of English Wools', pp. 119–125.
[75] Donkin, *Cistercians*, p. 17.
[76] E 327/541. *Advance Contracts*, no. 221. For Adam and John see: *CCR, 1237–42*, p. 322; *Calendar of the Liberate Rolls preserved in the Public Record Office, 1251–60* (London, 1959), p. 87. Subsequent references are to *CLR*.
[77] *Statuta*, I (1157: 48); III, 169, 175–176, 184 (1277: 30, 1278: 5, 1279: 2.)

On 20 March 1235, Henry III awarded Pipewell freedom from toll, passage, and pontage throughout the realm. This, of course, made carriage by road, river, and sea carriage, and thus export, much cheaper. Equally important was the exemption of sheep from distraint, if the abbey possessed other animals or chattels by which debts could be met.[78] This threw troubled abbots a critical lifeline in times of impending penury. Both, therefore, made them more attractive to buyers, and were privileges voraciously sought by many Cistercian houses as they became more deeply involved in selling wool.[79] But even without them, Pipewell's wool would always have suitors. After the gradual loss of Flemish custom in the wake of the crises of the early 1270s, it must have been reasonable to expect that the liquid capital accompanying Italian merchant companies into England would have found a home at Pipewell. The most successful company under Edward I, the Riccardi of Lucca, who had business connections in most counties, were active in Northamptonshire and Warwickshire.[80] But the evidence suggests that Pipewell was sought out by southern French merchants to the exclusion of all others.

THE CAHORSINS

Servat, Soliz, Redole, and Briole formed one of a number of fluid partnerships of merchants from the region round Cahors in southern France who had trading connections across Europe.[81] For a century, their predecessors had imported wine, cables, and cords into England in return for wool, cementing their involvement in the burgeoning woollen cloth trade of the North Sea world.[82] They had also penetrated the Northamptonshire wool market. In October 1259, Stephen Chaendut sold six sacks of wool '*de patria de Northamtonia*' to Imbert Delderoc, William Fresepayn, and Arnaud Griffun, merchants of Cahors.[83] Such men must have established long-term business contacts, information strands, and local knowledge in many parts of the country, and particularly so once they became resident. Griffun had lived in England since the 1250s and it is interesting to see

[78] *CCR, 1226–57*, p. 198.   [79] Donkin, *Cistercians*, pp. 85, 189.
[80] E 13/8, mm. 1d., 28; E 159/54, rot. 18, E 368/54, rot. 16; E 159/54, rot. 19, E 368/54, rot. 17d.; E 159/54, rot. 20; E 159/63, rot. 25d., E 368/61, rot. 29. *Advance Contracts*, nos. 31, 50, 55, 57, 58, 119.
[81] T. H. Lloyd, *Alien Merchants in England in the High Middle Ages* (Brighton, 1982), pp. 95–96.
[82] N.M. Fryde, 'Die Kaufleute aus Cahors im England des 13. Jahrhunderts', in *Kredit im Spätmittelalterlichen und Frühneuzeitlichen Europa: Quellen und Darstellungen zur Hansischen Geschichte* 38 (1991), pp. 25–38; *CLR*, pp. 116, 462.
[83] E 159/33, rot. 2d. *Advance Contracts*, no. 3.

him associated with Servat on his first appearance in English documentary evidence, both men receiving licence to export wool together in June 1272.[84]

Servat himself soon established residence in London, although he appears to have been equally active in the East Midlands.[85] Chancery recognisances between 1285 and 1291 show him as a creditor in Lincoln and Boston, lending money to individuals from Lincoln, Baston near Stamford, Holland in south Lincolnshire, and Nottingham.[86] A number of wool contracts confirm this impression. In 1283, he sued the abbot of Roche in south Yorkshire before the Exchequer over four sacks. Three years later he success-fully prosecuted a group of Stamford merchants for four sacks. In 1287, the Lincolnshire landowner Robert de Morteyn promised him and William de Averson one sack.[87] Much of his business was centred on Boston fair, the main centre for delivery and receipt, if not exchange, of wool, Servat apparently acting as the English anchor for his fellows. His colleagues, though, were active too. Arnaud and Jean sued the abbot of Biddlesden for one-and-a-half sacks in 1290.[88] Jean de Soliz, brother of Arnaud, and associated with Servat in two certificates for debt, was one of three mer-chants who had bargained for the wool of the Lincolnshire Cistercian abbey of Louth Park in 1275.[89] In 1280, he and Poncius de Mora, the most prominent Cahorsin in England, bought three sacks of Abbey Dore wool.[90]

It is obvious that these men knew how to source produce. Lincoln and Nottingham were important cloth towns at the heart of counties rich in producers of high-value wool. Baston sits close to the wool town of Stamford and the wool-producing area of the Deepings[91] on the fringe of the marshlands of Holland, where enormous monastic flocks grazed. Prolonged residence must have broadened business networks considerably. More importantly, it undoubtedly helped create networks of service and reward. Loans to the Crown during Edward I's Welsh wars garnered significant royal favours.[92] In 1281, Servat and William Tournemire, keeper of the Royal Mint, were permitted to render their accounts 'according to the custom of the exchequer',

[84] *CPR, 1266–72*, p. 689.
[85] F. Arens, 'Wilhelm Servat von Cahors als Kaufmann zu London (1273–1320), *VJSSWG* II (1913), pp. 477–514.
[86] C 241/9/238, 10/27, 12/3, 17/61, 31/93.
[87] E 13/12, mm. 6, 21; E159/60, rot. 12d., E 368/60, rot. 10d. *Advance Contracts*, nos. 81, 83, 88.
[88] E 13/14, m. 8d. *Advance Contracts*, no. 123.
[89] C 241/10/27, 31/93; C 54/93, m. 18d. *Advance Contracts*, no. 14.
[90] E 13/8, m. 14. *Advance Contracts*, no. 40.
[91] Arnaud Griffun had bought 70 sacks of the *collecta* of the Deepings and Spalding in Holland in 1259: E 159/32, rot.17. *Advance Contracts*, no. 2.
[92] *CPR, 1272–81*, pp. 214, 216; *CCh.R, 1277–1326*, pp. 215–216, 230; *CCR, 1279–88*, p. 36.

granting them the privileged access to speedy jurisdiction which some Italian merchants had acquired.[93] Servat and Averson were later entrusted with accompanying Anthony Bek, bishop of Durham, on embassies to Norway to negotiate a marriage alliance between Margaret, heiress to the Scottish throne, and Edward of Caernarfon, Edward I's son and heir.[94]

To have formed an association with such cosmopolitan, well-connected men must, then, have considerably appealed to the monks of Pipewell, offering access to a reliable source of capital and influential patrons. For the Cahorsins, the deal promised a steady stream of high-quality wool at a constant price. And yet, neither supply nor demand were so weak as to force them together. Both parties could surely have persuaded others to undertake such serious investment. This suggests that we should look more deeply into the reasons for their relationship.

Traditionally, Recognisances of the kind under discussion have been viewed as results of successful prosecutions by merchants desperate to recoup their investment against defaulters. In an era of recurrent sheep scab, a skin disease rendering fleeces useless, merchants used the mechanisms of the Exchequer either to compel monastic communities to honour their bargain by binding themselves, the house, and their successors, effectively mortgaging their future, or to submit to penalty charges.[95] This seems applicable to the arbitrated settlement of February 1291. Lloyd, however, argues that many such Recognisances were 'simple registrations of contracts' recording the mutual obligations of both parties.[96] This better fits the recognisance of November 1288 where the direct investment in sheep is unusual and, arguably, indicative of a longer-term commitment to a business association.

By the terms of the original contract, the merchants were to provide 733 sheep to be pastured with the monastic flock. At Kirkstall, Henry de Lacy, earl of Lincoln, stepped in to save the abbey after its flock had been utterly annihilated by scab by 1284, restoring it to a pre-disease level within twenty years. Similarly, at Pipewell, such large-scale purchases tend to be associated with restocking in the aftermath of epidemics.[97] Murrain struck in 1258, 1277, and 1283, decimating flocks nationwide, and bringing economic depression across the country for much of the 1280s.[98] While the effect of disease at Pipewell before 1296 is inestimable, twelve miles away at Wellingborough mortality reduced the flock of Crowland abbey by an

[93] Arens, 'Wilhelm Servat,' p. 485; Kaeuper, *Bankers to the Crown*, p. 21.
[94] *CPR, 1281–92*, p. 352; Arens, 'Wilhelm Servat,' pp. 486–491.
[95] Jamroziak, 'Rievaulx Abbey', p. 207; Ryder, 'Medieval Sheep and Wool Types'.
[96] Lloyd, *English Wool Trade*, p. 292.   [97] Barnes, *Kirkstall Abbey*, pp. 43–45.
[98] Kershaw, 'The Great European Famine', p. 27.

annual average of 15 per cent between 1280 and 1285, peaking at 20 per cent in 1281.[99] Young sheep were particularly badly affected: in 1282, 35 per cent of the manor's hoggets were slaughtered and in the following year, 23 per cent of lambs died. If such mortality was reflected at Pipewell, the flock might have struggled to meet the demands made of it.

To counter this, both parties aimed to create a breeding flock, conditions in the contract stipulating that the imported sheep were to be kept with the abbey's flock until they reached 2,000, whereupon they were to be divided equally and wool and issue sold to dual profit. The fleeces of animals dying during any year were to be sold and the receipts ploughed back into purchase of new sheep. Clearly, they had a vision of sustainable stock management to ensure a return on their investment. This, though, was not an overnight development. On 28 June 1280, the rectors of Elkington, Cold Ashby, and Thornby remitted to the abbey exaction of tithes on the produce of all sheep grazing in their parishes, whether the sheep belonged to the monks or to 'certain merchants'.[100] The dorse reveals that these were *'ovium mercatorum de Caturco'*. Although these sheep had never yet been pastured in their parishes, this implies that the abbot had negotiated a deal with the merchants and had persuaded the rectors by an advance of 40s to facilitate the plan. It is possible, therefore, that Cahorsin sheep grazed at Pipewell some years before the first official contract. Such sustained interest suggests that the merchants, far from engaging in transitory business, envisaged a relationship of mutual benefit to both parties.

In an atmosphere of declining production, the Cahorsin market share was threatened.[101] It had been squeezed by the Italian societies, whose international connections and greater liquidity had helped them wrest the majority of wool contracts formerly held by the Flemings. Financial difficulties may consequently have beset them. At Michaelmas 1287, Arnaud de Soliz received permission to have his debtors distrained to render their debts before the Exchequer. On 5 July 1289, moreover, Arnaud bound himself and his brother, Jean, to repay Jean de Redole the arrears of multiple debts he had incurred on their behalf in the Bar fair from 1285.[102] As his principal security for repayment, Arnaud pledged the wool he had recently bought from Pipewell, even though the date for the first delivery

[99]   *Wellingborough Manorial Accounts, AD 1258–1323*, ed. F. M. Page (Kettering: Publications of the Northamptonshire Record Society VIII, 1936), pp. 21–46.
[100] E 327/55.
[101] Wool exports in the late 1280s had fallen to around 25,000 sacks a year, a significant drop from over 33,000 recorded in 1273: Carus-Wilson and Coleman, *England's Export Trade*, pp. 36–37.
[102] E 159/61, rot. 1d; 62, rot. 9d.

was weeks away. More significantly, during Edward I's Welsh campaigns, Cahorsin merchants had advanced loans to the king of around £2,800, a considerable drain on resources.[103] Conversely, the capital investment required for the purchase of Pipewell's wool and in sourcing and buying sheep hints that the contract cannot wholly represent an attempt to buy themselves out of trouble.

Adoption of novel strategies defended the Cahorsins' niche in the market. At the Cistercian abbey of Gracedieu in Monmouthshire, Arnaud and his compatriot, Arnaud Jean, advanced 70 marks to have three granges for seven years, obtaining unfettered access to monastic produce.[104] Clauses in the Pipewell contract forbidding the monks from bargaining with any other merchants for their wool throughout the contract effectively gave them a fifteen-year monopoly. As importantly, it established a measure of stability during a period of price fluctuation. The imposition of an export duty of 6s 8d per sack in 1275[105] combined with wool scarcity through disease to push prices higher in the 1270s, though they were checked by a recoinage in 1279. Stagnation set in temporarily, but prices began rising again towards the end of the 1280s. Wool exports, which bottomed out in 1285–7, showed signs of revival in 1288.[106] It is possible, then, that the contract of November 1288 reflected increasing optimism that both sides would be able to garner good profit and within a reasonable timeframe. Graves, indeed, contends that the monks' ability to capture such sizeable loans 'suggests that their assets were promising in the eyes of creditors [for] . . . lending money to poor monks was not good business'.[107]

From the convent's viewpoint their relationship with the Cahorsins provided short- and long-term benefits. First, the initial investment perhaps resolved a long-term financial crisis. In August and October 1277, Pipewell was granted royal protection for one year. Combined with a simultaneous remission of the duty to provide carts for the king to convey victuals to supply his forces in Wales, this suggests that the king wished to shelter a struggling convent from unnecessary strains.[108] Secondly, the eventual contract gave the monks a guaranteed market for their best asset at a guaranteed price, a theoretical regular source of income facilitating more ambitious financial planning and exploitation of resources.

[103] *CPR, 1272–81*, pp. 214, 216; *CCR, 1272–9*, p. 535; *CCh.R, 1277–1326*, pp. 215–216.
[104] E 159/61, rot. 11.
[105] *Calender of Fine Rolls preserved in the Public Record Office, 1272–1307* (London, 1911), pp. 45–7. Subsequent references are to *CFR*.
[106] Lloyd, *Movement of Wool Prices*, p. 16.   [107] Graves, 'Economic Activites,' p. 45.
[108] *CPR, 1272–81*, pp. 224, 234.

MONASTIC SPENDING

The financial demands on monastic budgets grew exponentially during the thirteenth century and, as Jamroziak indicates, pressure arose from both within and without the monastic precinct.[109] As communities expanded, encompassing wider areas and more seigneurial units, the costs of administration and daily maintenance and the necessity for hired labour increased, particularly as the numbers of lay brethren staffing granges commensurately declined.[110] Pipewell was probably self-sufficient in meat, fish, dairy produce, some cloth,[111] and timber, and may have acquired iron utensils cheaply from local sources,[112] but the grain supply, as we have seen, was not wholly reliable. Medicinal spices and wine for consumption and ceremonial ritual, which could be purchased at fairs, were more exotic and demanded considerable outlay. Ordinary household consumption, however, was increasingly outstripped by the requirements of hospitality and charity.

Monastic communities were behoven to their founders and patrons. Late in the thirteenth century, Robert Botevileyn, a direct descendant of Pipewell's founder, William Botevileyn, enjoyed four annual blood-lettings and the right to a winter robe from the abbot. He claimed the right to stable his horse at the abbey whenever he pleased, along with his hunting dogs. When denied this right, Robert, a retainer of the earl of Gloucester and Hugh Despenser, two of the most powerful men at court, settled his claim by menaces, extorting a penalty of £40.[113] An equally pressing commitment to provide succour to the needy had to be met in the longer term. The distribution of alms and care of the sick slowly drained finances and proved nearly impossible in times of dearth. In a surviving fourteenth-century petition, the abbot and convent pray for relief from the king, lest the chantries and alms which their predecessors had committed them to should lapse.[114] Such stresses were only exacerbated when the king placed members

---

[109] Jamroziak, 'Rievaulx Abbey,' pp. 205–207.

[110] J. S. Donnelly, 'Changes in the Grange Economy of English and Welsh Cistercian Abbeys, 1300–1540', *Traditio* 10 (1954), pp. 399–458.

[111] The abbey possessed at least two fulling-mills at Long Lawford in Warwickshire and Great Barford in Bedfordshire: BL Cotton MS Otho B xiv, f. 189r.; *The Cartulary of Newnham Priory*, ed. J. Godber (Bedfordshire Historical Record Society Publications 43, 1963), p. 96.

[112] G. Foard highlights the proliferation of the iron industry in Rockingham Forest and it is possible, though evidence is lacking, that Pipewell manufactured most of its metal implements: Foard, 'Medieval Woodland, Agriculture and Industry'.

[113] BL Cotton MS Otho B xiv, f. 153r. Robert acted as attorney of Hugh Despenser in June 1314: *CCR, 1313–18*, p. 105.

[114] SC 8/66/3274.

of his household in convents, thus passing onto abbots the duty and expense of care for ageing royal servants, a practice which Edward II employed at Pipewell on two occasions.[115]

The impact of royal 'favour' was felt more acutely, however, when the king passed through the local area, which made Pipewell's proximity to Geddington Chase a liability. Purveyance – compulsory purchase of local produce for the king – could reduce stocks of foodstuff and fuel and might prove more costly, as under the first two Edwards suppliers battled to obtain swift and adequate repayment. Henry III visited Geddington in 1234.[116] In 1290, though, Edward I stayed for about four days at Pipewell itself.[117] Sadly, no victualling or household accounts survive for his stay, but a royal visit placed huge burdens on the monastic larder and purse, involving the accommodation, nourishment, and entertainment of the king, his family, and potentially dozens of retainers and servants, as well as stabling hundreds of horses.

Dignitaries often had to be accommodated too. Visitations by father abbots and diocesan bishops necessitated similarly large-scale spending. Royal and episcopal visits, though, were a signal honour and lavish hospitality would be expected and dutifully provided, especially when extravagant display and expenditure were occasioned by pride in achievement. On 5 April 1312, Thomas, earl of Lancaster, and William de Ros of Hamelake headed a huge gathering at Pipewell for the dedication of the abbey churchyard, close, and chapter-house. Commenting on this event twenty years on, Abbot Nicholas sardonically observes that 'no one knows how much was spent on this day except God'.[118]

This solemn celebration showed off the abbey's new buildings, the abbey church reconstruction having been completed a year earlier. Cistercian architecture progressed apace during the thirteenth century and many abbeys undertook expensive building projects. The sheer scale of such construction brought, as Jamroziak argues, both glory to God and the monastery itself, but equally fuelled those fires of indebtedness which gutted English Cistercian houses late in that century.[119] Lagging behind some of its contemporaries, the Pipewell convent nevertheless recognised that projects of such magnitude required long-term planning and financing, a primary part of which must have been founded on the relationship

---

[115] *CCR, 1307–13*, p. 257; *1313–18*, p. 446.   [116] *CPR, 1232–47*, p. 40.
[117] *CCR, 1288–96*, pp. 143–144; *CPR, 1281–92*, pp. 381, 406 (30 August – 2 September).
[118] '*Et expensas abbathie illo die factas nemo novit nisi Deus*': BL Cotton MS Otho B xiv, f. 197r.
[119] Jamroziak, 'Rievaulx Abbey', p. 206.

formed with the Cahorsins in the 1280s. This spirit also guided the construction and development of the abbey's principal grange at Cawston, which by the turn of the fourteenth century boasted dormitories and kitchens for the choir and lay brethren, a reredorter, frater, chapel, and chambers for the abbot and his guests. C. Platt has described Cawston as 'a resort, or rest-house, of the abbot, his monks and their servants'.[120] It must also have served as a guesthouse, as in 1307 a monk of Bruern had a chamber there. Situated close to some of the abbey's main sheep-stations, Cawston probably accommodated visiting merchants keen to assess stock and wool quality before purchase, its loss to fire in 1311 being deeply ingrained in the convent's memory.[121]

The potentially most debilitating, but most unpredictable drain on monastic finances was the growth of papal and royal taxation during the thirteenth century, which peaked in Edward I's reign. Desperate to supplement the resources available to fund prolonged campaigns in Wales in 1277, 1282, and 1287, the latter of which dovetailed with war in Gascony, and, therefore, to ensure that his most prominent financiers, the Riccardi, retained sufficient liquidity to advance money whenever necessary, Edward himself increased the national tax burden upon all his subjects.[122] Between 1279 and 1290, he taxed the English clergy on four occasions, to which the Cistercian Order made large contributions, although it was technically exempt.[123]

Early in their relationship with the English Crown, Cistercian abbots, in an attempt to defend liberties confirmed by Henry III in 1225 and 1244, set a precedent for the exaction of so-called 'compositions' – grants of money and, notably, wool to evade levies. In 1226, the Order secured exemption from a clerical fifteenth by a render of 2,000 marks.[124] In 1242, Henry III would have waived his request for a war subsidy if the abbots had agreed to grant one year's clip, which could easily have surpassed a fractional assessment of their moveable wealth.[125] Another year's clip was granted in 1258.[126] In 1275, £1,000 secured exemption from a fifteenth, in 1278 1,000 marks was paid to make up the earlier fine; in 1282, at least 1,000 marks was presented to escape a thirtieth; and in 1290,

---

[120] Platt, *The Monastic Grange*, p. 25.   [121] BL Cotton MS Otho B xiv, f. 154v.

[122] W. E. Lunt, *Financial Relations of the Papacy with England to 1327* (Cambridge, MA., 1939), pp. 311–418.

[123] H. S. Deighton, 'Clerical Taxation by Consent, 1279–1301', *English Historical Review* 68 (1953), pp. 161–162.

[124] *CPR, 1225–32*, p. 40.   [125] *CPR, 1232–47*, pp. 330, 336.   [126] *CPR, 1247–58*, pp. 515–516.

Cistercian abbots made fine in 2,000 marks to escape a fifteenth.[127] The extent of Pipewell's share of this burden is not easy to assess. The only evidence available comes from a breakdown of the Cistercian allocation of an undated, thirteenth-century exaction of £12,000, to which Pipewell was to contribute £33. This puts it on a par with Meaux, Kirkstall, and Louth Park, but shows it well adrift of more affluent houses such as Kirkstead and Fountains, which respectively contributed £54 and £66 16s.[128] Despite exemption from tithes on wool and milk and despite having secured freedom from distraint of sheep, the increased tax burden must have curtailed the monks' cashflow and their ability to fulfil wool contracts. Outside investment may well have been a temptation too great to resist, particularly in a period during which the local community involved the abbey in expensive litigation, perhaps the least obvious check on financial progression.

Throughout the latter half of the thirteenth century, Pipewell fell victim to numerous suits from local plaintiffs, asserting their seigneurial rights. The most serious plea was filed during the early 1270s, when the prior of nearby Monks Kirby temporarily obtained the valuable grange at Cawston. Though justices of the King's Bench intervened, the abbey was forced into a final concord and a fine of 200 marks to the prior for its return. The fine, of course, only exacerbated the costs of pleading, which involved the employment of lawyers, the journey to London, and payments to secure justice and the enrolment of the decision. Worse followed when the king pressed his claim for the grange in 1285 and the abbot had to defend himself before local Justices in Eyre. Only in 1292 could Abbot John de Hillun purchase the respite of the suit before the king at Westminster.[129] The processes of obtaining justice and defending rights and interests became part of the usual ebb and flow of monastic existence, particularly in the atmosphere of claim and counter-claim established by the English Justinian. Nevertheless, the legal travails of Hillun and his predecessor, Thomas de Grafton, 'slung a huge burden of debt around the necks of their successors'.[130]

Obviously the biggest such burden was the contract with Servat, Soliz and fellows. Possibly conceived at a moment of optimism from a myriad

---

[127] Graves, 'Economic Activities,' p. 46; *CPR, 1272–81*, p. 264; *CCh.R, 1277–1326*, p. 249.

[128] *The Coucher Book of Furness Abbey*, III, ed. J. C. Atkinson (Chetham Society, 1919), pp. 639–641.

[129] BL Cotton MS Otho B xiv, f. 154v.

[130] '*per huiusmodi placita angustiis et pressuris in tempore dicti abbatis supervenientibus creverunt debita diversa que postea in collibus successorum suorum ceciderunt onerosa valde*': BL Cotton MS Otho B xiv, f. 155v.

of mitigating factors, the fact remains that the monks reneged on the deal inordinately quickly. It is probable that problems were occurring only eighteen months after its inception. At nearby Wellingborough, the summer of 1290 saw the loss of 20 per cent of Crowland abbey's flock.[131] Signs that Pipewell had been blighted come as early as January 1291, when the abbot of Wardon (Beds.) mainperned to supply five sacks of *tayller* to the Cahorsins if Pipewell could not.[132] These negotiations may emanate from the arbitration which Edward I had initiated, possibly at the request of both parties – the merchants keen not to lose their investment, and the convent willing to come to terms to prevent penalties incurred through no fault of their own – which culminated in the enrolment of the arbiters' verdict on 28 February. The king's desire to secure the abbey's future and protect the interests of merchants with whom he had a close financial relationship can be seen in the verdict's enrolment in the Chancery and Exchequer, testament to the importance Edward gave to settlement.[133] It was perhaps this which persuaded him to stay at Pipewell in the previous September. Indeed, the renegotiation might originate directly in discussions taken at that time.

The resultant settlement seems skewed heavily in favour of the merchants. It retains the structure of the previous agreement, but includes a variety of apparently punitive clauses that point to the merchants' desire to obtain firmer control of their investment. Now, they were to receive *all* of the abbey's wool over thirteen years, presumably in recognition of the futility of their original deal for 360 sacks. *Tayller* wool, which had previously been sorted and packed separately, would be pressed among the remaining wool and, 'for divers trespasses and damages perpetrated against the merchants', two sacks each year would be taken from the woolsheds and given to the merchants *gratis*. The attached condition that, should the monks default, the merchants would be acquitted of 16 marks per sack suggests that these *gratis* sacks were taken as disguised interest. The same might be said for the 40 shillings and 3 sacks to be taken each year to make up for the merchants' loss of 1 sack over the previous two years. There is little doubt that the merchants were bitterly disappointed with the monks' investment of their money. Provisions permit them free access to their dresser, whose work is not to be criticised or rejected. They further dictate the construction of new storage facilities for wool in the abbey's sheds, ensuring that prepared wool is kept off the ground and well surrounded

[131] *Wellingborough Manorial Accounts*, p. 55.   [132] E 159/64, rot. 6d. *Advance Contracts*, no. 129.
[133] C 54/108, mm. 8d.–9d.; E 159/64, rot. 10; E 368/62, rot. 14. *Advance Contracts*, no. 133.

by walls, perhaps to ward off damp. The monks' failure to answer adequately for the issues of the 733 sheep originally purchased brought a redivision of the flock. Even though disease had probably intervened, 900 of the abbey's sheep were now to be separated from the remainder, marked with the signs of both parties and maintained wholly at the convent's costs as a breeding flock until the number of 2,000 had been reached. While the merchants would take half of the fleeces each year, any sheep dying were to be shorn and the fleeces sold. Profits were to be ploughed back into the purchase of new sheep at their agent's behest.

Despite such stinging criticism and an obvious desire to stamp their will on the agreement, there remains a willingness to compromise and maintain cordial relations for the benefit of both parties. The investment in sheep continued. The advances essentially remained as before, although it is questionable whether the £120 advanced upon the sealing of the contract really represented new money, rather than a deduction from the original advance. More importantly, the prices and the potential financial commitment remained stable. In analysing the contract, F. Arens contends that the merchants benefited by purchasing the wool at a preferential, discount rate (*Vorzugspreis*).[134] If Pegolotti's schedule indeed originates from the last quarter of the thirteenth century, this cannot be wholly correct. Even reduced by 20 per cent for costs of carriage to Flanders and a good profit, Pegolotti's price of 22 marks per sack of good wool would bring a domestic price of around 17 marks, making the Cahorsins offer of 21 marks for the bulk of the contract period more than generous.

Having attained a stake in the economic life of the monastery, the merchants possibly wished to enjoy the accompanying spiritual benefits. As in 1288, the merchants were to provide at least one, perhaps two, tuns of wine each year. While this may have been a sweetener to induce the abbot to agree to the merchants' monopoly, or simply a gift, the wine was explicitly presented for the celebration of Mass. Perhaps this was a symbolic offering to expiate the merchants' guilt in levying interest on their deal. Jamroziak has spoken of the Italians who dealt with Rievaulx as outsiders who 'never functioned as a part of the network of mutual obligations which existed locally'.[135] At Pipewell, however, the long-term commitment of the merchants to investing in the abbey and its produce perhaps involved the Cahorsins in ties of patronage. By 1314, and presumably sooner, William Servat acquired 5 stones of wool each year to put towards the robe he was to

---

[134] Arens, 'Wilhelm Servat,' p. 495.   [135] Jamroziak, 'Rievaulx Abbey,' p. 203.

receive from the abbey.[136] Resident in England for around fifty years, Servat had perhaps engaged himself in a more spiritual relationship as a patron of Pipewell, obtaining prayers and a place in the abbey's martyrology.

Unfortunately, this must remain speculation as such evidence does not survive. The same applies to the immediate consequences of their compromise. Nonetheless, the association of Pipewell with Servat and the Cahorsins continued until the summer of 1294. With war looming in Gascony and Edwardian finances stretched thinly by the demands of maintaining English hegemony in Scotland and Wales, Edward I not only banished all men of French blood in England, but also exiled many foreign merchants, seizing their wool stocks and trying to appropriate the wool they had contracted with monastic and lay producers for delivery after midsummer. A surcharge of 40s per sack was placed on the export of wool too.[137] Although the wool of Italian and Brabanter merchants was quickly released and the merchants rehabilitated, Edward persistently alienated French merchants. At a stroke, Pipewell had been shorn of the guaranteed market for its wool which the monks had hoped would maintain solvency and promote expansion. Worse still, this dovetailed with an economic slump and Edward I's battle to retain liquidity in pursuit of his military aims, which became the immediate catalysts for the collapse of Pipewell's finances.

The imposition of the 40s *maltote* and embargoes on trade with Flanders and other French territories enforced in 1294, together with the economic uncertainties flourishing in a period of incipient warfare, brought a significant fall in wool prices and a halving of exports in return for a large customs yield. Foreign demand for wool slackened and domestic merchants were hamstrung to an extent by the restrictions on their trade.[138] The wartime expansion of the national tax burden thus bit increasingly hard on communities struggling to find a profitable outlet for their main asset. In July 1294, Edward ordered an investigation into the contents of monastic and cathedral treasuries. Shortly thereafter, he successfully demanded the clergy grant half of their taxable income. Having encountered resistance and slow payment, Edward requested another tenth a year later and summoned individual monastic community leaders to attend a special parliament.[139] While agreeing to meet a national emergency with rebellion flaring in Wales and Scotland, the clerical convocation complained that by the increase in taxation 'the king has exhausted the treasure of the church'.[140]

---

[136] E 159/87, rot. 70. *Advance Contracts*, no. 190.   [137] E 159/68, rot. 82 (12 June 1294).
[138] Lloyd, *English Wool Trade*, p. 80.   [139] Deighton, 'Clerical Taxation,' pp. 172–173, 176–177.
[140] '*rex thesauros ecclesiae exhausit*'.

For few communities can this have been truer than for Pipewell, where the growing expense of daily life and estate administration combined with lofty architectural aspirations and the fiscal ambitions of the Crown to impose too great a burden on the monastic purse. There can be little doubt, however, that the spiralling debts owed to the Cahorsins provided the most severe strain. Despite the original potential perceived in their association, for the convent at least these negotiations had brought the abbey to its knees. It may be no coincidence that John de Hillun, the abbot who had overseen their relationship, was removed from the abbacy on 1 August 1294, a little over six weeks after the merchants had received orders to leave the country.[141] So onerous was this burden, indeed, that the impoverished convent petitioned the General Chapter for permission to disperse in 1296.[142]

PIPEWELL IN CRISIS

Ultimately, the convent does not appear to have been dispersed.[143] But, the petition is testament to the financial crisis at the abbey and may have been submitted as part of a plan of austerity introduced by the new abbot, Richard de Heyham, forced upon him by the king. Upon forfeiting foreign merchants in 1294, Edward assumed responsibility for the debts owed to them within his kingdom and demanded the abbey answer him for the Cahorsins' sheep, their issues and the sale of produce.[144] This perhaps introduced new urgency into combating debts. It is possible that Edward found the result unsatisfactory for he appears to have taken the abbey's goods into his hands late in 1296.[145] Whether he also took the abbey into his protection is, however, unclear. Certainly, a series of visitations between 1294 and 1296 had revealed crippling debts and allegations of financial irregularities and there must have been concerns over the abbey's short-term future.

Hillun's removal clearly caused a stir. An inquiry taken in the Exchequer at Michaelmas 1297 reveals that he had been removed at the behest of John

---

[141] BL Cotton MS Otho B xiv, f. 155v.; E 159/71, rot. 15d.   [142] *Statuta*, III, 286 (1296: 17).

[143] The chronicler remarks that by 1308 '*Sciendum est carissimi quod propter diversa debita, particula, placita et infortunia a prima domus fundacione usque ad cessionem abbatis Andree supervenencia nunquam fuit dispersio monachorum in Pipewella facta*'; 'It is to be known most beloved that dispersal had never been brought upon the monks in Pipewell on account of divers debts, pleas and misfortunes from the first foundation of the house until the death of Abbot Andrew.' BL Cotton MS Otho B xiv, f. 157r.

[144] E 159/72, rot. 23.

[145] E 210/8474 (letters of attorney for Brother Thomas de Hameye to plead in the royal court against the seizure – 5 March 1297).

of York, abbot of Newminster, head of the Cistercian Order in England and father abbot of Pipewell, in the aftermath of a visitation to ascertain the exact level of debt and establish a plan for repayment.[146] In the next three years, the abbey had endured visits from prominent abbots of the Order who had established the debt to the Cahorsins at £400. This suggests that the intervening years from 1291 had witnessed some attempt to meet the abbey's commitment to the merchants, an impression reinforced by Abbot Richard's answer to the royal inquiry in 1296 that his debt now stood at only £110. Bitter at his removal and ostracism, Hillun challenged this account, arguing that the established debt of £500 had thus been concealed from the king. Richard replied that his answer represented a fresh debt, he having accounted with the Cahorsins for the larger sum shortly after his elevation to the abbacy in October 1294. Sadly, though further inquiries were taken, the results are not known, and the case appears to peter out, although Hillun's failure to reappear before the Exchequer barons is suggestive that he had to be satisfied with his successor's riposte even if, ultimately, the merchants would not.

The years from 1294 to 1299 were *anni horribili* at Pipewell. A convent in turmoil headed by an abbot held 'in enmity'[147] by the Crown was forcibly bound to the king for debts he perceived as owing to him. Widespread proposed seizures of wool by prise at Lent 1297 stripped Pipewell of a further 5 sacks, 5 stones.[148] While the king's consequent debt of £29 5s 5d was offset against the £28 19s 8d owed by the abbey of the arrears of their debts to the king for the Cahorsins' wool and sheep, repeated petitions only secured the swift repayment promised by the king as early as October 1297 at Trinity 1312.[149] Dilatory repayment of this kind was another consequence of Edward I's rapacious quest for finances as his military campaign in Scotland again fed into renewed strife in Gascony. Repeated requests for taxes set at high rates in 1297 had provoked considerable opposition and had initially induced Edward to threaten his clerical opponents with outlawry and sequestration of their goods.[150] To avoid this fate, some had paid a fine equivalent to one fifth of their taxable income. Eventually, a compromise was negotiated and writs were issued for the collection of a fifth of clerical income or one third of their temporalities without exemption. By the summer of 1298, Edward had taken to begging Cistercian abbots to aid him in his urgent need and not to

---

[146] E 159/71, rot. 15d.   [147] 'de eius inimicicia hiis diebus': E 159/71, rot. 15d.

[148] Lloyd, *English Wool Trade*, pp. 87–89.

[149] *CPR, 1292–1301*, pp. 310–11; *1307–13*, p. 289 (23 October 1310); SC 8/297/14816, 315/E196; E 159/85, rot. 26 (Trinity 1312).

[150] Deighton, 'Clerical Taxation', pp. 177–187.

take money out of the kingdom to general chapters.[151] Murrain and a series of bad harvests, finally, contributed to the pre-famine nadir in the fortunes of the abbey. The accounts rendered to the king demonstrate that in 1296 and 1297, around 12 per cent–15 per cent of the Cahorsin merchants' sheep were slaughtered due to murrain, a figure which tallies well with the 15 per cent killed at nearby Wellingborough in 1296. Sheep sales were not strong either, Pipewell receiving only 8d per ewe compared with around 13d at Wellingborough.[152] On the other hand, the value of Pipewell's wool remained high. In 1296 and 1297, 289 and 322 fleeces were sold at 4s 4d (4.25s) and 4s 6d per stone respectively when the national average in these years has been calculated as 3.62s and 3.47s.[153] Disaster, though, struck in 1299. An inquiry taken in 1306 revealed that of 423 sheep pertaining to the Cahorsins' share kept in the abbot's custody in 1299, only 16 ewes survived.[154] Whether the remainder had been killed outright by disease[155] or had been slaughtered in winter when it became apparent that they had been afflicted with a form of scab is not clear, but the immediate consequences must have been devastating.

G. Barnes, in his study of Kirkstall abbey, however, remarks on the speed and relative completeness with which the monks were able to recover their fortunes after the utter devastation of their flocks and subsequent indebtedness.[156] Pipewell too, it appears, was able to weather such storms and, when the circumstances changed, flourish again. Old habits and necessities died hard and finances could perceptibly be rebuilt by employing the very measures that had led to the brink of disaster. But, even riding the crest of an economic boom, there remained an undercurrent of debt incurred through the advance sale of wool that would finally cast the abbey into catastrophe of worse proportions.

RECOVERY?

The abbacy of Andrew de Royewell arguably represented the apogee of Pipewell's economic fortunes in the Middle Ages. The ten years from his appointment in 1298 witnessed extensive building projects undertaken and

---

[151] *CCR, 1296–1302*, pp. 216–218.   [152] E 159/72, rot. 23; *Wellingborough Manorial Accounts*, pp. 67, 70.
[153] Lloyd, 'Movement of Wool Prices', p. 40. This may support Munro's argument that Lloyd's averages are on the low side, as his evidence centred on areas in southern England of low value: Munro, 'Wool Price Schedules and the Qualities of English Wool,' p. 129.
[154] E 159/80, rot. 37d.   [155] Five lambs had been killed by dogs.
[156] Barnes, *Kirkstall Abbey*, p. 40. The abbey's flock had been decimated in 1284, but had recovered to 4,500 by 1301.

completed and, unquestionably, the acceleration of the construction of the new abbey church, chapter-house, close and churchyard. Andrew presided over the construction and roofing of the stalls of infirmaries for the monks and lay brethren, the reredorter of the great chamber and its vaults. Lavish renovations at Braybrooke produced a new hall, chapel, kitchen, two chambers and a third '*ad purgacionem ventri necessaria*'. Although timber was plentiful in and around the abbey for construction, these achievements occurred during a peculiarly litigious period in the abbey's history. Nevertheless, Andrew impressed his successors by maintaining and winning crucial pleas at great expense, most notably over breaches of the abbey's millpond at Church Lawford and tithes at Rugby.[157] It is doubtful whether either could have been financed comfortably in the previous decade and an explanation is required.

Better climatic conditions and good harvests in the early fourteenth century enabled Andrew to create sizeable demesne flocks, herds and grain surpluses. At his death on 8 August 1308, Pipewell possessed 60 ploughs, 60 carthorses and horse-drawn carts, 120 affers, 311 plough oxen, 177 milch-cows and 126 calves, 10 bulls, 31 horses, 194 draught animals, 330 pigs, and 54 goats on the granges. According to an estimate made at the time, he bequeathed a surplus of 800 quarters of corn and malt to his successor.[158] This must have eased the task of feeding the convent and creating a surplus for sale. Most revealingly, he had apparently created a flock of 2,000 sheep of both sexes with 144 lambs. This would have left the abbey better placed to share in the present boom in the wool export trade.[159] A recoinage in 1299 lifted prices from the slump produced by Edward I's regulation of the trade, the *maltote*, and the prise. Before, but most especially after, the Flemish victory at Courtrai in 1302 and the Anglo-French peace agreement of Montreuil in 1303, annual demand for wool on continental markets rocketed to well over 40,000 sacks despite the imposition of a new custom on wool exports in 1303.[160]

Of course, it is difficult to take this particular flock size wholly at face value. Two thousand had been the exact number specified by the Cahorsins in the renegotiated contract of 1291. The suspicion lingers that the cellarer's account from which Abbot Nicholas received this information may have been invented to tally with the desired figure. Andrew himself apparently acted as cellarer and Nicholas himself suggests that Andrew 'had little

---

[157] BL Cotton MS Otho B xiv, f. 156r.   [158] BL Cotton MS Otho B xiv, f. 156v.
[159] For what follows, see Lloyd, *English Wool Trade*, pp. 99–100.
[160] *CFR, 1272–1307*, pp. 466, 470.

wool'.[161] On the other hand, with no corroborative evidence either way, this figure cannot be totally gainsaid. Indeed, it may even represent further investment in sheep by William Servat and his fellows. At the very least, it is probably indicative of a real recovery in flock strength at Pipewell. Andrew was apparently able to satisfy a group of Grantham merchants on a ten-year contract made with his predecessor for 100 sacks at 9 marks each.[162] There appears little reason to believe that this would have been the capacity limit. It is inconceivable, moreover, that the completion of the abbey church in 1311 could have been achieved without serious capital investment and the probability must be that this had been garnered from the monks' most marketable asset in advance contracts predicated on an expectation of a return on investment.

This period of buoyancy was, however, woefully short-lived and signs of another, more serious downward spiral in fortunes were present during moments of relative success. On 25 June 1310, just as wool exports were scaled back, the new abbot, Thomas de Thockrington, was summoned to appear before the Exchequer at the behest of William Servat and Jean de Redole to show why he should not be made to fulfil the obligations that his predecessor had entered into in February 1291.[163] When he appeared on 10 October, he claimed that he did not have to answer them as the merchants had been forfeited as enemies of the king, and that subsequently his predecessor had satisfied the king of all debts owed to them. Richard de Heyham, in his account with Edward I, had argued that *he* had satisfied the merchants before answering the king, but whether he had been acquitted of all such debts is debatable. The Exchequer barons adjourned the plea to take advice and scrutinise the rolls, but no result is recorded other than seven further adjournments until 1313. Whatever this implies, Thomas was in a rather weak position in comparison with Servat.

While Edward II shared his father's desire to shield monastic institutions from the worst consequences of economic distress, he too demonstrated great willingness to promote the interests of foreign merchants. Unlike the Frescobaldi, who were forced into exile by the Ordainers in 1311, or Antonio Pessagno of Genoa, his main financier thereafter, Servat did not court controversy, but remained a reliable financier worthy of reward. It is eminently probable that, due to his prior good service, Servat had enjoyed a much briefer period of alienation from Edward I in the late 1290s than other Cahorsins.[164] After the turn of the century he took on much greater

[161] '... *set lanas minime*'.   [162] BL Cotton MS Otho B xiv, f. 156r.
[163] E 13/34, m. 13.   [164] Lloyd, *Alien Merchants*, p. 96.

proximity to the Crown. Having been pardoned for clipping royal coins in 1300, he became one of the chief mercantile provisioners for the royal household, specialising in wine, spices and wax.[165] In return, he gained access to the issues of the new custom across a number of ports in 1303, the traditional method of royal debt repayment, though not before the king's leading financiers, the Frescobaldi had been paid off, a sinecure Edward II was only too happy to extend repeatedly.[166] In 1311, Servat was made responsible for the issues of the lands of the Templars in London.[167] It is doubtful, therefore, that recouping his investment made over twenty years ago at Pipewell was critical to his financial survival. Nevertheless, as we have seen, this had been no ordinary business association and Servat may well have exploited his position as 'king's merchant' in the favoured circles of Edward II to secure a return.

It is likely that the continued adjournments concealed negotiations between the two parties at the king's insistence, for Servat and Redole persisted in their attempts to broker a settlement. A petition submitted in April 1314 complained that, although they had been satisfied in £69 at the outbreak of Anglo-French hostilities in 1294, the monks claimed this during the merchants' forfeiture and concealed another £132 6s 8d which had been advanced to them.[168] However, requests for scrutiny of the Exchequer Rolls, which experience may have told them would turn up little, were soon reinforced by a direct plea to Edward II's father-in-law, Philip IV of France, who urged that the plea be settled.[169] Stung into action, Edward again called Thomas de Thockrington before the Exchequer and on 11 June, Servat and Redole acknowledged their satisfaction in all debts owed to them for sheep and wool.[170]

This, of course, was a neat legal fiction. No money changed hands, for in reality it entailed a second, far more realistic restructuring of the original wool contract of 1288. Such fictions had, indeed, become a common element in monastic debt settlement in the period. In 1315, for example, a similar final acquittance for a twenty-year contract originally made in 1298 with the Frescobaldi by Adam, abbot of Combermere, resulted in a second restructuring along more sensible lines.[171] At Pipewell, only 22 sacks were to change hands over eight years, 2 sacks in each of the first two years and 3 in the

---

[165] *CPR, 1292–1301*, pp. 557, 558; *1307–13*, p. 461; *CCR, 1302–07*, pp. 3, 8–9, 48; *CFR, 1272–1307*, p. 493; *1307–19*, pp. 50–51, 70, 133.

[166] *CFR, 1272–1303*, pp. 472–473; *1307–19*, p. 70 (August 1310); CPR, 1307–13, p. 270 (July 1310).

[167] *CPR, 1307–13*, p. 411.   [168] E 159/87, rot. 26d.; SC 8/279/13919, 318/E319, E327.

[169] SC 1/34/16.   [170] E 159/87, rot. 70. *Advance Contracts*, no. 190.

[171] E 159/72, rot. 45; 82, rot. 81; 88, rot. 140; 91, rot. 91. *Advance Contracts*, nos. 156, 182, 193, 195.

remaining six. The sack price of 15 marks probably represented both a penalty and a period of price deflation. Three stones of clack and locks were to be extracted from each sack and replaced by good wool, ensuring a delivery of higher than normal quality. An advance of £213 was paid, probably as a sign of the merchants' good faith, repayable in annual instalments of £26 12s 6d, while another £40 was to be made over in the quindene of Easter, which was to be allowed in the delivery of wool. Although the prepared wool was to be handed over at Pipewell, the monks were charged with carriage to Boston, possibly to make use of their exemptions from passage and pontage. Another 1,000 sheep of both sexes were purchased to be placed with the abbey's flock to create a breeding flock as before, but this time of only 1,500 sheep. Each year the fleeces were to be divided and sold to be ploughed back into the purchase of more sheep.

This is surely remarkable testament to both parties' continued faith in the potential profitability of their association whatever the past problems and ramifications. For William Servat, this was perhaps his closing gambit in a campaign he had been waging for over twenty years both to secure his own investment and to lift the monks out of trouble. Although they had been accused, and perhaps not without justice, of repeatedly trying to renege on the contract, they were still willing to deliver 5 stones of wool each year to William Servat for his robe, thereby tacitly recognising his position as one of their most important patrons with the mutual obligations that conferred. As on previous occasions, the monks may have been willing to accept cash at a time of crisis, praying that, with the investment in sheep, they would be able to deliver. In the final analysis, it may well have been partly this reluctance to cut its losses which brought at least Pipewell to disaster, though impending environmental catastrophe and dire necessity ensured that this could not ever be the case.

THE FOURTEENTH-CENTURY 'CRISIS'

The sealing of the contract presaged the most severe agrarian crisis within living memory at that time across much of the country.[172] Poor harvests at the end of the first decade of the new century had brought grain scarcity and higher prices. Thomas de Thockrington, appointed abbot in August 1308, had been compelled to purchase poor-quality grain widely at high

---

[172] For much of what follows, see Kershaw, 'The Great European Famine,' pp. 6–14. For other current literature of this subject see Jordan, *Great Famine* and Campbell (ed.), *Before the Black Death*.

prices (20s a quarter) as Pipewell's estates failed to meet demand.[173] Bread was rarely baked in the abbey's ovens and had to be carted in from Coventry at considerable expense. Indeed, the abbey's chronicler remarks that from the time of his appointment '*domus . . . peulatim cepit declinari*' (the house began gradually to decline).[174] By midsummer 1314, climatic indicators of such deterioration had multiplied. The subsequent harvest was unusually poor and crops may have been rotting in the ground after heavy downpours throughout spring. Crowland abbey, moreover, had apparently seen its flock shrink by 28 per cent – over 3,000 in number – in a new epidemic of murrain.[175] As in the 1280s, the deal with Servat could have been a pre-emptive gamble to combat the disease by slaughter of affected animals and consequent restocking.

The combination of virulent murrain and worsening famine caused by persistent rains and the consequent disastrous harvests over the next two summers ensured that the gamble failed. Flooding inundated fields and damaged mills, such as those at Roxton in Bedfordshire.[176] In the seven summers after 1314, only one produced corn good enough to be milled. In an attempt to resolve their dilemma, the abbot successfully petitioned Edward II for licence to assart, enclose, and bring into cultivation royal wastes in Rockingham forest.[177] Pipewell's abbots had long brought marginal lands under the plough.[178] But, by the fourteenth century, the fragility of their arable economy had repeatedly been exposed, implying that their search for fresh, cultivable land had increasingly taken them into areas less and less conducive even to subsistence-level agriculture. The monks were left to trawl local markets and producers, placing severe strain on the monastic budget. In 1316, the year of worst dearth, grain sold nationwide for upwards of 26s 8d a quarter, but at Leicester market, which John de Oudeby, the abbey's pantler, was forced to patronise, occasionally only one quarter of wheat would be sold, fetching 40s[179] A more general murrain also ravaged sheep flocks from 1315 to 1317, meaning that the monks could hardly generate income, could not fulfil contracts and were compelled to incur greater obligations to creditors.

Hamstrung, then, by inadequate demesne production, but bound by spiritual obligations to patrons and the poor in maintaining chantries and

---

[173] The national average for the first decade of the century was 5s 7¼d a quarter and had reached 8s by the autumn of 1315, which suggests this estimate may be an exaggeration: Kershaw, 'The Great European Famine,' p. 8.

[174] BL Cotton MS Otho B xiv, f. 157r.   [175] Kershaw, 'The Great European Famine,' p. 22.

[176] BL Cotton MS Otho B xiv, f. 159v.   [177] *CFR, 1307–19*, p. 235 (12 March 1315).

[178] BL Cotton MS Otho B xiv, f. 151v.   [179] BL Cotton MS Otho B xiv, f. 157r.

distributing alms, Pipewell abbey became trapped in a vicious circle of debt. It was not alone. I. Kershaw has calculated that in 1316 alone, over one hundred grants of royal protection were issued in favour of penurious monastic institutions.[180] Neither was it alone in the methods it employed to extricate itself. Despite Servat's purchase of *all* of the abbey's wool for eight years in 1314, Thockrington nevertheless finally and definitively flouted this monopoly and took money wherever he could find it. His wool attracted suitors from the elite of the Italian mercantile financier community and, although a swift recovery in flock numbers could hardly have occurred by 1317, more clement climatic conditions in that year and the next perhaps persuaded them that they could access a reliable source at a time of shortage. Indeed, over the next four years, Pipewell eased its cashflow crisis by negotiating sizeable advances on the back of its best asset.

On 20 July 1319, the English factors of the Bardi company of Florence purchased 18 sacks of wool from Thockrington, for which they offered £10 a sack – the same price as Servat had paid – and perhaps paid 120 marks in advance.[181] This connection continued a year later when Manento Francisci, former head of the company's operations in England, purchased 20 sacks at £10 a sack.[182] Of course, as with all wool contracts throughout the period in question, the possibility remains that no wool was intended to change hands and that the sum paid in advance was purely a loan which might be repaid in wool, but could often be repaid in cash. Although Francisci nominally contracted for 20 sacks, he would accept repayment of £200 in cash. At the same moment as the Bardi purchased 18 sacks, Banquino Bruneleschi of Florence loaned Pipewell 80 marks.[183] On 22 April 1320, the king's Italian leech Poncio de Controne, Peregrino Bonoditi de Controne, and Niccola Filippi of Lucca, forwarded £200. On the same day Bindo Gili, a Florentine merchant, advanced £73, while a day later the Francisci brothers had their Recognisance for £200 enrolled.[184] Two months on, Manento Francisci combined with another Florentine, Giovanni Marsopini, to lend £400.[185] None can be positively linked to sales of wool.

Nevertheless, the evidence suggests that contracts should be taken at their word and that the merchants were keen to exercise some claim to depleted monastic wool stocks. Pipewell apparently delivered 11 sacks to Francisci and 8 to the Bardi. Advances at this time may, in fact, have

---

[180] Kershaw, 'The Great European Famine,' p. 30. Pipewell is not amongst them.
[181] BL Cotton MS Otho B xiv, f. 158r. A Recognisance for this latter sum was enrolled in the Exchequer on 23 July: E 159/92, rot. 88d.
[182] BL Cotton MS Otho B xiv, ff. 157v., 195r. (13 April 1320).   [183] E 159/92, rot. 88 (21 July 1319).
[184] E159/93, rot. 59.   [185] *CCR, 1318–23*, p. 241.

established preferential delivery of high-quality wool if and when stocks recovered, and may even have been loans to accelerate the recovery process in the meantime. A year before their first wool contract, the Bardi had forwarded 100 marks, while just two months before he and his brothers purchased 20 sacks, Francisci had loaned the abbey £100.[186] On a national level, Italian loans to Cistercian and other notable wool-producing abbeys predominate and some Recognisances specify that advances are 'loans' to be put to the use of the convent.[187] While this is rather vague and may equally refer to simple sustenance, the quicker monasteries were able to right their finances and stock, the quicker the floundering wool trade might recover and debt could be serviced.

The European famine caused a dramatic slump in demand for wool and exports ran at under 20,000 sacks a year in 1315. It struck in the wake of English defeat at Bannockburn in June 1314 and mingled with Edward II's abortive attempts to regain hegemony in Scotland and Ireland, where Edward Bruce invaded and proclaimed himself king in May 1315, and subsequent rebellions in Glamorgan and at Bristol in 1316.[188] For many of the Italian financiers at court, these dual prongs strained finances, for he demanded larger loans and purveyances to fund his war efforts.[189] Between 1312 and 1315, for example, Manento Francisci had already received assignments from the Exchequer of issues worth over £15,000 in return for loans to the king as the chief Bardi factor in England.[190] In 1316, he was commissioned to provide 700 quarters of wheat for the Scottish campaign.[191] His successors, led by Roger Ardingelli and Francisco Balducci Pegolotti, both of whom dealt with Pipewell, kept Edward solvent for the remainder of the decade, making huge individual loans, such as the 10,000 marks advanced in November 1317.[192] Their rewards were tangible, chief among which was almost monopolistic assignment from the wool customs.[193] Assisting struggling monasteries, many of whom, particularly in the Cistercian Order,

---

[186] *CCR, 1318–23*, p. 94 (Bardi, 22 July 1318), p. 223 (Francisci, 28 February 1320).

[187] E 159/91, rot. 73d. – loan of £140 (18 October 1317) by Banquino Bruneleschi of Florence to Bruern '*ad ardua negocia domus sue inde expedienda*'; E 159/92, rot. 60d. – loan of 80 marks (1 August 1319) to Combe '*pro arduis nostris negociis domus et ecclesie nostre inde expediendis et promovendis*'.

[188] R. M. Haines, *King Edward II: His Reign and its Aftermath, 1284–1330* (Montreal, 2003), pp. 98–101, 289.

[189] The mission of Roger Mortimer to Ireland in April 1317, for example, was partly financed by Antonio Pessagno of Genoa and the Bardi: *CPR, 1313–17*, p. 608.

[190] *CCR, 1307–13*, pp. 403, 405–406, 407; *1313–18*, pp. 33, 114, 118, 121–122, 144–145; *CFR, 1307–19*, pp. 158, 168, 178, 186; *CPR, 1313–17*, pp. 11, 19, 106–107.

[191] *CCR, 1313–18*, p. 383.

[192] *CPR, 1317–21*, pp. 55, 59.

[193] *CPR, 1313–17*, pp. 608, 672–673; *1317–21*, pp. 9, 11, 15–16, 127; *CCR, 1313–18*, p. 492.

were among the leading producers of the best-quality wool in the British Isles, thus made obvious sense.

Indeed, Pipewell, was merely one link in these extending chains of credit. The Bardi were certainly prominent creditors in Northamptonshire and Warwickshire, lending 70m 6s 8d to Sulby shortly after its first surviving loan to Pipewell and 80 marks to Combe in August 1319.[194] They were also active elsewhere, Francisci advancing 200 marks to Vaudey on the day before he loaned Pipewell £200.[195] Bruern in the Cotswolds, an abbey with some of the most prized wool in England, took £154 17s 4d from the Bardi on 20 October 1317, two days after it had received £140 from Banquino Bruneleschi.[196] Bruneleschi himself loaned at least £430 to Sawtry (Hunts.), Wardon and the Gilbertine house of Chicksands (Beds.) in November 1317.[197] What overall effect such a flow of credit in the direction of wool-producing houses had can only be guessed, but between 1319 and 1321, wool exports revealingly rose again to over 30,000 sacks.[198]

So acute were the financial problems at many houses, however, that the expansion of credit created as many problems as it attempted to resolve. Loans had to be repaid and often at harsh terms. Pipewell's loans from Controne and Gili had to be met within eight months, for example. Debts were increasingly incurred to service other credit obligations and the consequences could be drastic, particularly when the better harvests of 1317 and 1318 and the retreat of the sheep murrain proved to be false dawns as the rains returned and with them rinderpest, which decimated stocks of draught animals across the country.[199] Crops, which damp had not destroyed, rotted in the fields and once more a crisis of subsistence set in.

In January 1320, Pipewell endured a visitation from its father abbot, John of Whelpington, abbot of Newminster.[200] He established Pipewell's debt at £469 20s 10d, around the level it had been in 1296, permitting the monks to sell the abbey's goods to meet debts. The abbey chronicle reveals that this would have availed them little, for the full extent of their debts had been concealed from their visitor, a marginal note estimating the true total at £1,118 3s 4d, which does appear a more accurate assessment. Whether such deceit or more general despair at his decision-making

[194] E 159/92, rots. 60d. (28 July 1318), 89. [195] E 159/93, rot. 58 (12 April 1320).
[196] E 159/91, rots. 73d., 74.
[197] E 159/91, rots. 75d., 77, 77d. This small list, however, does very little justice to the large number of Recognisances surviving on the Memoranda Rolls in 1317–20, which demonstrate monastic credit relationships across most orders and in most counties of England and Wales.
[198] Lloyd, 'Movement of Wool Prices', p. 18. [199] BL Cotton MS Otho B xiv, f. 160v.
[200] BL Cotton MS Otho B xiv, ff. 157v.–158r.

brought about the deposition of Thomas de Thockrington on 1 January 1321, is difficult to say.[201] His strategy of taking Italian silver did bind the abbey to outside forces and made extricating it from ever-decreasing circles of debt increasingly problematic. In an effort to meet contract obligations to foreign merchants, the abbey had purchased wool worth 100 marks from Roger Belers, a local Leicestershire landowner and retainer of Thomas earl of Lancaster, cousin and most prominent critic of Edward II. After Lancaster's defeat at Boroughbridge in March 1322, Belers became one of the architects of Exchequer reform during the 'tyranny' of Edward II. He proceeded to extort a £100 annuity from the abbey and a pledge of the granges of Elkington and Cold Ashby.[202] Furthermore, in November 1321, Giovanni Marsopini and Asselino Simonetti of Lucca loaned 200 marks to have first refusal on the abbey's goods that were to be sold off to meet its debts.[203] The vultures, it appeared, were now circling to pick over the abbey's carcass.

Despite an initial determination to meet his predecessor's obligations, William of Lawford, the new abbot, soon succumbed to the yoke of burden (*jugum oneris*) of debt. In the first month of his rule, he procured the cancellation of the Recognisances to Poncio de Controne and Bindo Gili, wiping £273 from the calculations.[204] He was also able to deliver 11 sacks to Manento Francisci and 8 of the 18 sacks owed to the Bardi. It is worth remembering, though, that such cancellations did not necessarily imply full payment. Francisci only finally agreed to annul his agreement three years after it had technically been settled in August 1323. The Bardi, moreover, exacted a penalty of £40 for a false weighing of the delivered wool and for failing to carry it to the delivery point at Stamford, although they were willing to loan a further £50 on 9 February 1321.[205] This last loan highlights the quandary into which every abbot of Pipewell had fallen over the past forty years – no matter how straitened the circumstances, the repeated acceptance of liquid capital to sustain the brethren and their obligations made the light at the end of the tunnel seem closer irrespective of the likely consequences. For Lawford, though, these consequences brought scandal and lasting infamy.

---

[201] BL Cotton MS Otho B xiv, f. 194r.

[202] BL Cotton MS Otho B xiv, f. 186r.: '*ad opus domini Rogeri Boler cui domus tenebatur in c marcis . . . pro lanis ab eodem emptis ad opus mercatorum*'. For Belers, see N. M. Fryde, *Tyranny and Fall of Edward II, 1322–6* (Cambridge, 1979), pp. 101–104.

[203] E 159/95, rot. 39d.; BL Cotton MS Otho B xiv, ff. 159r., 196r.

[204] BL Stowe MS 937, f. 143r.   [205] BL Cotton MS Otho B xiv, f. 158r.; E 159/94, rot. 67d.

He was singularly unfortunate that his elevation to the abbacy coincided with perhaps the worst of all of the crisis years. Another deluge had ruined the harvest in 1320, while drought brought renewed crop failures and famine in 1321.[206] Even in Norfolk, England's most prosperous county, the failure of the barley harvest and the return of sheep murrain created unrivalled destitution.[207] Wool exports slumped to only 18,000 sacks.[208] The only solution apparent amidst this desolation was that proposed by the abbot of Newminster in 1320. The abbey's assets had to be sold off, even if only temporarily, to raise enough money upon which the brethren could survive.

Historians have long viewed the early fourteenth century as a watershed in the Cistercian and national agrarian economy. D. Knowles commented that the monks were 'gradually going over from direct exploitation . . . to rents and leases'.[209] Certainly, in 1293 the General Chapter legislated to permit land exchanges and alienations without its licence and in 1315 it authorised leases to laymen for life if the benefits would be manifest.[210] J. Donnelly has argued that leases of granges at Fountains, Furness, Meaux and Whalley helped finance debt repayments without incurring further charges.[211] On broader social levels, B. Harvey believes that land transactions took place in times of greatest dearth, as sellers attempted to gain sufficient liquidity to survive crises.[212] At Pipewell, however, the impression lingers that the loss of the keystones of the monastic economy, whatever the short-term financial benefit, proved insufficient to improve the abbey's finances.

The abbey chronicle details goods sold off to service debts[213]: wool worth £30; the produce of fishponds worth £19; five large basins for £7; the produce of felling trees worth £110. More seriously, demises for immediate profit reduced the income-generating capacity of the abbey's demesne and seigneurial rights and brought in less than expected. Two barns at Braybrooke and Dunchurch were sold for £20, while 20s accrued from the

---

[206] Kershaw, 'The Great European Famine,' p. 15.
[207] P. Nightingale, 'Norwich, London, and the Regional Integration of Norfolk's Economy in the First Half of the Fourteenth Century', in *Trade, Urban Hinterlands and Market Integration c. 1300–1600*, ed. James Galloway (London: Centre for Metropolitan History Working Paper Series 3, 2000), p. 94.
[208] Lloyd, 'Movement of Wool Prices', p. 18.   [209] Knowles, *Religious Orders* II, p. 126.
[210] *Statuta*, III, 261 (1293: 2), 330 (1315:4).
[211] Donnelly, 'Changes in the Grange Economy,' pp. 426–442.
[212] B. Harvey, 'Introduction' in Campbell (ed.), *Before the Black Death*, p. 14.
[213] BL Cotton MS Otho B xiv, f. 158v.

sale of a cowshed at Dunchurch. A windmill at Rugby fetched £5 6s
8d. William de Bromwyk, moreover, paid £10 to have a long-term
reduction in rent. At Marham, the monks intended to demise their
land to Robert of Lawford for 26s 8d, but *propter sterilitatem* at Easter
1321 he would only pay 20s. Conversely, Robert purchased the mill at
Church Lawford for 8 quarters of grain and an annual mulcture, a sign
perhaps of the monks' desperate need for foodstuffs, but he was able to
make material improvements in spending more than the monks on its
repair.

The most instantly profitable demise came on 3 November 1321, the very
day upon which Simonetti and Marsopini asserted their right to first refusal
on the abbey's goods.[214] After considerable wrangling in London and a
dispute with the convent over its sale, Augustine le Waleys received pos-
session of the grange of Cold Ashby, rendering £180 in advance, for an
annual render of a rose (token payment). Apart from this large lump sum,
this sale is significant as it perhaps marks a sea-change in the abbey's attitude
to finance and a longer-term search for more local patrons who would be
better placed to reduce the charges on the monks. On 14 February 1321,
Abbot William demised the grange at Elkington to William Tekne, burgess
of Northampton.[215] Elkington suffered badly during the famine years and
could no longer support more than a handful of the abbey's beasts.[216] More
importantly in the immediate short term, by a loan of £100 worth of grain,
malt, and ale, the grange was demised to him rent-free for a term of nine
years. Disquiet in the convent about the generosity of this sale prompted the
negotiation of a new lease. In return for establishing the abbey's debt to him
for foodstuffs at £200 in the court of the King's Bench, William received
the grange for nine years at an annual render of 90 marks, as well as 40
quarters of corn in the first year, 50 quarters in the second and 60 year on
year for the remaining seven years. Throughout this term, moreover,
William was to find pasture and fodder for 300 ewes and their issue at
Calewelhilcote for the abbot and convent. Sheep, after all, were the lifeblood of Pipewell's economy. William Servat died in 1320 and with him any
hope of further Cahorsin investment in the abbey's stock at a time of real
desperation. Nevertheless, this does not appear to have deterred Pipewell

[214] BL Stowe MS 937, f. 22v.; Cotton MS Otho B xiv, ff. 186v.–187r.
[215] BL Cotton MS Otho B xiv, ff. 160v., 187v.
[216] 'nec fuit tunc aliquis monachus vel conversus qui voluit scivit vel potuit custodiam dicte grangie adviter
sine auxilio magno bursa communis et sumptuoso'.

from seeking patrons willing to enter into a business relationship of the kind practised by Servat.

On 8 June 1321, Abbot William demised the grange of Newbold-on-Avon to John and Henry, sons of Hugh de Merynton, merchant of Coventry, at an annual rent of £8.[217] By July 1322, he appears to have granted Hugh £20 of annual rent from the granges of Cawston and Dunchurch. He also leased the manor of Cawston for £40 on condition that Hugh managed grain production and pasture, but only took his profit in corn, hay and grass after the abbey had repaid him this sum, thereby passing the costs of production on to a party with greater liquidity, but without prejudicing their subsistence needs.[218] Coventry, of course, lay a very short distance from some of Pipewell's most valuable Warwickshire granges and Hugh had moved into the abbey's orbit over a number of years.[219] Around the time of the initial demise of Newbold, Hugh received from the Bardi the abbey's as yet unfulfilled obligation for 12 of the 18 sacks that Thomas de Thockrington had agreed to deliver in July 1319.[220]

Sometime shortly thereafter, Abbot William agreed to sell Hugh sixty sacks of wool and sixty fleeces over the next ten years.[221] This may equate in part with the contract related in the abbey chronicle for 45 sacks, at 10 marks a sack, over seven-and-a-half years.[222] Revealingly, this contract committed the monks to paying Hugh and his wife an annuity of 40s in return for his purchase for them of 100 sheep. An advance of 20 marks was made on condition that the monks reinvested it in the purchase of more sheep. As with the contract, which overshadowed all of Pipewell's financial dealings during this period, they did not. For all Merynton, le Waleys, and Tekne could offer the monks, the level of their investment in the short term could not offset climatic catastrophe and the crippling level of long-standing debt, as it necessitated the removal of production units from the monastic economy and the consequent obligations for further debts. On 28 April 1322, Edward II took Pipewell into his protection. Just under a year later, on 24 April 1323, William of Lawford, presumably pressured by monks nourished only by black bread and potage and despairing of a revival in the abbey's fortunes, resigned his rule. Only four months later, on

---

[217] BL Cotton MS Otho B xiv, f. 190r.   [218] E 326/8934.
[219] For analysis of Coventry's merchant community and its relationship with its hinterland, see R. M. Goddard, *Lordship and Medieval Urbanisation: Coventry, 1043–1355* (Woodbridge, 2004).
[220] *CPR, 1317–21*, p. 410.
[221] Two letters of acquittance drawn up in 1324 attest to this agreement, the second stating that the monks had satisfied Hugh for the third year: E 326/8934, 11541.
[222] BL Cotton MS Otho B xiv, f. 161v.

13 September, '*per . . . pondera oneris domus sancte Marie pervenit ad ultimum punctum inedie ac paupertatis*',[223] and was dispersed for three years, as it finally acknowledged defeat in its struggle to stay afloat, a struggle that had endured for over forty years.[224]

EXONERATION OR BLAME?

In her study of the bankruptcies of Rievaulx abbey in the late thirteenth century, E. Jamroziak not only dispels the notion that the monks' ill-fated forays into the wool market represented a significant and growing departure from the Cistercian orthodoxy, but she also goes a long way in exonerating the convent of the charge of 'mismanagement'.[225] Cash-strapped monasteries were drawn into marketing their primary saleable asset – wool – in order to sustain higher living costs, royal taxation, and to fund projects to the greater glory of God and their own community. When environmental calamities and endemic outbreaks of disease combined to decimate flocks, indebtedness became a 'way of life'. Nowhere else would appear better able to corroborate this argument, but can an assessment of recurrent financial crisis conclude by similarly exonerating its monks?

It is undeniable that the four decades either side of the turn of the fourteenth century represent one of the most turbulent periods in the economic history of England and of Cistercian involvement in that economy. Pipewell, whose monks repeatedly struggled to raise sufficient surpluses of grain from its increasingly marginal lands, experienced the wide fluctuations between dizzying booms of buoyant demand and good prices for its wool, on one hand, and spiralling lows marked by bovine and ovine pestilence and famine on the other. Taxation too, in adding to the rising burden of debt, threatened to swamp the community with commitments that it could not hope to fulfil. It is probably best to let the monks describe what the combined effects had been.

A petition from the abbot and convent of Pipewell speaks of the decimation wrought by the recent years of dearth and by murrain and of the recurrent threat of dispersal.[226] In response to the latest tax demand,

---

[223] 'By . . . the weight of this burden the house of St mary reached its ultimate end of starvation and poverty'.

[224] BL Stowe MS 937, f. 143v.; Cotton MS Otho B xiv, f. 150r.

[225] Jamroziak, 'Rievaulx Abbey,' pp. 215–217; R. H. Snape, *English Monastic Finances in the Later Middle Ages* (Cambridge, 1926), p. 128.

[226] SC 8/66/3274: '*la dite meson seyt si enpouery par le [. . .] annees qe avaunt ses heures ount este e par morine des bestes . . .*'

they claim that their old assessment now exceeds what could be spent from the revenue of the lands still in their hands in one year and request they be taxed on what they have at least until the king has received what is due to him from a lay twentieth and other tallages and customs. Without such a reassessment they would not be able to maintain the chantries and alms with which their founders and patrons have charged them and would have to disperse.[227] Of course, the monks know exactly which buttons to press and their plea is calculated to appeal to the royal duty of protection for struggling religious institutions. Exaggerating their case or the possible consequences might tug more firmly at the royal heartstrings and be more likely to evince a positive response. Sadly, this was definitely not the case, the king refusing the request as he '*ad tant a faire de ses deners qil ne les puisse mie respiter*' ('had so much to do with his money that he cannot respite this'). References to the concurrent clerical tenth and lay twentieth and the ravages over the years date it most probably to 1327/8, making it doubtful in this case that they were cynically manipulating Edward III.[228] Nightingale has shown that the years 1325–9 represented one of the worst periods in the economic history of Norfolk, with a return of heavy rains and disease.[229] It is likely that even after its reconstitution, which probably occurred simultaneously with the cancellation of long-standing Recognisances to the Bardi in June 1326,[230] Pipewell abbey continued to suffer from chronic indebtedness.

It is hard, though, to believe that the monks who submitted this petition could have been wholly forgiving of their predecessors. Indeed, their plea emphasises that previous abbots had leased lands and possessions in return for money paid in advance in order, so they said, to evade dispersal.[231] The convent had witnessed the loss of many of their most valuable units of production. Early in Edward III's reign, they negotiated with Thomas

---

[227] '*la quele demaunde amounte a plus qils ne pount despendre par an de totes lour terres en lour mayn demorauntz, par quey sil payent tute la dite demaunde de disme ils ne pount recoverir a longe temps ne lour chaunteries ne autres almoygnes dount yl sount chargez par lour foundours et feffours a meyntenir ne pount mes covent qils mettount lour covent en dispercion*'.

[228] W. M. Ormrod, 'The Crown and the English Economy, 1290–1348', in Campbell (ed.), *Before the Black Death*, p. 161; *Lay Taxes in England and Wales, 1188–1688*, ed. M. Jurkowski, C. L. Smith and D. Crook (Richmond, 1998), p. 36. The only other plausible year would appear to be 1316, but references to the demises discussed above, which mainly occurred towards the beginning of the 1320s, militate against this.

[229] Nightingale, 'Norfolk, London, and the Regional Integration of Norfolk's Economy', p. 94.

[230] BL Stowe MS 937, f. 143r.

[231] '*les predecessours le dit abbe ount lesse lour terres, rentes e possessiouns en [. . .] mayn ascunz a terme de vye ascuns a lunge terme des annz e pristrent lour deners devaunt la mayn pur lour sustenaunce e pur escure la dispercioun de[..] covent*'.

Latimer to quash a demise made to him in 1318 of lands in Braybrooke.[232] Moreover, William of Lawford's penitent confession of guilt and submission to temptation in entering into the Recognisances which caused the abbey's dispersal served as a salutary reminder to the monks of their forebears' actions and their consequences. Jamroziak questions whether Rievaulx's monks, in simultaneously taking on wool contracts for over eighty sacks a year, an impossible burden, were 'risk-loving investors', unscrupulously taking Italian lucre in the knowledge that they could fall back on royal protection.[233] While she answers in the negative, even a fraction of the commitments that Thomas de Thockrington and William of Lawford entered into from 1317 to 1323 would have been impossible to meet, stock levels falling to terrible lows. In January 1321, Thomas bequeathed to his successor only 45 per cent of the affers, 15 per cent of the plough oxen, 7 per cent of the milch-cows and, most importantly, 33 per cent of the sheep which he had received in 1308 from Andrew de Royewell. By April 1323, William of Lawford possessed only 54 per cent of the affers, 21 per cent of the plough oxen and 43 per cent of the sheep that Thomas had left to him.[234] Were they deceitfully taking money and not employing it for the purposes it was intended?

Abbot Nicholas, or his apologist, certainly looked back on his experiences in the convent during this period with considerable regret. Remarking on the deal with Hugh de Merynton, by which the abbey received an advance of 20 marks, he argues that, had it been used to buy more sheep as specified in the contract, the church of Pipewell would have felt considerable benefit.[235] Accusations of deceit pervade accounts of the abbey's recent history. After all, at least three abbots resigned, or were forced to resign, their office shrouded in debt and controversy. Richard de Heyham, Andrew de Royewell and Thomas de Thockrington, moreover, were accused of concealing the full nature of their debts, while secret alienations, gifts, and private sales of timber against the convent's consent are attributed to most of Nicholas's predecessors.[236] Shortly before the dispersal, too, the abbey apparently succeeded in having the contract with the Cahorsins quashed for as little as two marks 'per viam dexteram sinistram' after the death of Servat's executor, John de Stoketon.[237] Even accounting for the abbey chronicle's slanted view of history to exonerate

---

[232] BL Stowe MS 937, f. 72v.   [233] Jamroziak, 'Rievaulx Abbey,' p. 214–215.
[234] BL Cotton MS Otho B xiv, ff. 158r., 161r.   [235] BL Cotton MS Otho B xiv, f. 161v.
[236] BL Cotton MS Otho B xiv, f. 151r.   [237] BL Cotton MS Otho B xiv, f. 155v.

Nicholas from blame, casting off the shackles of this most pressing of debts had long been the aim of successive abbots.

There can be little question that the association with the Cahorsins was the single most important factor behind the financial difficulties faced by Pipewell abbey. As the relationship matured, it hung in a Damocletian manner over the heads of the monks who repeatedly took the Cahorsins' investment, but persistently reneged on fulfilling their obligations, even on occasion trying to backtrack and have it quashed by dubious means. And yet it is unlikely that it was a relationship founded on deceit, being instead intended to give both parties long-term security and stability. Even the hostile abbey chronicler is forced to admit that 'if Abbot William had not reduced the debt during his time, the house of Pipewell would have incurred irreparable damage'.[238] Formed at a time of stock shortages and disease, the business relationship between the abbey and the Cahorsins offered the possibility of establishing a breeding flock both to survive the current crisis and a firmer foundation for future prosperity.[239] The quality of their product enabled the monks to attract investors who were clearly not solely interested in a quick return on their outlay. Regardless of the drain subsequent defaults and legal entanglements had on their resources, investment in sheep purchases and large advance payments suggests that the Cahorsins were not prepared to forgo the potential profitability of this arrangement, frequently bailing out the monks. William Servat, moreover, in obtaining a stake in the future direction of the abbey, had perhaps even become bound in the abbey's network of patronage, entering into a series of reciprocal economic and spiritual obligations. Intriguingly, after the convent's dispersal, a visitation decreed that as the Cahorsins had not been satisfied, the monks would offer daily prayers for them and the rest of their benefactors at the altar of St Michael.[240]

Throughout its recent history, therefore, there was unrivalled evidence at Pipewell for a desire to establish a sustainable economy centred on wool production and to attract patrons from a wider community. The Cahorsins

[238] BL Cotton MS Otho B xiv, f. 159v.: '*Pro certo dico quod nisi abbas Willelmus in tempore suo debitum Servat declinasset, domus de Pipewell dampnum irrecuperabile incurrisset*'.

[239] Whilst Pipewell took a risk with its most valuable asset, wool, to attempt to survive, other European monasteries used other creative financial techniques to keep solvent during this period of crisis. For example, a German-Danish house, Klosster Reinbek, sold a village to a lay donor in 1316, and numerous other houses were forced to alienate their property, either for limited periods or in perpetuity: Jordan, *Great Famine*, 65–67. In modern finance terms these institutions were mortgaging, or on occasion liquidating, their real estate portfolios to access the cash they needed for daily survival.

[240] BL Cotton MS Otho B xiv, f. 195r.

were eventually replaced in this scheme by Hugh de Merynton. The downside, of course, was that this always had the potential to throw the monks into the hands of outside forces who did not have their best interests at heart. A combination of bad luck and unrealistic expectations of their flocks had driven them into a vicious circle, where their original need for money for monastic subsistence and future expansion became subsumed by the desperate desire to counter increasing poverty and new debts, whether in wool or in cash, taken to service old debts; as the circle constricted, so they fell further and further into trouble. But although it became 'easy to take, but hard to give', the end justified the means.

CHAPTER 4

Modern finance in the Middle Ages? Financial Aspects of the Advance Contracts for the Sale of Wool

The objective of this chapter is to use valuation techniques from 'modern' finance theory to analyse the large number of advance contracts for the sale of wool that were described in previous chapters. Specifically, we conduct two separate pieces of empirical analysis. We first calculate the implied interest rates for these transactions, which can then be compared with those for similar transactions documented in extant secondary sources. Second, we examine the efficiency of the wool market, which relates to how quickly relevant information is reflected in the wool market prices. To anticipate our main findings, we observe that plausible rates of interest were charged and that the wool market appears to have been efficient.

SOURCES OF DATA, CONTRACT DETAILS AND WOOL PRICING

As discussed in detail in Chapter 2, the unique data employed in this study are the details of recorded contracts between sheep farmers and, generally, foreign merchants seeking wool to export for textile manufacture. To summarise our previous discussion, information from over 200 contracts has been collected from the National Archives for the period 1200–1330, although the vast majority were enrolled between 1270 and 1310. Simple registrations of debt and more complex arrangements are found in the Memoranda Rolls of the Exchequer, longer, more detailed contracts in the Close Rolls of the Chancery, while the Plea Rolls of the Exchequer detail disputes over, and attempted resolution of, instances of default. Most contracts were written in medieval Latin, though a handful survive in medieval French. The contracts are highly detailed[1] and give information

---

[1] It should be stated at the outset that any study of medieval source data from a modern finance perspective is fraught with difficulty. The techniques that are in common usage today for the pricing of financial assets can typically rely on large quantities of readily accessible data of high quality. However, the records that were kept in the Middle Ages were far from complete, and there was no

on the purchaser and seller, the quality and amount of wool to be delivered, the due dates and conditions for delivery, and the amount of money per sack to be paid, together with information on any advance and miscellaneous payments towards the costs of preparation or carriage. Contracts could technically remain in force from just a few months to as long as twenty years. In total, they record arrangements for the delivery of around 5,300 sacks of wool between both a small number of individual, lay producers and all of the major monastic orders (though the Cistercians predominate, contracting for exactly half of the total wool sold) and wool merchants from England, France, Flanders, Germany, Spain, and, most especially, the Italian city states of Florence, Lucca, Piacenza, and Pistoia.

A first question that arises from a financial perspective is whether these contracts are best termed 'futures' or 'forward agreements'. In the former case, the contracts would be highly standardised (for example, in terms of the delivery dates and wool amounts, qualities and prices) and the contracts could be bought or sold on to a third party after their inception. So, in the case of a futures contract, a wool-grower could 'close out' an agreement that he had made to sell wool in the future by buying the same amount for delivery on the same date. However, these contracts were individually tailored by the counterparties since no formalised secondary market existed (so that the contract agreements could not subsequently be sold on to another party), and thus it is evident that these are forward agreements of sorts rather than futures contracts in financial parlance.

WHY WERE THESE AGREEMENTS FORMED AND WHAT WAS THE NATURE OF THEM?

What did the monks and the merchants have to gain from entering into agreements to exchange wool for so many years in advance? For the monasteries, their gains from the contract could be two-fold. First, they would have known in advance how much money they would obtain for their wool for several years into the future, which would have enabled them to plan financially. Indeed, both parties would have benefited from the

---

international standard in terms of wool quality, quantity or even exchange rates, all of which combine to make comparisons across different transactions difficult. For example, Lloyd, 'Movement of Wool Prices', p. 2, argues that, 'a stone . . . might weigh almost anything from 6 to 28 pounds'. Therefore, the calculations performed below will necessarily require a number of assumptions that would be unnecessary for research using modern data.

certainty of price paid/received for the wool since neither would be able to predict with any reasonable accuracy whether the price would rise or fall between contract signing and delivery date. In exploiting their single most marketable asset, their flock, community leaders would have been able to make a reliable estimate of their potential income. In addition, by constructing a broader network of business contacts they might also hope to obtain longer-term security and bask in the reflected glory of those lining the monarch's coffers. Also, in brokering advance contracts for their wool, monasteries could hope to stave off the worst effects of disease and impoverishment, either by servicing other debts on the backs of the sheep, or by reinvesting the advances into fresh stocks, so attaining a measure of solvency, however temporary.

Second, and almost certainly more importantly, they obtained large up-front payments (known as '*arra*') that could be put to immediate use for building works, providing hospitality for visitors, and the dual burden of royal and papal tax payments, as shown in the example of Pipewell in Chapter 3. Of the contracts that we have identified, around half contain details of advance payments[2] and of those, 75 per cent involve advance payment of the full value of wool to be delivered. Most of the remainder of contracts leave one quarter to one half of the total unpaid in advance, to be rendered on the requisite delivery of the promised wool.

Large architectural projects were highly prized by the monks for the greater glory of God, and their incomes could not cover such expenses. Even though they were usually asset-rich in land, buildings and ceremonial items, the abbots had few reliable sources of liquid capital with which to meet the charges on their revenue. Whitwell[3] suggests that in some cases, the abbeys' financial positions were so weak that they were unable to afford to replenish their stocks of sheep, resulting in declining wool yields and putting their very livelihoods at risk. For example, Richard de Barton, Abbot of Meaux, was only able to pay off the debts of more than £2,000 incurred by his predecessor by selling wool in advance, leasing some of the abbey's property, and by allowing the quality and number of sheep to decline.

While the advance payments associated with the agreements had obvious benefits for the monasteries, they would not have known in advance whether their sheep would be hit by disease. Rather than

---

[2] The likelihood is that most of the other contracts also incorporated advance payments, but these were not explicitly stated.
[3] Whitwell, 'English Monasteries and the Wool Trade', p. 31.

conservatively estimating their ability to produce wool and contracting accordingly, it appears common for the monks to have contracted to supply in excess of their anticipated capacity. Outbreaks of disease would imply that the wool-grower would have to buy wool on the open market to make good his obligation to the merchants. If disease was widespread, this is likely to have pushed up the price so that the monks would have to pay considerably more to purchase the wool on the open market than they had sold it for in advance. The risks involved with advance sales combined with a lack of diversified sources of income often led to financial hardship for the monasteries and occasionally forced dissolution, as discussed in detail in Chapter 3. Incidences of scab in the 1270s and 1280s led to near bankruptcy for several Cistercian houses.[4] There is evidence that senior members of the religious orders were aware of the difficulties that these contracts could entail. For example, the Chapter General of the Cistercian order attempted in 1181, largely unsuccessfully, to forbid any wool sale agreements of more than a year in duration.[5]

Little imagination is needed to ascertain why Italians and other Europeans became involved in the English wool trade. Short-stapled English wool was a commodity of immense value to the Flemish and northern Italian luxury cloth industries for the unrivalled fineness it gave to the finished product, and thus wool merchants were keen to ensure a continual supply of high-quality wool to fuel cloth production in the rapidly expanding urban, industrial centres of Flanders and northern Italy.[6] Italian societies, in particular, sought out, and had the capacity to pay very high prices for, the highest quality wools, committing their financial resources to producers over prolonged periods to secure them. Just two societies, the Riccardi of Lucca and the Frescobaldi of Florence, for instance, took over 50 per cent of the total contracted wool, investing around £20,000.[7] In 1294, moreover, Italian merchants were buying from forty-nine out of the seventy-four Cistercian monasteries, which produced the best-grade wool. In the twelfth and thirteenth centuries, English wool was considered to be of the finest quality, whereas wools from the Netherlands and France were of lower quality and could only be used for coarser grades of cloth.[8] Upland flocks of, particularly, the more isolated

---

[4] J. E. Burton, *Monastic and Religious Orders in Britain, 1000–1300* (Cambridge, 1994), p. 260.
[5] *Ibid.*, p. 258.
[6] For clarification on the length of staple and its degree of fineness, see P. J. Bowden, 'Wool Supply and the Woollen Industry', *Economic History Review* 9 (1956), pp. 44–58.
[7] And this represented only a fraction of their total outlay in trading operations in England.
[8] Power, *The Wool Trade in English Medieval History*.

Cistercian houses produced perhaps the finest grade and were subject to more refined, professional preparation techniques. Driven by the highly lucrative nature of the trade, merchants from England and overseas competed to increase their share of a continual supply of high-quality wool and they were prepared to pay well to receive it.

The wool trade was extremely profitable for the Italian merchants. At its peak, the wool and clothing trade accounted for over half of the Bardi's earnings between 1330 and 1332.[9] Further, since the Bardi and Peruzzi were both papal bankers, part of any transfer of money from the papacy to the English wool-growers would inevitably find its way back to the bankers' coffers when the monasteries paid their papal dues. By 1318, the Bardi alone had assets in England of over £12,000, and the majority of this resulted from advance payments to English wool-growers.[10]

The protracted diplomatic wranglings between the kings of England and counts of Flanders throughout the thirteenth century, culminating in the expensive series of export bans and export licensing schemes of the early 1270s, ousted the Flemings from their position of dominance and paved the way for new entrepreneurial parties to take their place.[11] Moreover, in dealing directly with the leaders of monastic institutions at source – most societies had multiple agents traversing the country buying up wool in huge quantities[12] – they could also tap the produce of smaller-scale lay growers seeking an outlet for their wool.

On the other hand, of course, the prevalence of disease appears to have cast producers into the hands of the merchants, who could offer hard cash in advance for wool perhaps thus bought at a significant discount compared to the cost of buying on an ad hoc or year-by-year basis. Not only was this sound economic sense, but, in tying producers to long-term deals, merchants who had found a source of high-grade wool at a time of dearth could secure themselves an important advantage at market for many years to come at the expense of their rivals. Naturally, in this prevailing atmosphere of desolation, they were taking huge risks, but it appears that for both parties these were risks worth taking whether out of necessity or of a drive for profit.

Through the contracts, we would anticipate that the merchants should typically receive the wool at a significant discount compared to the prices

---

[9] Lopez and Raymond, *Medieval Trade in the Mediterranean World*, pp. 370–371.
[10] Hunt, 'A New Look at the Dealings of the Bardi and Peruzzi with Edward III', p. 152.
[11] Lloyd, *English Wool Trade*, pp. 28–39.
[12] As is evidenced in the Exchequer Schedules: E 101/126/7, mms. 14, 20, 22, 23, 24, 25; *Advance Contracts*, nos. 206, 211, 213, 214, 215, 216.

prevailing at that time, and thus the merchants received an implicit interest payment on their 'loans'. Ignoring any 'time value of money',[13] the average value per sack of wool specified in the contracts is some 20 per cent lower than the monks would have received if they sold their wool at the prevailing price at the time that the contract was signed. Of course, this average figure masks enormous variations in the differences across contracts. An extreme example is where William, abbot of Flaxley (Gloucs.) contracted on 21 November 1281[14] to sell eight sacks of wool (six of good wool, one of middle wool and one of locks) for delivery on 9 July 1291 to Thomas de Basinges, citizen of London. The prevailing price for a sack of good wool at that time was 4,178d,[15] but the abbot received only 1,120d, representing a 73 per cent discount, although the contract suggests that there had been postponement of an earlier delivery. As one would expect, previous default seems to reduce the amount that an abbot could expect to receive for his wool by selling it in advance. Examining only those contracts where there is renegotiation following default, the typical discount relative to the market price rises to 27 per cent. As well as a substantive discount on the fair value of the wool, it was common for the merchants to take 'an extra sack or two gratis'.[16]

Examining the size of these discounts is simply another way of looking at the large interest payments that the merchants received on their loans to the monasteries. Although it is impossible to separate the impact of the quality of wool from the implicit loan interest (aside from information on the broad quality categorisations described below), given the vast differences between the prevailing market prices and the prices that the abbots received by selling in advance, it cannot be said on the whole that the merchants were paying over the odds for their wool. On the other hand, there were instances of the monks receiving larger payments per sack than the prevailing prices, although these were rather rare and the differences were usually very small. The most extreme example that we have been able to uncover is when Reyner, prior of Coxford (Norfolk), contracted on 17 October 1287[17] to sell eight sacks of wool to the Riccardi for delivery on 24 June 1288 at a

---

[13] The time value of money is a financial term referring to the tendency for people to value a given sum now more highly than they would value the same sum to be delivered in the future. The time value of money is almost invariably positive due to inflation, higher risks for future payments, and the fundamental human desire for immediate gratification.

[14] E 159/55, rot. 6; *Advance Contracts*, no. 64.

[15] For simplicity, when analysing the contracts for the financial calculations employed in this chapter, we subsequently convert all values into old pence (d). To remind readers of the conversion rates, one shilling = 12d, £1 = 240d, 1 mark = 160d.

[16] Power, *The Wool Trade in English Medieval History*, p. 43.

[17] E 159/61, rot. 12; *Advance Contracts*, no. 100.

price of 1,760d per sack when the prevailing price was 1,323d – a premium of 33 per cent.

Another interesting feature of the majority of contracts is that, no matter what their duration, the payments per sack for a given grade of wool remained fixed. For example, the agreement enrolled on 29 September 1298 between Abbot Adam of Combermere (Cheshire) and the Frescobaldi, stipulated that four sacks of good wool would be delivered annually on 8 July for twenty years for a fixed price of £9 6s 8d per sack.[18] This contrasts with many modern financial situations, although there are several instances of 'level term' cashflows – for example, the monthly repayments on a mortgage are constant over its lifetime (assuming no change in the rate of interest). One possible explanation for the fact that the prices per sack specified in the contract do not increase over the lifetime of the contract is that these amounts per sack were purely notional figures 'for the records'. That is, the merchant had said, 'I will pay you the sum of £500 now, and I want to receive five sacks of good wool per year for the next ten years'. It would not matter whether the contract stipulated that the sacks were all worth £10, or whether they were worth £8 per sack for the first five years and £12 per sack thereafter. Thus fixing the amounts specified per sack through time was done purely for mathematical simplicity.

An alternative explanation is that wool prices had no predictable patterns or trends, and the counterparties were aware of this and set the contract details accordingly. The stability of the prices within the contracts stands in stark contrast to the highly volatile series of actual wool prices. Figure 4.1 plots the mean annual prices of wool, in shillings per stone of 14 lb, from Lloyd (1973, table 1) for part of our sample period, 1275–1322.

This figure shows that while wool prices fluctuated a great deal from one year to the next around their mean value (dashed line) of 4.7[19] shillings per stone (£6 2s 2d per sack), there was indeed no underlying upward trend in prices. Therefore it was sensible, when viewed *ex post*, for both parties to assume that prices would not rise over the contract period. Examining the other main features of the wool price series, there were recoinages in 1274 and 1299. A fall in wool prices resulted from the latter but not the former, with prices in 1300–05 lower than they had been in the recent past. An

---

[18] Usually, forward prices move towards the spot price as the contract matures, but since there was no secondary market for these forward contracts, there would therefore be no expectation that this would happen.

[19] Note that both Lloyd and Munro use decimals to denote prices (e.g. 10s 6d would be written 10.5s).

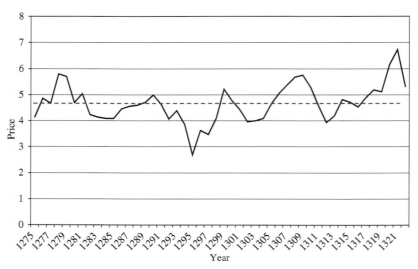

Figure 4.1: Wool Spot Prices 1275–1322.

outbreak of scab occurred in 1268, and this did not abate until after 1283, and there was also a general economic depression beginning in 1279 which further reduced prices.[20] Lloyd alleges that this led many abbeys to with-draw permanently from sheep farming, which, based on the evidence presented in Chapter 3, cannot universally have been the case by any manner of means.

As with any commodity, the price of wool would be expected to have been generated by the interaction of demand and supply factors in the market. However, there were also a large number of impediments to the free running of the medieval wool market, including the monopolistic power of the small groups of sellers and royal taxes on wool, manipulation of the market and attempts at price fixing in the fourteenth century. There is also evidence of restrictive practices occurring in the luxury textile market, including quotas on output and restrictions on employment in the profession, and these are bound to have affected the prices of their raw material. Lloyd[21] argues that wool prices were affected more by demand than supply. He suggests that political interference from the Crown and

---

[20] Waites, 'Monasteries and the Wool Trade in North and East Yorkshire During the 13th and 14th Centuries', p. 117.
[21] Lloyd, 'Movement of Wool Prices', p. 10.

changes in the fortunes of the cloth production industry had greater impacts than changes in supply caused principally by disease.

A major influence on the wool price soon after the end of the period covered in Figure 4.1 was the English Wool Company set up in 1336 by Edward III together with a set of English businessmen. The king established an embargo on all exports of wool to the Netherlands in 1336 that lasted into 1337. He allowed his associates in the Wool Company to compulsorily purchase wool from English wool-growers and then to act as the sole exporters. The Wool Company expected to sell 30,000 sacks of wool abroad, obtaining monopoly sellers' prices from the raw material-starved Flemish merchants. The scheme ultimately collapsed, largely as a result of dishonesty on the part of the king's nominated merchants and associates. They used the king's orders to compulsorily purchase wool, often at well below fair market prices, and smuggled large quantities of wool abroad for their own profit rather than that of the king. As well as causing great resentment among the growers, this resulted in the Company being unable to deliver the agreed amounts to the Netherlands. A failure on the part of the king and his associates to understand the law of supply and demand also contributed to the scheme's downfall, since when the wool was eventually released to the market, its price fell, probably back to the value it would have had in the absence of royal interference.[22]

The demand for English wools of the highest quality was particularly strong, and in the late thirteenth century, increasing transactions costs (including taxation and the physical costs of safely transporting the wool to its destination) led to the development of a luxury textile market based on such wools. Wools of lower quality and the fabrics produced from them were essentially viewed as commodities where an almost identical product would be widely sold in circumstances approximating perfect competition[23] where sellers would have had no ability to bargain or raise prices.

Pricing

One of the most elusive elements in the medieval English wool trade is the pricing of wool as expressed in the contracts. As T. H. Lloyd argued, the prices in most bargains made with foreign merchants are for good-quality

---

[22] See Fryde, *William de la Pole, Merchant and King's Banker*.
[23] J. H. Munro, 'Urban Regulation and Monopolistic Competition in the Textile Industries of the Late-Medieval Low Countries', in Erik Aerts and John Munro (eds.), *Textiles of the Low Countries in European Economic History*, Proceedings of the Tenth International Economic History Congress: Session B-15, Studies in Social and Economic History 19 (Leuven: Leuven History Press, 1990).

wool and therefore will not really reflect national averages.[24] Moreover, regional and even local differences in the standard by which wool was graded, as well as the variety of weights and measures and methods of preparation (or the lack of it), the proximity of markets or places of export, and debts already owing to merchants, might create any number of price permutations.[25] Wool was also particularly susceptible to the influence of disease and climatic extremes. The late thirteenth and early fourteenth centuries witnessed numerous harsh winters and wet summers, epidemics of sheep scab and murrain, culminating in the great European famine of 1315–17, which was followed by further widespread murrain in England.[26] Perhaps more importantly in the present context, however, the body of material from which prices can be drawn is relatively small and in a number of individual contracts, only one or two pricing figures have survived, making conclusions impossible. This means that other information has to be drawn from the schedules of 1294, which themselves are open to question – how accurate were the figures given by the merchant houses when it might be in their interests to inflate their losses? The treatise of Pegolotti must also, of necessity, be consulted, but here too the prices he quotes are those on the Flemish market, from which he himself deducts a good profit and costs of carriage and transport. Moreover, as Bischoff points out, much of his information must have come from the accounts of other societies that had come to him second hand.[27] How reliable is his information? Indeed, at present it is not within the realms of possibility to decipher, for example, whether prices really did vary greatly within the years immediately following the scab, or whether competition between merchants forced up prices. Only impressionistic suggestions can be made from a small number of chosen examples, which again means that any suggestions will be made rather artificially.

Most apparent is that, in general, there is some stability in prices for the wool of many religious houses over the whole span of the period, which, if Lloyd is correct, was the natural concomitant of merchants and monks wishing to establish stable prices both to ensure long-term profits and to combat the inevitable fluctuations brought by the scab, international crises and inflationary and deflationary pressures. This, however, should not be taken to imply that contract prices are worthless, for there is considerable

[24] Lloyd, 'Movement of Wool Prices', p. 10.
[25] Denholm-Young, *Seigneurial Administration*, p. 60.
[26] See, for example, C. McNamee, *The Wars of the Bruces: Scotland, England and Ireland, 1306–28* (East Linton, 1997).
[27] Bischoff, 'An Honest Merchant?', p. 104.

importance in the level at which prices were set in anticipation of crises or recovery and in renegotiations of deals to account for the price of previous failure. The monks of the cathedral priory of St Swithun's, Winchester received a set price of six marks per sack throughout the period. The Riccardi, their sole patrons, may have wished to establish this incredibly low price due to the paucity of high-grade wool among their flocks or due to the huge nature of the first three of their surviving contracts for 240, 200 and 170 sacks respectively. Nevertheless, when, in the fourth contract of 1291, the Riccardi scaled back their demands to thirty sacks, possibly in recognition of the difficulties in delivering vast quantities at that time, the price remained six marks, as it did in 1294.[28] At Meaux in the East Riding, despite two contracts with Hugh Pape and the Cerchi in 1278 and 1280, which priced their good wool at just 12 and 10 marks respectively, three remaining contracts and Pegolotti agree that the value stood at 15 marks per sack throughout the years from 1287 to 1321.[29] One slight anomaly comes in 1294 when the Riccardi, who had made all of the contracts with the monks of Meaux since 1287, claimed that the abbey's wool was valued at only 12 marks. Whether this is explicable by a drop in quality or an increase in volume produced is difficult to say, however.

Elsewhere, prices showed a gradual climb to their peak in 1318–21 under Pegolotti.[30] Combermere in Cheshire, for example, saw the value of its good wool rise from 11 marks per sack in a contract covering 1279–98 to 14 marks in the renegotiation of two contracts covering 1299–1318 and 1309–28, before finally reaching 21 marks in Pegolotti's list.[31] It can only be assumed that the frequent failure of the monks brought about by disease, combined perhaps with a trend towards a slight rise in the price of wool which both sides anticipated, might have contributed to this phenomenon. On the other hand, however, the values given to the abbey's middle-grade wool and locks stagnate throughout the period. Locks fluctuate between 7 and 8 marks and middle-grade, beginning at 10 in 1279 drops back to 9 in 1299 and 1309, before rising considerably to 13 marks according to Pegolotti. Byland, though, shows a slight fall over about a

---

[28] E 159/58, rot. 16, E 368/58, rot. 19; E 159/59, rot. 4 and schedule; E 159/64, rot. 22d, E 368/62, rot. 27; E 101/126/7, m. 12. *Advance Contracts*, nos. 78, 82, 122, 205.

[29] E 13/6, m. 10d.; E 159/53, rot. 12d., E 368/53 rot. 14; E 159/60, rot. 18; E 159/61, m. 14; E 159/62, rot. 15; E101/126/7, m. 12. *Advance Contracts*, nos. 21, 43, 95, 103, 109, 205. *La Pratica Della Mercatura*, p. 260.

[30] If we accept the dating argued by Munro, 'Wool price schedules and the Qualities of English Wools', pp. 129–135.

[31] E 159/52, rot. 15, E 368/52, rot. 15; E 159/72, rot. 45; E 159/82, rot. 81. *Advance Contracts*, nos. 28, 156, 182. *La Pratica Della Mercatura*, p. 261.

mark over the twenty years from 1279 to 1299. The prices paid for the wool of the Cistercian abbey of Biddlesden show similar trends. From a base of 12 marks in a contract for 21 sacks with Reginald de Plesance in 1276–8, the Riccardi were willing to pay 15 marks in 1284 for ten sacks, while Cahorsin merchants agreed to pay 16 marks for 1½ sacks in 1290. By 1318–21, Pegolotti was suggesting that merchants would have to pay 21 marks per sack, which even with deductions probably represents another increase.[32] Whether such increases should be attributed to an element of competition in which successive foreign merchants upped the price to ensure supply, or whether they represent a more general trend towards rising prices in the disease years of the 1280s, is equally difficult to fathom. One factor to be thrown into the equation is the purchase in 1284 of the advance for the entire wool crop of the abbey by the Mozzi of Florence.[33]

Stability and upward movements are not the only trends visible in the contract material. At Flaxley in the Forest of Dean, there seems to have been a trend towards marked fluctuation in prices per sack. In his first recorded contract with the monks, Thomas de Basing was willing to pay 10 marks per sack of good wool and 6 for each sack of locks. In the renegotiation of this contract in 1281, the value had fallen to 8 marks across the board for good, middling and locks. Nevertheless, by 1299, James Pilate of Douai agreed to pay 15 marks per sack for good wool, 10 for middling and 8½ for locks, a considerable increase.[34] On the one hand, such fluctuation might be attributed to the willingness and capacity of foreign wool merchants to pay more for the product to ensure a steady supply. On the other, Thomas was contracting with the monks at Flaxley at the time of their two bankruptcies of 1277 and 1281, and was even awarded custody of the abbey at some point during this period. It would be in his interests to deflate the prices, and he would perhaps also be justified in offering a markedly lower price as damages for the monks' repeated default on earlier bargains, a price sanctioned by the Exchequer officials trying to reach a compromise in their dispute.

Such a possibility begs the question as to whether other merchants were able to manipulate wool prices in their favour during times of bankruptcy. Though the evidence is inconclusive, the valuations offered for the wool of

---

[32] E 13/4, m. 8–8d., 14, m. 8d; E 159/58, rot. 13. *Advance Contracts*, nos. 17, 75, 123. *La Pratica Della Mercatura*, p. 262.

[33] *Della Decima*, p. 325.

[34] E 159/51, rot. 20d, E 368/51, rot. 13d. and schedule (1278); E 159/55, rot. 6 (1281); E 159/73, rot. 35 (1299–1300). *Advance Contracts*, nos. 23, 64, 163.

Rievaulx abbey perhaps suggest that they might have. Rievaulx was bankrupted twice, in 1276 and 1288.[35] Sadly, no pricing information is available for any year before 1287 when the Mozzi paid the extravagant price of 18 marks per sack for good wool, 12 for locks and 17 for *collecta*.[36] Rievaulx's wool was clearly worth the Mozzi venturing so much capital in a wholly unrealistic deal for 168 sacks, which suggests they may have wished to muscle in on such a lucrative trade. It may well be, indeed, that the Mozzi's ambition has skewed the perception of the true value of Rievaulx's wool, for in the year of the second bankruptcy the Riccardi, who may have been the abbey's long-term business partners, were able to garner a much less ambitious slice of the abbey's business at a reduction, contracting for 30 sacks of wool and paying 16 marks for good quality and only 12 for *collecta*.[37] By 1294, the Exchequer Schedules reveal that 12 marks were being paid for a sack of good wool by the Riccardi and only 10 marks for four sacks by the Spini of Florence. The Cerchi Neri, who had clearly grasped the abbey's trade by this point, paid just 13 marks per sack on a contract for 54 sacks.[38] For Pegolotti, 17½ marks was the going rate for good wool and only 9 marks for locks.

A final question which can be tentatively answered is the relative value of wool within regions, or at least within and among the three Ridings of Yorkshire, a comparison which is possible, for all of the abbeys which appear in the contracts belonged to the Cistercian Order and were therefore subject to the more rigorous dressing and packaging practices of the Order. It is clear, first of all, that the wool of the East Riding, which is solely represented by Meaux abbey, was the lowest in quality, though an average of 15 marks speaks of wool of a high standard. It is debatable whether the wool of the West Riding, as represented by Fountains Abbey, or that of the North Riding, differed greatly in the excellence of the finished product. As stated above, the value placed on Rievaulx's wool by the Mozzi may conceal a product of comparatively lesser grade. However, throughout the period it generally holds its own with that of Fountains, which fluctuates from a low of 12 marks in 1280–4 to a high of 17½ marks in 1287. This latter figure is again provided by the ambition of the Mozzi, who seem to have arrived fairly fresh on the scene with huge amounts of liquid capital to invest. By 1294, the Riccardi were apparently content to give 15 marks, but by

---

[35] Jamroziak, 'Rievaulx Abbey', pp. 206–207.
[36] E 159/59, rot. 9d, E 368/59, rot. 19d. *Advance Contracts*, no. 86.
[37] E 159/61, rot. 11d. *Advance Contracts*, no. 99.
[38] E 101/126/7, mm. 12, 18, 23. *Advance Contracts*, nos. 205, 209, 214.

the 1320s, Pegolotti suggested 21 marks, which with deductions probably approximates to the Mozzi's pricing.[39]

Multiple deals

The Mozzi's capacity for paying high prices on huge contracts of wool is one of the most striking elements of the surviving body of evidence. But, by 1294 they were paying the lowest average sack price in comparison to other Italian companies, some 10½ marks per sack. The Pulci-Rembertini and Spini paid around 13 marks per sack, the Cerchi Bianchi 13½ and the Frescobaldi Neri 14.[40] What might account for this? Perhaps quite simply the Mozzi were dealing with more growers who produced lesser-quality wool. Alternatively, it is possible that in the mid-1280s they were keen to establish themselves upon a firmer footing in England and felt forced to pay inflated prices as a sweetener or retainer to secure sufficient supplies at a time when many producers were apparently struggling. In light of these contracts, and those taken over from the Cerchi, perhaps their position near the top of the English wool market had stabilised by 1294 and it was their competitors who were being forced into paying slightly higher average prices to secure their supply. It is doubtful, moreover, that there were any distinct lines of demarcation within the English wool market. While not entirely a free-for-all, it was a market apparently open to all, in which producers might occasionally play one party off against others to gain the best deal for themselves.

CALCULATING THE INTEREST RATE FOR THE WOOL TRANSACTIONS

A further important issue is the question as to whether the advance wool contracts are best analysed as forward agreements or loans. R. M. Eldridge and R. Maltby[41] have investigated one particular thirteenth-century contract between Fountains Abbey and a group of Florentine merchants for the advance sale of wool, arguing that this is equivalent to a modern forward contract. As they point out, these agreements certainly have many of the characteristics of forward contracts as the term would be

---

[39] E 159/52, rot. 13, E 368/52, rot. 12d.; E 159/60, rot. 16d., E 368/60, rot. 14d.; E101/126/7, m. 12. *Advance Contracts*, nos. 26, 93, 205. *Della Decima*, p. 324; *La Pratica Della Mercatura*, p. 260.

[40] Lloyd, 'Movement of Wool Prices', p. 9.

[41] Eldridge and Maltby, 'On the Existence and Implied Cost of Carry', pp. 36–49.

understood by financial market practitioners – they are an agreement for the purchase/sale of a particular quantity of wool of specific quality grade. The dates and places where the wool will be delivered, and the payment schedule are also specified meticulously in the contracts.

However, most historians would argue that such transactions were in fact loans in disguise, motivated by the illegality of usury (charging of interest) at that time. The key point appears to be that no money would change hands on the contract signing date in the case of a forward contract, but the monasteries often received large up-front payments. As early as 1941, Eileen Power demonstrated that the advances paid in the contracts could very well constitute 'loans made on the security of wool'.[42] In November 1274, the prior of Thornholme in Lincolnshire admitted that he had agreed to sell 75 sacks to Master William of Louth in 1269–70 and had received 900 marks 'as a loan'.[43] Most contracts upon which an advance was paid expressly stipulated repayment in wool, advances being allowed to the merchants upon delivery of the wool.[44] While there is plenty of evidence to suggest that in many cases wool was actually delivered, repayment in wool may have been nominal in a number of cases. During the Michaelmas term of 1276, for example, the abbot of the Cistercian house of Thame in Oxfordshire acknowledged that he owed Bertram Cappdemayle and his fellows 7 sacks of wool, for which he had already received 70 marks. He agreed, though, that repayments would be in two parcels of 35 marks. Money had clearly been forwarded to the abbot but it is not clear whether it was to be wool or cash which was to be repaid, as, of course, the 35 marks could be made up of 5 sacks of wool worth 7 marks each. It is also the case that by this time, wool stocks may have been low and it may have been necessary for money to change hands. Perhaps, though, wool had never really been on the agenda in this case.[45]

In making and accepting such loans, if that is what they indeed were, both parties would be desperate to escape any taint of charging interest, though in practice they probably recognised the necessity of some kind of usurious agreement. From the merchants' point of view the extension of credit facilities to leading monastic wool producers, whose own lack of capital made them more receptive to their overtures despite their submission to strictures against participation in trade and commerce, had the

[42] Power, *The Wool Trade in English Medieval History*, p. 43.
[43] ' . . . *mutuo receperat*': E 13/3, m. 5d.
[44] See for example the Pipewell contract with the Cahorsins at C 54/108, mm.8d.–9d; E 159/64, rot. 10; E 368/62, rot. 14. *Advance Contracts*, no. 133.
[45] E 13/5, m. 2. *Advance Contracts*, no. 18.

potential simultaneously to increase their share of the most prized commodity on the market and augment further any profits which might be gleaned. After all, the desire to gain as much of the best-quality wool as possible at the best possible prices over the longest period and, in so doing, perhaps restrict the access of competing companies to the best sources, would be paramount. The stigma attached to usury meant that strategies had to be developed to conceal any interest. This, of course, when combined with the fluctuations of wool prices in the period under consideration, is difficult to discern.[46]

It is possible that interest might be charged in deflated valuations of sack prices, the merchants thus getting more for their money over an extended period. This was certainly the case with the abbot of Bordesley in Worcestershire. The chapter of this Cistercian house complained to the king that he had contracted with the Cerchi in 1275 without their assent for a loan of 300 marks repayable over six years. The debt was to be repaid in 42 sacks of the abbey's wool. The abbot claimed that he had made delivery of 12 sacks for which he had received payment, but the convent disagreed and wanted the unfinished contract annulled. Lloyd believes that the advance paid represented the full value of wool priced at 9 marks per sack, whereas they should actually have been valued at 13 marks, making an interest payment by the abbot of 78 marks.[47] The lack of comprehensive, nationwide and regional pricing information makes any conclusions about the charging of interest in this way less than firm. It is possible that the Florentine merchants who dealt with the Cistercian abbey of Combermere in Cheshire garnered some profit in lower sack valuations over time. In *La Pratica Della Mercatura*, Pegolotti lists Combermere wool at 21 marks for good quality, 13 for middling and 10½ for locks.[48] While his valuations are those payable on the Flemish market, include carriage and shipping costs, and were recorded at a time when English wool prices reached their peak during the Middle Ages, they are still significantly higher than the 11 marks, 8 marks and 7 marks respectively offered by the Florentine merchants Guido Chuffanatalis and Guido Amaduri for 300 sacks of the abbey's wool from 1279 to 1298.[49]

---

[46] For an unsurpassed survey of wool prices in the late thirteenth and early fourteenth centuries, see Lloyd, 'Movement of Wool Prices'.

[47] Lloyd, *English Wool Trade*, p. 291.   [48] *La Pratica Della Mercatura*, p. 261.

[49] E 159/52, rot. 15; E 368/52, rot. 15; *Advance Contracts*, no. 28. Two other deals made with the Frescobaldi, which covered the years 1299–1318 and 1309–28 priced the abbey's wool at 14 marks for good quality, 9 for middling and 7 for locks: E159/72, rot. 45; 82, rot. 81. *Advance Contracts*, nos. 156, 182.

At Pipewell in Northamptonshire, a contract of 1288 specifies that in the first five years of a fifteen-year deal the monks will receive 18 marks per sack of good wool. In compensation for this low price they will give the Cahorsin merchants with whom they have contracted one sack as it comes out of the sheepfold (*exit' de Ouili*), while in the fifteenth and final year they will give one sack of good wool. Is this evidence of double hidden interest?[50] Certainly, there is evidence that such alternative solutions to the problem of usury were tried elsewhere. An agreement made during Hilary term 1280 with four Banbury merchants, who are known from other documents to have acted for the prior of Wroxton, specifies that each of the 4 sacks of wool to be provided for the Riccardi is to contain 1 stone of wool gratis as profit (*de avantagio*).[51] A similar provision is made in a bargain between the Yorkshireman, Robert Ughtred, and the Frescobaldi at Michaelmas 1300.[52] In a contract made with the Cistercian abbey of Ford in Dorset, the Riccardi demand that 4 stones of extraneous wool be pressed into each of the 11 sacks to be delivered three weeks from the Nativity of St John the Baptist in 1293 and 1294.[53]

Conversely, it does appear in several cases that Prestwich's assertion that the Italians' loans were not imbued with interest rates is largely the correct view.[54] Several contracts reveal merchants seemingly willing to pay what looks to be over the odds for a long-term contract. The Spaniard, Peter Mundenard, offered 19½ marks per sack to obtain 6 sacks of the wool of the Cistercian house of Wroxton in Oxfordshire from 1280 to 1286, each sack containing 260 fleeces valued at 12d each, whereas Ricardo Bonaventure, an Italian domiciled in London, had offered only 7½ marks per sack in 1271 for 8 sacks.[55]

Nowhere is the inclination to pay seemingly inflated sack prices more visible than in the contracts entered into by successive abbots of Pipewell with merchants of Cahors.[56] In 1242 and again from 1315 to 1322, Cahorsin merchants were willing to pay 15 marks per sack for Pipewell's best wool, which despite the effects of inflation might be taken as an acceptable level

---

[50] E 159/62, rot. 9d. *Advance Contracts*, no. 110.

[51] E 159/53, rot. 12d; E 368/53, rot. 14; E 13/8, m. 3d. *Advance Contracts*, nos. 41, 33.

[52] E 159/74, rot. 41d. *Advance Contracts*, no. 165.

[53] E 159/66, rot. 43; E 368/64, rot. 35. *Advance Contracts*, no. 145.

[54] Prestwich, 'Italian Merchants in Late Thirteenth and Early Fourteenth Century England', p. 95. For an opposing view that 'usurious loans were general and the rate of interest high, in spite of the rising tide of protest from theologians', see Denholm-Young, *Seigneurial Administration*, p. 65.

[55] E 13/8, m. 15d. (Mundenard); E 159/45, rot.18; E 368/44, rot. 11d (Bonaventure). *Advance Contracts*, nos. 44, 12.

[56] For more in-depth discussion of Pipewell and wool, see Chapter 3.

for pricing purposes.[57] However, in a contract covering the years 1288–1302 and in the renegotiation of this contract from 1291 to 1303, good wool was valued at 18 marks for the first five years and then at 21 for the remainder, middling wool similarly increased from an initial 12½ marks to 14 and locks from 10 to 13.[58] Although, as stated, these deals may conceal hidden interest payments, both cover a period when, if Lloyd's price indices at least represent fluctuating trends in wool prices, a stone of wool varied in value from 2.69s in 1295 and 5.22s in 1301.[59] Ultimately, it is likely that in sealing long-term contracts for monastic wool, merchants sought to ensure a constant supply of wool of the highest available quality and to ensure artificially that price fluctuations would not adversely affect profits for bulk orders. From the monks' point of view, establishing a reasonable and, in some cases apparently high, price for their product and a reliable outlet would likewise negate the fluctuations of the market. This was crucial in combating the effects of disease at a time when many monasteries had fallen into severe financial strife. It would also enable them to plan for the future and invest the capital in whatever was deemed necessary. It was precisely these difficulties and opportunities which made the advance contract so attractive, but so problematic, for the monastic producers at least.

Equally, these agreements are not pure loans since the 'repayment' was stated as being in wool rather than cash. Thus we conjecture that the transactions have both loan and forward contract features, and given the kind of data available, it appears impossible to separate the two parts. We are therefore able to calculate a rate of interest implied in the transaction, which will be a composite rate made up of both loan interest and the cost of carry. The core formulae for valuing forwards on commodities are known as the 'cost of carry' relations, which stipulate that the fair price to pay today for delivery of the commodity in the future is equal to the spot price adjusted for the cost of storage of the commodity plus the cost of funding it. In theory, for the case of wool forwards, there is also a 'convenience yield' to consider, since physical ownership of the wool would have been valuable in case of wool shortages during the lifetime of the contract. If shortages are deemed likely, the convenience yield will be high, although if the wool-growers already have large inventories, this yield will be small.

[57] E 327/541; E 159/87, rot. 70. *Advance Contracts*, nos. 192, 221.
[58] E 159/62, rot. 4 (1288); C 54/108, mm. 8d.–9d.; E 159/64, rot. 10; E 368/62, rot. 14 (1291). *Advance Contracts*, nos. 110, 133.
[59] Lloyd, 'Movement of Wool Prices', pp. 39–40.

Wool in the thirteenth century had very poor keeping qualities and therefore a very short shelf life. Lloyd notes that 'when a clip had to be held over from one year to the next it was often sold at a lower price than fetched by new wool'.[60] Additionally, while the cost of storage would probably not have been significant because many abbeys had such facilities, in the cases that we are interested in there would have been no incentive to hold the wool back. Even if the current market price is below that which had been expected or that likely to prevail in the future, the monasteries had already agreed the prices that will be received through the contracts. Given the monasteries' precarious financial positions, it would have made no sense for them to store wool when it could have been used to generate cash immediately. Therefore, while it would not be possible for us to separate out the storage cost and the convenience yield parts of the interest rate, we would argue that the former would be small and the latter would be negligible.

The cost of carry formula cannot apply in this case as a result of the loan component of the transaction and the associated up-front payment. Therefore, in order to estimate the interest rate for the transaction, an alternative approach that focuses on the loan component must be employed. Following Eldridge and Maltby, we use a present value calculation and then we solve the resulting equation to give the interest rate. A present value calculation is one that expresses all of the amounts to be paid or received at today's prices. This is achieved by 'discounting' the future payments (i.e. reducing them) to their present-day equivalent. To give one illustration of how this operates, consider the contract sealed on 16 October 1288[61] by John de Bosco and Edmund Trussel with the Riccardi of Lucca for the supply of 2 sacks of good wool per year at the feast of the Nativity of St John the Baptist (24 June) for three years starting in 1289. The merchants paid the full 11 marks per sack in advance upon signing the contract. The details of the contract are given in Table 4.1, and this information is used to calculate the implied rate of interest.

The present value formula for this contract would be

$$adv = \frac{P_{1289}}{(1+r)^{t_1}} + \frac{P_{1290}}{(1+r)^{t_1+1}} + \frac{P_{1291}}{(1+r)^{t_1+2}}$$

[60] Lloyd, 'Movement of Wool Prices', p. 3.　　[61] E 159/62, rot. 14. *Advance Contracts*, no. 108.

where *adv* is the advance payment received, i.e. the full payment of 11 marks (1,760d) per sack × 6 sacks, t_1 is the time from enrolment (contract signing) to due delivery for the first batch. This equation would then be solved for *r*, which is then the interest rate. Note that the prices, $P_{1289} \ldots P_{1291}$ to be employed in the present value calculation would not be the prices specified in the contract, since using these would give a calculated interest rate of zero by construction. Given the illegality of usury at the time, the transaction would have shown an implicit rather than explicit return for the merchants on lending the money. Instead, following Eldridge and Maltby, we employ the 'spot' prices (i.e. the prices for immediate delivery) that actually prevailed on those dates.

Determining the spot prices

In order to be able to calculate the implied interest rate underlying these transactions, it is necessary to know the prevailing spot price. Unfortunately, this information is considerably harder to obtain than that for advance delivery because most straightforward direct exchanges of cash for wool would not have been recorded. The classic source of spot prices is T. H. Lloyd, who provides information on wool prices by year and by region.[62] But a casual examination of his Table 1 suggests significantly lower valuations than those in the forward contracts we consider. Munro, indeed, has argued that Lloyd's prices for 1294 are only 57 per cent of the mean English abbey wool price in the Exchequer Schedule of that year.[63] This schedule, arising from the seizure of the goods of foreign merchants by Edward I, details the merchant inventories of wool confiscated by the king and also provides the spot prices for monastic wool prevalent in England and Wales in that year.[64] The Exchequer Schedule contains a much broader span of prices – both geographically and in terms of numbers of growers – than the alternative Douai schedule of prevailing English wool prices on the continent (*c.* 1270), leading Munro to term it 'the most important of the earlier price lists'. The Exchequer figures cover 125 monastic houses in 25 counties.[65]

Munro argues that Lloyd's prices are biased for that year since they are based on an equal weighting of only five districts that produced relatively

---

[62] Lloyd, 'Movement of Wool Prices'.
[63] Munro, 'Wool Price Schedules and the Qualities of English Wools in the Latter Middle Ages'.
[64] E 101/126/7. *Advance Contracts*, Appendix 1.
[65] Munro, 'Wool Price Schedules and the Qualities of English Wools', p. 127.

low-quality wool. Additionally, Lloyd takes an average of the wool prices over quality grades. However, Lloyd's prices for 1294 are lower than those for previous years, and none of them are close to those contained in the forward contracts. The prices contained in Munro, drawn from the Exchequer Schedule, look more plausible, but also have drawbacks. Most importantly, the data are only available for this single year, and not for the range of years that we wish to consider. The other prices presented in Munro, Table 1 are obtained from a further two sources: the Douai Schedule and the Pegolotti Schedule, a ready reckoner of monastic wool production and prices around the turn of the fourteenth century compiled by a Florentine merchant who worked for the Bardi and who had experience of English market conditions.[66] The Pegolotti Schedule incorporates information on wool prices from 194 abbeys and from non-monastic growers – more than either the Exchequer or Douai Schedules. However, there has been some doubt concerning the accuracy of the Pegolotti Schedule since he is unlikely to have had full access to the accounts of other companies (only those of the Bardi), and there may have been incentives to distort the figures (for example, to avoid tax duties). Yet an extensive study by J. P. Bischoff could find no significant biases in the figures presented.[67] The Douai Schedule presents only one wool price per abbey, representing only some of the wool sold by the abbeys.

The average difference between the Douai and Pegolotti Schedules is around 8 per cent, while the Exchequer Schedule averages about 13 per cent less for English wool. These differences are probably attributable to the costs of transportation, taxes and so on since the Douai and Pegolotti Schedules refer to prices in Flanders for variable dates. While no single source is clearly superior, we will adopt the Exchequer Schedule as our point of reference, representing the spot wool price in 1294. We then make an adjustment to these prices based on the difference between the average price for good-quality wool that prevailed in 1294 according to Lloyd (£3.86 = 926d) and Lloyd's price for good-quality wool in the year that the contract was enrolled and in that region. To give an illustration, suppose that the Exchequer Schedule price for wool from a particular abbey is 1,200d and the contract is enrolled in 1275. The mean wool price from Lloyd for that year in that region is £4.15, and so the adjusted price that we use as a proxy for the price that would have prevailed for immediate delivery of good wool in 1275 is 1,200d × £4.15 / £3.86 = 1,290d. We are

---

[66] The dating of the Pegolotti Schedule is controversial: *ibid*, pp. 129–135.
[67] Bischoff, 'An honest merchant?', pp. 103–108.

thus implicitly assuming that while Lloyd's average prices are too low, the proportional variations in prices between regions and across years are accurate. We will also assume that prices did not vary within a year. According to T. H. Lloyd, this assumption held in reality since both the supply of and the demand for wool were known by the time that the sheep were to be sheared.[68]

A number of contracts were necessarily excluded from this part of the statistical analysis. A contract had to be removed from the sample if it did not specify the wool quality, if the abbey was not listed in the Exchequer Schedule and there was no nearby comparator abbey, if there were ambiguities in the contract (for example, if a contract states that 12 sacks are to be delivered but the sum of the sacks of good wool, middle wool and locks is 14 sacks), if a price per sack is not quoted, if no delivery date is specified in the contract, or if there is no advance payment. The statistical analysis focuses mainly on good wool since it is this grade that is discussed in the Exchequer Schedule. However, the spot prices for lower grades of wool are scaled down for inclusion in the calculation – this is discussed in greater detail below. We also removed from the analysis any contracts with a lifetime of less than nine months, to exclude any contracts covering wool from the same season (which one could argue are not really forward contracts at all). Finally, for the calculation of interest rates (but not for the other statistical analysis), we only examine contracts where the advance payment constituted the entire amount to be remitted by the merchants to the wool-growers. Sometimes, the contracts make vague references to complex miscellaneous payments. This restriction was imposed to avoid the need to make assumptions about when the additional payments from the merchants would be made during the lifetime of the contract, unless the contract also specified this, in which case it was included in the analysis.

An examination of the contracts clearly shows that the merchants were sensibly willing to pay more for wool of higher quality. Wool quality varied substantially by region according to the breed of sheep, the climate, and the quality of the land for grazing. The best wool typically originated from moderate to cool climates where feeding was relatively sparse.[69] There is also significant evidence in these contracts that religious orders obtained more for their wool than non-monastic sellers. The average discount of the contract price per sack from the prevailing market price is 18 per cent for religious orders but 25 per cent for others. It also appears that some

---

[68] Lloyd, 'Movement of Wool Prices', p. 3.
[69] Munro, 'Wool Price Schedules and the Qualities of English Wools', p. 118.

religious orders were systematically able to obtain more for their wool than others. It is commonly thought that Cistercian wool was particularly highly valued because it was not only of good quality as a result of better breeding techniques, but it was also subjected to highly skilled preparation and packaging before delivery.[70] The Cistercians were also one of the few wool-growers to grade their wool – the Benedictines, for example, sold fleeces of mixed quality together.[71] Indeed, in sixty contracts – predominantly, though not exclusively, made with Cistercian monks – merchants demanded thorough washing, drying, sorting, weighing and specialised packaging of the purchased wool. This was a time-consuming and costly process in which Cistercian abbeys excelled. The Exchequer Schedule[72] explicitly states the expenses of the wool dresser, which usually amounted to around 2 per cent–4 per cent of the total value of the wool.

In the context of modern-day futures contracts, there would be no 'counterparty risk',[73] but in the present context, it is likely that not only did such risks exist, but there could also have been differential levels of risk between the merchants and the abbots. The lack of storability of medieval wool beyond a few months implies that it would not have been possible to hedge a long-dated forward position. In other words, neither party could insure against the risk that the other party would default. Therefore, both the suppliers of wool and the purchasing merchants would have faced risks when entering into a contractual agreement for the exchange of wool for cash, and these risks are likely to have been reflected in the prices paid or received for the wool and also in the implicit interest rates that the monasteries were charged.

On the abbots' side, the only real risk was that they had contracted to supply something that they later found themselves unable to deliver. Lloyd argues,

Despite the fact that the contracts provided a guaranteed outlet for the wool and a fixed price, they were of dubious advantage to the grower. If his flocks were hit by disease then the grower would have to buy wool to fulfil his quotas, and if disease was general, he might have to pay more for the wool than the price at which he had contracted to sell it.[74]

---

[70] Jamorziak, 'Rievaulx Abbey'.
[71] Burton, *Monastic and Religious Orders*, p. 257.
[72] E101/126/7, mm.14, 17. *Advance Contracts*, Appendix 1.
[73] 'Counterparty risk' is defined as the risk that one of the counterparties (i.e. the growers or merchants) would renege on his obligation. Modern futures contracts are traded on an official exchange, and each individual transaction is always with the exchange rather than with other traders, and thus there is no risk of failing to honour an agreement.
[74] Lloyd, 'Movement of Wool Prices', p. 8.

Since the abbots could have no idea whether their flock would be diseased in ten years time, this was a significant risk that they had no way to hedge or insure against.[75] The abbeys are unlikely to have faced any risk that the merchants would default because they had usually received much of or all of the specified money due at the time of signing the contract. However, as discussed previously, the wool market was subject to royal interference that is likely to have had significant short-term impacts on prices and on the monks' abilities to deliver the agreed wool. For example, wool was seized from Cistercian and Premonstratensian monasteries in 1193 to pay King Richard's ransom and then again in the following year even though much of this wool would have already been committed to foreign merchants.[76]

On the merchants' side, the potential risks are more numerous, but arguably less catastrophic in most cases. The merchant societies were frequently large and wealthy; they typically transacted with many wool-growers and thus they were able to spread their purchases and therefore the risk of default. In many instances, the wool trade was so profitable that they were able to weather the minor storms caused by disease or other reasons for default. The merchants' risks include: defaults on the contracts due to disease or dishonesty on the part of the abbots; the imposition of an unexpected tax by the Crown or worse, a seizure of the wool; an abbey declaring bankruptcy in order to obtain royal protection.[77]

The contracts that have been investigated give some indication of whether default occurred. Of the 215 contracts documented, only 49 state that the delivery was made in full. Removing contracts in the Pleas Rolls of the Exchequer, which by their very nature imply non-delivery, from the figures, the proportion of contracts where delivery has clearly been made in full rises to 30 per cent. Satisfied contracts relate to 45 per cent of the volume of wool transacted, according to the evidence that we have, a higher proportion than in pure numbers of contracts, suggesting that large contracts were more likely to be honoured. We cannot make any assumptions concerning the outcomes of those contracts that do not specify either that the delivery occurred in full or that there was a default. Therefore, the default rate appears to be around 10 per cent–15 per cent. However, particularly in times of widespread sheep disease, the probability of default is likely to have been much higher than this. In the case of default, the

[75] Apart from entering into a forward agreement of the sort we investigate and then defaulting.
[76] Whitwell, 'English Monasteries and the Wool Trade'.
[77] See Eldridge and Maltby, 'On the Existence and Implied Cost of Carry', for further discussion of these risks.

records suggest that the 'recovery rate' for the merchants was about half of the volume of wool specified in the contract. More often, though, the king's willingness to protect ailing monasteries coupled with the merchants' desire to maintain a grip on the sources of best-quality wool led in most cases of default to a renegotiation of the original contract, frequently skewed more in the merchants' favour but giving the abbot a more practical timetable for delivery. The ultimate indirect penalty, of course, could be dissolution of the monastery, although this would not help the merchants since an amount equivalent to the value of the default would be paid to the Crown from monastic assets, not to the merchants. While short-term bankruptcies did occur at Flaxley, Kirkstall and Rievaulx, for example, the general pattern tended towards renegotiation and survival rather than this most severe of consequences.[78]

The impact on the merchant of the wool seller defaulting is unclear and would depend on whether the merchant had already sold the wool on to a third party, as in the example of Arnaud and Jean de Soliz detailed above.[79] Damages to cover default were sometimes specified in the terms of the contract. If the merchant had not already contracted to sell the wool on, the maximum potential loss would be the advance payment made, plus any forgone return on the sum that could have been earned between payment of advance and default. But if the merchant was also obliged to deliver the wool, and had to purchase the wool at the prevailing spot price, the loss could be more substantial. In summary, the possibility of one of the counterparties defaulting on the contract agreement will only affect the prices if either one party is more risky than the other or if one party would be affected more adversely by a default than the other. Both parties faced risks and it is not obvious which were the greater.

One would have expected that the probability of default would be higher the longer the contract, and therefore that the merchants would have been prepared to pay less per sack for longer contracts implying a higher rate of interest on the loan component. However, there seems to be no evidence for this among the contracts that we studied. Thus slightly higher prices per sack were paid on average for longer contracts, perhaps suggesting that the merchants valued a continuing supply of wool more highly than they did the additional risk. There is also evidence that merchants were sometimes willing to pay inflated prices in a deliberate attempt to preclude rival merchants from obtaining wool supplies.

---

[78] For Flaxley and Rievaulx, see Lloyd, *English Wool Trade*, p. 290, and for Kirkstall, see Barnes, *Kirkstall Abbey*, pp. 43–44.

[79] E 159/62, rot. 9d. *Advance Contracts*, no. 112.

Penalty clauses were also sometimes built into the contracts to protect the merchants against the possibility of default. Typically, there would be a charge of a fixed amount of money or the value of one sack of wool in the event of delivery of the full contracted amount not occurring. The Mozzi, for example, charged the monks of Rievaulx £10 per sack, while the Riccardi who contracted with Meaux in 1280 for 53 sacks of *collecta* charged 12½ marks, the price of one sack.[80] In the most extreme case, Giles de Ayre, on behalf of John Wermond of Cambrai, inserted a clause into his contract with Darnhall, charging the monks £20 for each day that they defaulted.[81]

Results of interest rate calculations

Table 4.2 gives summary information and calculated interest rates for the contracts that we have examined. All prices quoted in the table are in old pence.

It is not immediately obvious whether the spot prices used in the interest rate calculations should relate to those prevailing at the times when the wool was to be delivered, or whether they should be the prices quoted at the time that the contract was initially signed. A present value relationship would usually use the former, while the latter also makes sense in this case in order to use only the information that would have been available to the counterparties at the time when they were establishing the contract details. We employ (separately) both methods for determining the spot prices, and this almost always makes little difference to the calculated interest rates.

The fourth and sixth columns of Table 4.2 show the total number of sacks to be delivered over the life of the contract, and the number of sacks per year respectively, while the fifth column gives the delivery dates for each batch of wool. The third column from the right of the table shows the forward prices per sack as specified in the contracts, and the last two columns give the interest rates for each spot price measure, calculated by solving the present value relationships of the form given in the equation above to find the interest rate for each contract.

Of course, there will be situations where our spot prices are somewhat inaccurate (for example, if Lloyd's prices are based on a very small sample for a particular region in a particular year), or where the spot prices changed substantially between when the contract was enrolled and when the wool was due for delivery. There may also be case-specific details of which we are unaware (for example, a monastery being unable to secure a

---

[80] E159/53 rot. 12d., E368/53, rot. 14 (Meaux); E159/59, rot. 9d (Rievaulx); E368/59, rot. 19d. *Advance Contracts*, nos. 42, 86.
[81] C54/92, m. 2d. *Advance Contracts*, no. 13.

Table 4.1 *Sample Contract Details used for Interest Rate Calculation*

Estimated date of enrolment	Seller	Counterparty	Total sacks	Location for delivery	Due dates for delivery	Good	Price (d/sack)
16 October 1288	John de Bosco, Edmund Trussel	Riccardi	6	Thorpe	24 June 1289	2	1760
					24 June 1290	2	1760
					24 June 1291	2	1760

Table 4.2 Results of Interest Rate Calculations

Estimated date of enrolment	Spot at date wool due	Spot at date contract signing	Total sacks over contract	Due dates for delivery	Sacks each year	Quality	Price (d/sack)	Interest rate% – spot at wool due	Interest rate% – spot at contract signing
17 November 1259	1595	1311	10	1 July 1261	10	Good	800	53	36
15 October 1276	2904	3022	62	9 July 1277	17	Collecta	1800	22	17
	3606	3022		9 July 1278	17	Collecta	1800		
	3544	3022		9 July 1279	14	Collecta	1800		
	2922	3022		9 July 1280	14	Collecta	1800		
5 February 1280	2338	2338	53	9 July 1280	25	Good	2000	0	0
	2109	2338		9 July 1282	28	Good	2000		
20 May 1280	1802	3117	20	24 June 1280	10	Good	1600	31	448
	1932	3117		24 June 1281	10	Good	1600		
9 October 1281	2109	1462	3	2 July 1282	3	Good	1760	22	0
21 November 1281	3277	4178	8	9 July 1291	6	Good	1120	9	12
12 October 1282	1888	1933	3	1 August 1283	1.5	Good	1280	34	34
	1865	1933		1 August 1284	1.5	Good	1280		
9 October 1284	2882	3730	10	9 July 1285	10	Good	2400	28	28
8 July 1286	2174	2126	23	24 June 1287	13	Collecta	2080	28	28
	2193	2126		24 June 1288	10	Collecta	2080	0	0
12 May 1287	2343	2268	11	9 July 1289	11	Good	2400	0	0
25 June 1287	2288	2268	30	9 July 1288	30	Good	1600	45	44
27 June 1287	2288	1323	19	24 June 1288	13	Good	1760	30	30
				24 June 1288	6	Good	1760		
13 October 1287	2288	2268	26	9 July 1288	10	Collecta	1920	0	0
	2288	2268		24 June 1288	8	Good	2560		
	2343	2268		24 June 1289	8	Good	2560		
17 October 1287	2288	1323	8	24 June 1288	8	Good	1760	48	48

24 November 1287	3432	3402	5	1 September 1288	5	Collecta	1360	160	157
27 November 1287	1525	1512	400	2 February 1288	80	Collecta	1000	12	11
	1562	1512		2 February 1289	80	Collecta	1000		
	1655	1512		2 February 1290	80	Collecta	1000		
	1542	1512		2 February 1291	80	Collecta	1000		
	1350	1512		2 February 1292	80	Collecta	1000		
16 October 1288	2148	2097	6	24 June 1289	2	Good	1760	14	11
	2275	2097		24 June 1290	2	Good	1760		
	2120	2097		24 June 1291	2	Good	1760		
3 November 1288	2343	2288	11	9 July 1289	2	Good	2400	0	0
	2482	2288		9 July 1290	4	Good	2400		
	2313	2288		9 July 1291	5	Good	2400		
27 November 1290	1156	1241	30	24 June 1291	5	Good	960	0	9
	1012	1241		24 June 1292	5	Good	960		
	1092	1241		24 June 1293	5	Good	960		
	960	1241		24 June 1294	5	Good	960		
	669	1241		24 June 1295	5	Good	960		
	900	1241		24 June 1296	5	Good	960		
9 October 1292	1820	2868	11	15 July 1293	6	Good	1920	6	62
	1600	2868		15 July 1294	6	Good	1920		
29 October 1292	2730	2531	10	22 July 1293	10	Good	2240	31	18
7 April 1293	2730	3457	12	9 July 1293	6	Good	1280	231	510
	2400	3457		9 July 1294	6	Good	1280		

good price for its wool owing to previous defaults). These factors may result in negative calculated interest rates, which we set to zero in the table, or implausibly high rates of interest. Examining the last two columns of Table 4.2, there are evidently some zero rates and some implausibly high rates. But for the majority of contracts that we investigated, and that were amenable to this analysis, the implied rates of interest are not only plausible, but are also in accordance with other historical studies detailing interest rates on alternative types of transactions at that time. Employing the spot prices that prevailed when the contract was signed for the whole lifetime of the contract gives a median interest rate per annum of 22 per cent; using the spot prices that prevailed at each delivery date gives a median rate of 18 per cent per annum; the majority of implied interest rates are between 10 per cent and 40 per cent. For comparison with existing evidence, Eldridge and Maltby cite Mate, who studied loans to Canterbury Cathedral Priory, where interest rates ranged from 15 per cent–24 per cent per annum.[82] J. Gilchrist suggests that 'distress loans' or emergency funds obtained from pawnbrokers or money lenders, and which were needed to ensure subsistence, would command interest rates equivalent to 43 per cent per annum. Even for secured loans, the rate would be 20 per cent–25 per cent.[83] He also suggests that loans to the Church typically commanded interest rates of 15 per cent–38 per cent. For example, Canterbury Cathedral Priory agreed a number of long-term loans from Jews and Italians at rates of 15 per cent–20 per cent.[84] We are also able to make comparision with prevailing interest rates in continental Europe, such as for forced loans from big individual lenders in Italy; at Siena these were repaid at a rate of 15 per cent–40 per cent, at Pisa between 1280 and 1350, interest rates ranged between 12 per cent and 20 per cent and at Florence between 10 per cent and 15 per cent. This shows that the interest rates we have calculated are not out of line with those in the Italian creditors' home cities.[85]

Eldridge and Maltby's study used data from a contract made between Fountains Abbey in Yorkshire and a consortium of Florentine merchants, enrolled on 15 October 1276 (the second contract in Table 4.2). They calculated interest rates of between 40 per cent and 60 per cent per annum, depending on assumptions made concerning the spot rate. However, they used a different approach to determining the spot prices

---

[82] M. Mate, 'The Indebtedness of Canterbury Cathedral Priory 1215–1295', *Economic History Review Second Series*, 26 (1973), pp. 183–197.
[83] Gilchrist, *The Church and Economic Activity.*   [84] *Ibid*, p. 105 and p. 298.
[85] L. Martines, *Power and Imagination: City-States in Renaissance Italy* (Baltimore: Johns Hopkins, 1988), pp. 177–178.

(that we would argue is less accurate than the method employed here). They assumed that the time until delivery of the first batch of wool was a year when in fact it was nine months, and they did not allow for the fact that *collecta* wool was to be delivered under the contract rather than the monastery's own wool, whereas we account for this. Our calculated interest rates for this contract are 17 per cent and 22 per cent (depending on the dates used to determine the spot prices), figures much closer to those usually quoted for financial transactions during the thirteenth century.

Was the medieval wool market efficient?

A further issue worthy of investigation is the extent to which the forward rate unbiasedness (FRU) hypothesis held in the medieval wool market. This hypothesis states that (in the absence of transactions costs and other impediments to the effective functioning of the markets), the forward price should be an unbiased predictor of the subsequent spot price. Such analyses have been conducted extensively in the context of exchange rates.[86] While the medieval wool market is unlikely to have been frictionless and available data are limited, if the market is functioning properly, there should be no information from previous spot prices or previous values of the discount (the amount that the merchants paid for the wool below the prevailing market price) that could be used to predict the next period discount.

To test this, we first determine the average value of this discount, and we find that, ignoring all other influences, the typical price per sack received by the sheep breeders is 417d lower than they would have received on the open market. Next, we reduce the sample to consider only the first year of any contract. We do this firstly because the forward prices per sack in the agreements are almost always identical for the life of the contract, and secondly, because we want to ensure that when we test for efficiency, we are only employing current and lagged prices that would have been in the information sets of those forming the agreements. This reduces the number of available observations to sixty-three. We also want to examine formally the relationship between the discount and the length of the contract and between the discount and the size of the contract (the total number of sacks to be delivered). Finally, we are also interested in determining the impact of

---

[86] See L. P. Hansen and R. J. Hodrick, 'Forward Rates as Optimal Predictors of Spot Rates: An Econometric Analysis' *Journal of Political Economy* 88 (1980), 829–853, or C. A. E. Goodhart, P. C. McMahon and Y. L. Ngama, 'Does the Forward Premium/Discount Help to Predict the Future Change in the Exchange Rate?', *Scottish Journal of Political Economy* 39 (1992), 129–139.

the monastic order on the discount. Unfortunately, we have insufficient numbers of contracts for the individual orders after some contracts are removed from the sample, as discussed above, to be able to examine this within a regression framework. So instead we consider the impact of belonging to any religious order on the size of the discount.

Comparing the sizes of the discounts for all sellers and for monastic sellers only, it is again evident that the latter obtained a slightly worse deal, with heavier discounts relative to the high price that their good wool could have obtained if sold in the year it was sheared. There seems to be virtually no relationship between the contract size (total number of sacks to be delivered) and the discount, or between the length of the contract period and the discount. Sellers of larger quantities who were to deliver quickly (i.e. short contracts) would generate the smallest forward pricing discounts relative to market prices, as one would expect.

In summary, this chapter has discussed the results of a financial examination of the agreements, with the aim of addressing two issues. First, to consider the interest rates that were implicit in the transaction details, and second, to examine the forward pricing efficiency of the advance contracts. On the first question, we find that the calculated rates of interest are, in the main, not only plausible, but also broadly concurrent with those described in related studies of loans (implicit or explicit) made at that time. As to the question of market efficiency, this is eqivalent to asking whether there was information that would have been available to the counterparties at the time the contract was signed that was not incorporated into the deal. Our results suggest that only to a limited degree could old information from the spot market have been used to predict the subsequent discount. It would therefore be concluded that, by comparison with studies on modern-day financial markets, the medieval wool markets were fairly efficient. In particular, there is no evidence that the discount could have been predicted using this stale information when the sellers were abbots. Comparing these results with existing studies on the efficiency of modern wool markets suggests that broadly the same conclusions were reached.[87] Thus, even for these modern contracts that are very frequently traded on a formal exchange, the evidence for efficiency is mixed. When considered in this light, the medieval wool forward market was remarkably well functioning and orderly.

---

[87] See B. A. Goss, 'The Forecasting Approach to Efficiency in the Wool Market', *Applied Economics* 22 (1990), 973–993, or J. Graham-Higgs, A. Rambaldi and B. Davidson, 'Is the Australian Wool Futures Market Efficient as a Predictor of Spot Prices?', *Journal of Futures Markets* 19 (1999), 565–582, who both examine the Australian wool spot–futures price relationship.

CHAPTER 5

Conclusions

This book is a review and analysis of the data contained within a unique body of evidence, concerning advance contracts for the sale of wool in medieval England. The nature of these contracts tells us much about the early use of sophisticated financial instruments on not just a domestic but also a European-wide scale. We have been able to delve into the contracts to look at why they existed and what form they took. In turn, we have been able to further focus on one particular monastery and to investigate the reasons for its eventual dispersal, determining how the advance wool contracts were linked into this event. We have also attempted to analyse the contracts from a modern finance perspective, probably for the first time. We have looked at whether the market was efficient and whether these contracts were forwards or loans, by calculating the interest rates charged.

This book benefits from the survival of a wealth of contract evidence but not the contracts themselves. We are able to discover the details of the bulk of the contracts because of the legal processes of the Exchequer (Memoranda Rolls and Plea Rolls) and Chancery (Close Rolls).[1] We are not therefore able to undertake a survey of all advance contracts that may have been in existence – we can only analyse those that survive because of the legal process. We can see from the Exchequer Schedule of 1294,[2] for instance, that the wool market was much bigger than the wool exchanged in the contracts that we have found. Therefore, throughout what follows, the nature of the material we have used must temper our conclusions.

So what have we discovered about the advance contracts? The sellers include the monastic orders of the Cistercians, who have long been known to have been involved in this practice, and who are the most active in this trade, and also the Augustinians, Benedictines, Cluniacs, Premonstratensians and the Knights Templar. There are also a large number of contracts with

[1] E 159, E 368, E 13, C 54.
[2] E 101/126/7, mm. 11–25. *Advance Contracts*, Appendix 1.

lay growers, but the volume of wool sold is biased heavily in favour of the monasteries. The buyers come from Flanders, France, Germany, and predominately on this evidence from Italy. This includes societies from Florence, Lucca, Piacenza and Pistoia. It can be shown that despite some contracts showing evidence of full or partial payments in advance, such payments are unusual rather than being the norm. One such contract of 1287 between the Cluniac house of Lewes and the Riccardi, included a full advance payment of £1,666 13s 4d for 400 sacks of *collecta* wool for delivery over five years, and all of the wool was delivered as promised.[3] Although a minority event, this type of advance payment does show how keen the Italian merchants were to get hold of high-quality wool.

Have we been able to discover why advance contracts were made? It is possible that the outbreak of sheep scab from around 1272 onwards[4] had a significant effect on the predominance of the advance contracts from this date to 1327. The merchants were probably more likely to use the full support of the English legal apparatus to protect their investment in the light of the ravages of disease. In contrast to this, it may have been that the shortage in wool production, perhaps as a result of the sheep scab, encouraged the buyers to attempt to secure the best wool by tying the monasteries into long-term contracts – a large number of long-term contracts were negotiated in this period and many monasteries delivered in full on their promises of wool. Indeed, it has been shown that the Cahorsin merchants involved with Pipewell Monastery even went so far as to provide the monks with the sheep they would need to deliver on renegotiated wool deals.[5] It would also appear that another contributory factor was the financial difficulties many monastic houses found themselves in – sometimes with the very Italian merchants negotiating the advance wool purchases. It is entirely possible that some of the advance payments described in the contracts were not payments that had been made at all, but instead were reductions in debt payments already due to the merchants. In this instance, the advance contracts would have been an imaginative method of gaining repayment, perhaps with interest, from debts previously incurred. The Cistercian General Chapter itself only licensed longer-term wool deals so that urgent debts could be paid off.[6]

We have been able to show that, when possible, the legal solution for non-delivery, both advised and preferred by the Crown, was renegotiation and

[3] E 159/61, rot. 14. *Advance Contracts*, no. 104.
[4] Donkin, 'Cistercian Sheep Farming and Wool Sales', p. 6.
[5] C 54/108, mm. 8d.–9d.; E 159/64, rot. 10; E 368/62, rot. 14. *Advance Contracts*, no. 133.
[6] Denholm-Young, *Seigneurial Administration*, p. 55.

restructure. This was in the monasteries' and the King's interest – and was perhaps even in the best interest of the merchants, especially with the periodic threat of exile and thus a complete loss being incurred in that event. It does seem that the merchants were willing to restructure and even to throw greater sums of money at their counterparties. For instance, the Riccardi and the Benedictine priory of St Swithun in Winchester took around twenty years and numerous restructurings to settle an original contract for 470 sacks of wool from 1285 onwards.[7] It is clear from this that the King did not want his monasteries to go bankrupt with the strain of debt from foreign merchants. The monasteries were a great source of taxation and spiritual wealth and the King would therefore use his powers of persuasion to ensure that deals could be done in the majority of cases.

In the event of non-delivery of the promised wool, the merchants could obtain redress in a number of ways. As we have mentioned, the reason that the contract evidence exists is because the merchants were able to make use of the available legal procedures to protect against predicted or actual default. Two outcomes were generally possible, the first being an encouragement to renegotiate a new structure for the delivery of wool between the two parties.[8] The second outcome would be used if a settlement was not possible, normally due to non-attendance by one party, and in these cases distraint could be used against the wrongdoers. However, it has to be said that cases exist when both buyers and sellers end up on the wrong side of the law during a dispute. Perhaps to avoid such drawn-out disputes, occasionally the merchants would instead structure their original contract in order to protect themselves against future non-delivery. In this way merchants could still make profit from late delivery[9] by ensuring that they were protected against default by the monasteries. The merchants could structure their payments, year on year – thus lowering their overall exposure to risk – or place penalty clauses on non-delivery. For instance, Darnall Abbey was to be charged £20 per day of default in a contract with Gyles de Ayre.[10] We are not able to judge with precision the percentage of actual agreements that ended in legal dispute, as we only have the legal evidence to consider. But if we accept that the wool export trade was running at approximately 25,000 sacks annually,[11] it would seem that only a small percentage ended up in the courts.

[7] This was finally settled in 1305, E 159/62, rot. 4; *Advance Contracts*, no. III.
[8] E 13/4, mm. 8 –8d.; E 13/8, m. 3d.; E 13/8, m. 9d. *Advance Contracts*, nos. 17, 33, 34.
[9] Prestwich, 'Italian Merchants in Late Thirteenth and Early Fourteenth Century England', p. 95.
[10] C 54/92, m. 2d. *Advance Contracts*, no. 13.
[11] Carus-Wilson and Coleman, *England's Export Trade*, p. 122, table, England: Raw Wool Exports.

Despite only accounting for a minority of the actual wool exported in any particular year, the evidence from the contracts provides us with a valuable insight into the English wool market as a whole. If payments actually changed hands, this was likely to occur in London, or at one of the many regional fairs during the summer months. It is not too much of a leap to imagine that such payments may have sometimes taken the form of deductions on existing debt or as discounts on other products at such established local centres of exchange. It would seem that the heads of houses would on the whole broker the deals themselves – with the agreement of their convent – since it is generally their name on the top of the Recognisance, but we also have evidence that deals may have been made by a lay brother of the house.[12] We can also find agents or middlemen acting as both buyers and sellers – perhaps taking their own cut from such deals. The contracts give us much detail regarding the preparation and dressing of the wool and it can be seen that it is this, as well as the inherent wool quality, that the merchants are willing to pay highly for. It would seem that the monasteries had become expert in the technique of dressing and this led to them being able to broker high prices for *collecta* wool – sometimes higher than their own wool[13] – if they prepared it. This would therefore seem to indicate that they had some awareness of the importance of the marketability of brand – and that the merchants themselves were also extremely brand aware.

We can also comment on the existing delivery and distribution network which appears to be working within England at this time. A number of established centres for delivery are identified. For instance, the importance of York is clearly shown, with distant houses such as Calder from Cumberland, and Cartmel and Furness in Lancashire making their deliveries here.[14] Other regional centres were also important, as was London, but it was Boston in Lincolnshire to which much of the wool was delivered. This would confirm Lloyd's contention that Boston was the hub for wool throughout the period.[15] It is also clear that the wool trade was highly localised – with the merchants knowing exactly where to find the best-quality wool.

We have been able to show that the two main local regions for the wool market were Yorkshire and Lincolnshire – and whereas Yorkshire has

---

[12] E 13/4, m. 8–8d. *Advance Contracts*, no. 71.
[13] E 159/53, rot. 12d., E 368/53, rot. 14. *Advance Contracts*, nos. 42, 43.
[14] E 101/126/7, mm. 14, 16, 18, 20, 23, 24, 25. *Advance Contracts*, nos. 206, 207, 209, 210, 214, 215, 216.
[15] Lloyd, *English Wool Trade*, p. 64.

been well covered by local studies of the wool market[16] – historians have neglected Lincolnshire. As we have mentioned, Boston was the key place for the delivery of wool identified in the contracts and it exported more wool than London in this period.[17] Whilst we are unable to make any statement regarding the relative value of the wool from Lincolnshire, there is no doubt that it was highly prized, with every Italian merchant society trying to get their hands on it. This included wool produced by the Augustinian abbey of Thornton, the Cistercian nunnery of Nun Cotham, the Premonstratensian priory of Newsham and the Templar House at Temple Bruer.[18] It is clear that the question of the importance of Lincolnshire in the wool market would benefit from some more intensive local research.

In order to gain a fuller understanding of the background of the advance contracts we concentrated on Pipewell abbey in Northamptonshire and their series of agreements made with Cahorsin merchants.[19] The evidence from the wool contracts is supported by the words of the Abbot of Pipewell himself, William of Lawford, written onto a blank folio in the abbey's cartulary, alongside a list of fifteen Recognisances for debt. That Pipewell fell into indebtedness and eventual dispersal in 1323, following a forty-year struggle, is clear. What we have been able to show is that the most important factor in Pipewell's financial difficulties was indeed the advance contracts for wool – which had been continually renegotiated and restructured since 1288. That this relationship had not led to prosperity for the monks and their patrons can be seen to be a result of bad luck and an over-optimistic view of their potential wool production. It does not appear that the agreements were entered into in bad faith. Rather, we would say that Pipewell attempted to use its resources creatively to drag itself out of a mess created by external forces. It is also of no doubt that the methods employed by Pipewell were risky, but were also by no means unique at this time or indeed more recently. Unfortunately for Pipewell, the risks did not pay off and instead led the abbey further into trouble. This situation parallels that of 'rogue trader' Nick Leeson, who attempted to overcome his financial losses in futures contracts by buying more, a technique known as 'doubling up', where the size of holding is doubled but the average loss per unit of holding is halved.

---

[16] Denholm-Young, *Seigneurial Adminstration*, pp. 53–63; Waites, 'Monasteries and the Wool Trade in North and East Yorkshire during the 13th and 14th Centuries'; Jamroziak, 'Rievaulx Abbey'; Platt, *The Monastic Grange*.

[17] Lloyd, *English Wool Trade*, p. 64.

[18] E 101/126/7, mm. 17, 18, 20, 22, 24, 26. *Advance Contracts*, nos. 208, 209, 211, 213, 215, 216.

[19] See Chapter 3.

One of the innovative parts of our study concerns the use of modern financial formulae in an attempt to investigate the nature and sophistication of the advance contracts. This book therefore adds to the growing body of evidence that those transacting in the medieval economy were much more financially aware than many modern commentators give them credit for. We have calculated the interest rates implied in the advance wool transactions typically to be of the order of 10 per cent–40 per cent. We also conducted an examination of the efficiency of the medieval English wool spot and forward markets, finding little evidence of inefficiencies in the sense that stale information could be used to predict future market outcomes. It seems that 'modern finance' is perhaps not so modern after all, and that valuation formulae developed in the past few decades were implicitly in use over 700 years ago.

Our research involving the financial aspects of the contracts suggests several potentially fruitful avenues for further study. First, it would be of interest to examine in greater detail the relationship between financial positions of the abbeys and the forward price discount on their wool. It may be that knowledgeable merchants were able to exploit the monasteries in trouble that were the most desperate for cash. Indeed, Munro[20] suggests that the huge discounts that the merchants were able to obtain in part reflected 'distress sales'. Second, is there a relationship between the likelihood of default and the size of the forward price discount? Clearly, monasteries that had sold their wool the most cheaply relative to prevailing prices would have the strongest incentives to renege on the deal when the wool became available. Third, the only existing wool futures market is the Sydney Futures Exchange, Australia. Wool futures have been trading there since May 1960, with the principal aim of assisting market participants in managing their price risk – that is, the risk to growers that prices will fall and the risk to wool users that prices will rise. It would be of interest to compare comprehensively the current Australian wool futures market with the English medieval wool market.

Finally, the existence of the advance contracts for the sale of wool that we have investigated appears to be a historically unique phenomenon as they are confined to a short period at the close of the thirteenth century. As well as investigating other aspects of these contracts in greater detail, such as the credit risk that the merchants faced when they made up-front payments to the monasteries, future research may investigate why the forward agreements died out almost as quickly as they arose. A casual examination of the available

---

[20] Munro, 'Wool Price Schedules and the Qualities of English Wools', p. 129.

secondary sources suggests that there were several factors that encouraged the demise of these early derivatives contracts. First, the quality and quantity of available English wools deteriorated. Throughout the thirteenth and fourteenth centuries, English wool was highly prized for its quality, but by the end of the sixteenth century, it had been surpassed by Spanish wool as the finest in the world.[21] The lack of long-woolled sheep in England in the Middle Ages meant that wool yields per sheep were relatively small and therefore that the wool was more costly to produce than was the case for some foreign producers. Second, as international demand for English wool declined, domestic demand increased to fuel the rapidly growing domestic textile industries. J. H. Munro argues that England overtook the Low Countries as the prime source of cloth from the late thirteenth century in part as a result of a move towards higher-quality textile production.[22] As we have also observed, the taxation of the export of raw wool also contributed to the growth of this domestic industry, and exports increased 140-fold between 1349 and 1539. Finally, the impacts of royal taxation and manipulation of the market, European and civil war, and attempts by the religious orders to ban such agreements must also have taken their toll. While wool exports had been subject to a heavy burden of duties, exports of finished cloth had not. Taxation on cloth had averaged 3 per cent over the twelfth and thirteenth centuries until 1373. Even then, the rate of taxation on cloth exports increased to just 5 per cent.[23] By 1340, the golden age of English raw wool export via sophisticated advance contracts had passed and a period of stagnation lasting more than a century then ensued.

The story that has emerged from this enormous body of evidence is one of a dynamic market economy, which was able to be reactive to national and international politics and also to the ravages of disease. We have discovered a society that was able to be imaginative in their financial dealings, using what we would term 'modern' techniques to solve their solvency issues – even if sometimes, just as happens today, these dealings often led to the courts and eventual bankruptcy.

---

[21] Bowden, 'Wool Supply and the Woollen Industry'.

[22] J. H. Munro, 'The Symbiosis of Towns and Textiles: Urban Institutions and the Changing Fortunes of Cloth Manufacturing in the Low Countries and England, 1270–1570,' *Journal of Early Modern History: Contacts, Comparisons, Contrasts* 3(1999), pp. 1–74.

[23] J. M. Murray, *A History of Business in Medieval Europe 1200–1550* (Cambridge, 1999), pp. 166–167.

Appendix 1: Sample contract

This appendix details one of the earliest known indentures for an advance sale of wool between Pipewell Abbey and two prominent Londoners.[1] We believe that this contract has not been previously identified or discussed in the literature. We have presented the original contract, photographed at the National Archives, Kew, the Latin transcription and English translation.

LATIN TRANSCRIPTION

Notum sit omnibus Christi fidelibus presentibus et futuris quod hec est convencio facta Anno gracie m° cc° xlij° ad Purificationem beate Marie inter Abbatem et Conventum de Pipewell', ex una parte, et Johannem Tolosanum et Adam de Sorisdich', Cives London', ex altera, scilicet quod predicti Abbas et Conventus vendiderunt pre manibus predictis Johanni et Ade totam Lanam suam venalem anni sequentis, scilicet unumquemque saccum de bona pro quindecim marcis et unumquemque saccum de media pro decem marcis, unde debent predicti Johannes et Adam vel alter eorum sive sui assignati reddere predictis Abbati et Conventui vel suo certo nuncio ad proximas Nundinas sancti Ivonis post istam Convencionem factam infra Octavas clausi Pasce Lx marcas, et infra Octavas exaltacionis sancte Crucis proximo sequentis apud London' Lx marcas sub pena decem marcarum. Et residuum pacamenti reddent ad sequentes nundinas sancti Botulphi quando et ubi Lanam predictam recipient. In cuius Rei testimonium predicti Abbas et Johannes et Adam hoc Cirographum sigillis suis alternatim roboraverunt. Hiis testibus Fratre Ricardo de Norhampton monacho, Fratre Ricardo de Assele monacho et Fratre Roberto Converso et aliis.

---

[1] E 327/541. *Advance Contracts*, no. 221.

An early advance contract: Pipewell Abbey, 1242 (TNA E327/541, Crown Copyright).

ENGLISH TRANSLATION

It is to be known to all faithful in Christ, present and future, that this is the agreement made in the year of grace 1242, at the Purification of the Blessed Mary, between the abbot and convent of Pipewell, on the one hand, and John of Toulouse and Adam of Shoreditch, citizens of London, on the other, namely that the aforesaid abbot and convent have sold in advance to the aforesaid John and Adam all of their saleable wool produced in the year following, namely each sack of good wool for 15 m. and each sack of middle-grade for 10 m, wherefore the aforesaid John and Adam, or either of them or their assigns, ought to render 60 m to the aforesaid abbot and convent, or to their certain nuncio, at the next fair of St Ives held after this agreement has been made within the octaves of the Close of Easter [4 May], and 60 m. within the octaves of the Exaltation of the Holy Cross [21 September] next following in London under pain of 10 m. And they are to render the remainder of the payment at the following fair of Boston whenever and wherever they receive the aforesaid wool. In testimony of which thing, the aforesaid abbot and John and Adam have validated this chirograph alternately with their seals. Witnessed by Brother Richard of Northampton, monk, Brother Richard de Assele, monk, and Brother Robert the lay brother, and others. [2 February 1242.]

Appendix 2: Summary facts and figures of contracts

This appendix provides a summary of the data we have drawn from the contract evidence.

The Contract Evidence [215–113 monastic, 102 lay]:
(C54, 11–9 monastic, 2 lay); (E13, 64–27 monastic, 37 lay); (E159/368, 128 – 70 monastic, 58 lay); (Common Pleas, 4 – 1 monastic, 3 lay); (Ancient Deeds, 4 – 3 monastic, 1 lay); (KB/26 – 2 monastic); (KB/27 – 1 lay); (SC1 – 1 monastic).
Exchequer Schedule 1294 [220 – all monastic]:
(E101/126/7, mm.12–28).
Della Decima [23–20 monastic, 3 lay]
Documents/Texts [151]:
Chancery, Close Rolls, 11 [C54/92, 93, 102, 105, 106, 108, 111, 118, 130, 131] King's Remembrancer's Memoranda Rolls, 66 [E159/37-102 inclusive]; Treasurer's Remembrancer's Memoranda Rolls, 28 [E368/37-64 inclusive]; Exchequer Plea Rolls, 36 [E13/2-37]; Exchequer Miscellanea, 1 file, 19 membranes [E101/126/7, mm. 11–29]; one roll, 5 mm. [E163/5/17]; Ancient Deeds, 4 [E210/7015 and E327/541]; Ancient Correspondence, 1 [SC1]; Justices in Eyre, 1 [JUST 1]; King's Bench, Curia Regis Rolls, 2 [KB 26]; King's Bench, Coram Rege Rolls, 1 [KB 27]; *Della Decima*; Francisco Balducci Pegolotti, *La Pratica Della Mercatura*.
Contracts by Religious Order [123]:
Augustinian (19); Benedictine (8); Cistercian (77); Cluniac (9); Gilbertine (0); Hospitaller (0); Premonstratensian (7); Templar (3)
TOTAL SACKS [5330 sacks, 12 stone and 28 whole crops and wool worth £1304. 13s 4d]
Sacks by religious order
TOTAL: 4432 sacks, 4 stone and 28 whole crops and wool worth £1304 13s 4d

- Augustinian (379 and 6 whole crops)
- Benedictine (363 and 3 whole crops)
- Cistercian (2662 sacks, 4 stone and 13 whole crops)

- Cluniac (963 and 1 whole crop)
- Gilbertine (0)
- Hospitaller (0)
- Premonstratensian (65 and 5 whole crops)
- Templar (wool worth £1304 13s 4d)

Sacks purchased from ecclesiastical growers
55 sacks and 1 whole crop from 4 contracts.
Sacks purchased from lay growers
843 sacks, 8 stone.
Contracts by county:
Bedfordshire (4); Berkshire (3); Buckinghamshire (8); Cheshire (5); Cumberland (1); Dorset (3); Essex (4); Gloucestershire (4); Hampshire (7); Herefordshire (6); Huntingdonshire (2); Kent (1); Lancashire (1); Leicestershire (14); Lincolnshire – county (6); Holland (6); Kesteven (13); Lindsey (17) – [41]; Norfolk (8); Northamptonshire (9); Northumberland (2); Nottinghamshire/ Derbyshire (17); Oxfordshire (13); Shropshire (1); Staffordshire (2); Surrey (2); Sussex (7); Warwickshire (12); Wiltshire (1); Yorkshire – county (4); East Riding (11); North Riding (17); West Riding (11) – [43]; ENGLAND [county unknown] (1); WALES (1); IRELAND (2); unidentified (5).
Contracts per company/nationality of merchants (with number of sacks):
Total Contracts (223)
Total Sacks (5282, 15¼ stone, 28 whole crops and Templar wool worth £1304. 13s 4d)

CAHORS
Contracts (14)
Sacks (572 sacks, 17 stone and 1 whole crop)

ENGLISH
Contracts (38)
Sacks (1110 sacks and 2 whole crops)

FLANDERS
Contracts (7)
Sacks (49 sacks, 20 stone and 1 whole crop)

FRANCE
Contracts (1)
Sacks (7)

GERMANY
Contracts (3)
Sacks (3 sacks and 1 whole crop)

ITALY
Contracts (157)
Sacks (3529 sacks, 4¼ stone, 23 whole crops and Templar wool worth £1304. 13s 4d)

Florence
Contracts (74)
Sacks (1959 sacks, 20¼ stone, 23 whole crops and Templar wool worth £1304. 13s 4d)
- Bardi (Contracts 1, £475. 6s 8d of Lincolnshire Templar wool)
- Cerchi (Contracts 7; Sacks 274)
- Falconeri (Contracts 3, Sacks 24)
- Frescobaldi (Contracts 28, Sacks 1208, 12¼ stone and 4 whole crops and 1100 marks worth of Templar wool)
- Mozzi (Contracts 28, Sacks 322, 18 stone and 19 whole crops)
- Peruzzi (Contracts 1, Sacks 8)
- Pulci-Rembertini (Contracts 3, Sacks 69)
- Scala (Contracts 2, Sacks 3, 16 stone)
- Spini (Contracts 1, Sacks 50)

Lucca
Contracts (78)
Sacks (1511, 23 stone)
- Baroncino Galteri and his sons, Ricardo and Burnetto (Contracts 2, Sacks 24½)
- Bellardi (Contracts 2, Sacks 20)
- Riccardi (Contracts 72, Sacks 1461, 10 stone)
- Unidentified others (Contracts 2, Sacks 6)

Piacenza
- Scotti (Contracts 4, Sacks 55½)

Pistoia
Contracts (1)
Sacks (2)

SPAIN
Contracts (2)
Sacks (11)
Contracts explicitly mentioning an advance payment 78
Contracts for which a payment of the advance was made in full 53
Contracts in which full delivery was made 49
Contracts in which the growers are to dress the wool 60

Appendix 3: List of contracts

This appendix contains a summary listing of the main body of contract evidence drawn from Chancery and Exchequer records. The numbered contracts refer to the listing within the volume produced for the List and Index Society, where a full transcription and translation is available.[1]

---

[1] *Advance Contracts*, also accessible at the UK Data Archive, study number 5325: www.data-archive.ac.uk

No.	Reference	Date	Seller	Buyer	Summary
1	E159/10, rot. 6d	11 April 1231	Walter de Lacy, Lord of Meath	Richard, son of John, citizen of London	12 sacks for delivery later the same year
2	E159/32, rot. 17	1 July 1259	Robert de Tateshale, Lincolnshire, Holland	Arnold Griffun and associates (Cahors)	70 sacks for delivery in following year, 1260
3	E159/33, rot. 2d	6 October 1259	Stephen de Chaendut, Northamptonshire	Arnold Griffun, Imbert Delderoc and William Frescepayn (Cahors)	6 sacks for delivery in following year, 1260
4	E159/33, rot. 5	17 November 1259	John de Burgh, Derbyshire	Adam de Basinges	10 sacks for delivery in 1261
5	E159/33, rot. 5	17 November 1259	John de Burgh, Derbyshire	Arnold Griffun and associates (Cahors)	23 sacks for delivery in 1260
6	E 159/34, rot. 2	4 October 1260	John de Burgh and William Blund, Derbyshire	Adam de Basinges	10 sacks for delivery in 1261 (see 4)
7	E159/34, rot. 1d	3 October 1261	John de Burgh and William Blund, Derbyshire	Adam de Basinges	10 sacks for delivery in 1261 (see 4)
8	E159/36, rot. 17	3 July 1262	John de Burgh, Derbyshire	Adam de Basinges	50 m. to be levied from the goods of John de Burgh (see 4, 6 and 7)
9	E159/37, rot. 8	Michaelmas, 1262–3	Reginald Maniword of Hereford	Peter Berard (Cahors)	13 sacks and 16 stones of lambswool. 4 sacks to be delivered in 1263; 4 sacks in 1264; 5 sacks and 16 stones to be delivered in 1265.
10	E159/44, rot. 12	Michaelmas, 1269	John de Burgh, Derbyshire	Bernard Nicholas, Arnaud Griffin and Imbert Rok (Cahors)	Receipt of 430 m. in lieu of 52 sacks of wool.
11	E13/1E, m. 14d	Candlemas 1269	Thornholme priory, Lincolnshire (Augustinian)	William of Louth	75 sacks for delivery 1269–1270. This contract comes to light as a result of the prior's breach in selling much of this wool to another party.

No.	Reference	Date	Seller	Buyer	Summary
12	E159/45, rot. 18; E368/44, rot. 11d	Michaelmas 1270–1	Wroxton priory, North East Oxfordshire (Augustinian)	Ricardo Bonaventuri, citizen of London	8 sacks for delivery in 1271
13	C54/92, m. 2d	8 November 1275	Darnhall abbey, Cheshire (Cistercian)	John Wermond of Cambrai, via his attorney, Giles de Ayre	12 sacks for delivery in following year, 1276.
14	C54/93, m. 18d.	25 November 1275	Louth Park abbey	Herbert Wermond, via his attorney Giles de Ayre	14 sacks and 20 stones of wool to be delivered in the following year, 1276
15	E13/4. m. 5	27 March–2 April 1276	Thomas son of Robert, Roger le Shipwrihcte and Andrew Motty Kirkstall abbey	William Frescenade	2 sacks of wool
16	E13/4. m. 6	13 April 1276		Teglario Amatour and Gentyl de Lyvary, merchants of Florence	2 sacks and three stones of wool to be delivered later that year.
17	E13/4. m.8-8d	7 June 1276	Biddlesden abbey, North Buckinghamshire (Cistercian)	Scotti of Piacenza	21 sacks for delivery in the same year. This contract arises as a previous arrangement for the delivery of 21 sacks at an unspecified date in the recent past had not been adhered to by the monks. This original agreement had been made by Ralph de Laneria, a lay brother of the abbey, apparently on his own authority. The merchants claim that the default has cost them room in damages.

No.	Reference	Date	Seller	Buyer	Summary
18	E13/5, m. 2	Michaelmas 1276	Thame abbey, Chilterns (Cistercian)	Bertram Cappedemayle, Bertram de Cruser and Peter Donde, merchants of the Treasurer, Joseph de Cauncy	7 sacks of wool
19	C54/93, m. 3d	15 October 1276	Peter de Aling (abbot), Fountains abbey, West Riding Yorkshire (Cistercian)	Dunelanus Jonte and Bernard Thecdaldi (Florence)	62 sacks for delivery over the next four years, i.e. 1277–1280
20	E13/5, m. 12d	21 January 1277	William de Len, Ingram the Merchant of Louth and Robert de Elington'	Reginald of Piacenza	Dispute over 2½ sacks of wool
21	E13/6, m. 10d	10 February 1278	Meaux abbey, Holderness (Cistercian)	Del Papa (Florence)	105 sacks of wool. This contract is revealed by the failure of Hugh Papa to make full payment to the monks. He is also bound to acquit the merchants of 1800m which they appear to have subsequently paid for the wool. There is no reference to the period during which this contract ought to have run.
22	E13/6, m. 20d	27 June 1278	Clement son of Elias, William son of John and Robert Alzun of Pontefract, West Riding Yorkshire	Scotti of Piacenza	4 sacks of wool – never delivered.

No.	Reference	Date	Seller	Buyer	Summary
23	E159/51, rot.20d; E368/51, rot.13d. and schedule	22 June 1278	Flaxley abbey, Gloucestershire (Cistercian)	Thomas de Basing, citizen of London	130 sacks of wool for delivery over the next 13 years, i.e. 1278–1290. A recognisance for the repayment of the advance at the rate of £20 a year for eight years and £50 in the final year was entered into on the same day and resulted from a previous 12-year contract which the monks had apparently been unable to fulfil, but which Thomas was willing to remit to them in return for this new contract. The wool is to be carried to Thomas's chambers in London at the costs of the convent in each of only the final five years. The monks, however, are not to receive any payments for wool delivered in the last four years unless they deliver the wool.
24	E159/52, rot. 11; E368/52, rot. 10	Michaelmas 1278–9	Welbeck abbey, Nottinghamshire (Premonstratensian)	Falconeri	5 sacks for delivery over the next five years (1 sack per year), 1279–1283;
25	E159/52, rot. 12; E368/52, rot. 11d	Michaelmas 1278–9	Roger le Bret de Sopwort, Robert le Blund of Lacock, Wiltshire	William de Frescenade, merchant	1 sack of wool for delivery the following year.
26	E159/52, rot. 13; E368/52, rot. 12d	Hilary 1279	Fountains abbey, West Riding Yorkshire (Cistercian)	Cerchi/Bardi	27 sacks for delivery over two years, i.e. 1279–1280

No.	Reference	Date	Seller	Buyer	Summary
27	E159/52, rot. 13; E368/52, rot. 12d	Hilary 1279	Byland abbey, North Riding Yorkshire (Cistercian)	Frescobaldi	120 sacks of wool for delivery over the next seven years, i.e. 1279–1285.
28	E159/52, rot. 15; E368/52, rot. 15	Easter 1279	Combermere abbey, Cheshire (Cistercian)	Frescobaldi	300 sacks over the next 20 years, i.e. 1279–1298
29	E13/8, m. 1d	30 September 1279	Robert son of Alice, Pontefract, West Riding Yorkshire	Riccardi	10 sacks for delivery later that year
30	E13/8, m. 1d	30 September 1279	Merchants of Grantham	Riccardi	Resolving dispute
31	E13/8, m. 1d	30 September 1279	Merchants of Leicester and Coventry	Riccardi	Resolving dispute
32	E13/8, m. 1d	30 September 1279	Robert Son of Alice et al.	Riccardi	Resolving dispute
33	E13/8, m. 3d	30 September – 6 October 1279	Merchants of Banbury	Riccardi	5 sacks of wool for delivery the following year. The wool is specifically to be ewes' wool [bona lana matricia] from the collecta of Banbury.
34	E13/8, m. 9d	19 November 1279	Burgesses of Northampton	Riccardi	6 sacks of wool
35	E13/8, m. 9d	19 November 1279	Juliana, Widow of Adam le Bretun of Chipping Norton	Riccardi	5 sacks of wool
36	E159/53, rot. 9; E368/53, rot. 10	Michaelmas 1279	Swineshead abbey, Lincolnshire (Cistercian)	Falconeri	12 sacks for delivery from 1283–1289 (the contract definitely states that 12 sacks are involved, but when the sacks are broken down into individual instalments 13 are mentioned).

No.	Reference	Date	Seller	Buyer	Summary
37	E368/53, rot. 12	Michaelmas 1279	Fountains abbey, West Riding Yorkshire (Cistercian)	Frescobaldi	130 sacks for delivery from 1280 to 1284
38	E368/53, rot. 12d	Michaelmas 1279	West Acre priory, Norfolk (Augustinian)	Cerchi	48 sacks for delivery from 1281 to 1284
39	E13/8, m. 11	14 January 1280	Wroxton priory, Oxfordshire	Peter Mundenard of Spain	6 sacks of wool. These sacks are to be delivered to Peter in part payment of a debt he owes Queen Eleanor. The sheriff is to raise the wool from within and without the liberty of Banbury.
40	E13/8, m. 14	28 January, 3 February 1280	Abbey Dore, Herefordshire	Poncio de Mora and John de Soliz (Cahors)	3 sacks for delivery later that year
41	E159/53, rot. 12d; E368/53, rot. 14	Hilary 1280	Merchants of Banbury	Riccardi	4 sacks and a poke of wool
42	E159/53, rot. 12d; E368/53, rot. 14	Hilary 1280	Meaux abbey, Holderness (Cistercian)	Riccardi	53 sacks for delivery in 1280 and 1282. The wool is to be taken from the *collecta* of the lands between Bridlington, Kirkham and York. The abbot is to find sarpliers each year and is to accommodate the merchants' dresser.
43	E159/53, rot. 12d; E368/53, rot. 14	Hilary 1280	Meaux abbey, Holderness (Cistercian)	Cerchi	90 sacks of wool for delivery over three years, i.e. 1280–1282
44	E13/8, m. 15d	17 February 1280	Wroxton priory, Oxfordshire	Peter de Mundenard of Spain	6 sacks (1820 fleeces) of wool for delivery over seven years, i.e. 1280–1286

No.	Reference	Date	Seller	Buyer	Summary
45	E368/53, rot. 13	Hilary 1280	Tilty abbey, Essex (Cistercian)	Frescobaldi	100 sacks for delivery over ten years, i.e. 1280–1290.
46	E368/53, rot. 14d	Hilary 1280	Pontefract priory, West Riding Yorkshire (Cluniac)	Frescobaldi	80 sacks of wool for delivery over eight years, i.e. 1280–1287
47	E368/53, rot. 14d	1280	John of Walton	Riccardi	1050 fleeces for delivery that year
48	E368/53, rot. 15	Easter 1280	John de Reddemere of Appleby in Lindsey, Lincolnshire	Riccardi	20 sacks over two years 1280–1281
49	E13/8, m. 21	6 May 1280	John Caritas of Leicester	Riccardi	1½ sacks of wool
50	E13/8, m. 28	25 June, 2 July 1280	Thomas de Fakenham, Henry the Baker of Coventry and Adam Russel	Riccardi	10 sacks of wool
51	E159/54, rot. 11d; E368/54, rot. 11	Michaelmas 1280–1	Stone priory, Staffordshire (Augustinian)	Falconeri	7 sacks over three years 1281–1283
52	E159/54, rot. 11d: E368/54, rot. 11	Michaelmas 1280–1	Castle Acre priory, Norfolk (Cluniac)	John Donedeu and William Jon (Cahors)	20 sacks over four years 1281–1284
53	E159/54, rot. 12d; E368/54, rot. 12	Michaelmas 1280–1	John son of Arnold de Bosco, William de Stok, William de Aston and Martin the Merchant of Hinckley.	Gilbert de Cestretone and William son of Walter of Melton.	30 sacks over five years 1281–1285. Each sack is to contain 28 stone of wool.
54	E159/54, rot. 15	Hilary 1281	Ralph de Wodeberg	Riccardi	5 sacks for delivery later that year
55	E159/54, rot. 18; E368/54, rot. 16	Easter 1281	John de Say of Warwick	Riccardi	2 sacks for delivery later that year
56	E159/54, rot. 18; E368/54, rot. 16	Easter 1281	John de Say and Henry de Kynton'	Riccardi	16 sacks for delivery later that year

No.	Reference	Date	Seller	Buyer	Summary
57	E159/54, rot. 19; E368/54, rot. 17d	Easter 1281	Robert of Skifington, Leicestershire	Riccardi	4 sacks for delivery over two years 1281–1282
58	E159/54, rot. 20	Easter 1281	Robert of Skifington, Leicestershire	Riccardi	4 sacks for delivery later that year
59	E368/54, rot. 16	Easter 1281	John de Gatesden'	Baldwin de Gaunt, merchant	2 sacks for delivery later that year
60	E13/9, m. 2d	30 September, 6 October 1281	Robert le Franceys of Banbury	Riccardi	3 sacks for delivery in the following year. The sheriff reported that he had been hindered in distraining the wool by men of the liberty of Banbury. He himself was amerced 100s and ordered to have the men before him on 7 December 1282.
61	E159/55, rot. 9; E368/55, rot. 8	Michaelmas 1281	Roger de Toftes, Norfolk	Riccardi	3 sacks for delivery in 1282. The wool is to come from his own store at Bircham Tofts and Pedale in Norfolk and is to be weighed according to the Lynn weight and then carried to Boston at his costs in the merchants' sarpliers.
62	E13/9, m. 7	14 and 21 October 1281	William le Mire of Northampton	Robert of Acre	1 sack of wool. This plea arose as there was a dispute as to the verity of a tally by which William and Reginald claimed they had acquitted themselves of the wool. They were to appear in court on 27 January 1282.

No.	Reference	Date	Seller	Buyer	Summary
63	E159/55, rot. 10	Michaelmas 1281	Norman Darcy	John Bonquer	1 sack of wool for delivery the following year. The wool is to come from Lindsey and the sack is to contain 30 stones of wool, no specification being made as to the quality required.
64	E159/55, rot. 6	21 November 1281	Flaxley abbey, Gloucestshire (Cistercian)	Thomas de Basinges, citizen of London	8 sacks of wool for delivery in 1291. The original delivery date of 9 July 1281 had been postponed by Thomas in order to relieve the monks of an irksome burden. Although the wool is reckoned at 56 marks, a sum which is to be made over to them upon full delivery, the monks agree to repay 63 marks which they admit to have received in advance, in case of their default. The merchants' dresser is to be accommodated at their charge and the wool is to be carried to his chamber likewise.
65	E13/9, m. 10d	7 December 1281	Robert de Ocham and Stephen Bulke of Stow Thetford priory	Stephen de Cornhulle, citizen of London	1 sack of wool
66	E159/55, rot. 14; E368/55, rot. 13d	Easter 1282		Merchants of Florence	59 sacks of wool for delivery over 10 years
67	E13/10, m. 2	Michaelmas 1282	Humberston abbey, Lincolnshire (Benedictine)	Riccardi	1 sack of wool for delivery the following year
68	E159/56, rot. 4; E368/56, rot. 4	Michaelmas 1282	Robert of Skeffington	Merchants of Lucca	4 sacks of wool
69	E159/56, rot. 4; E368/56, rot. 4	Michaelmas 1282	Thomas Luard, vicar of Wellington, Shropshire	Richard Borrey	3 sacks for delivery over the next two years 1283–1284

No.	Reference	Date	Seller	Buyer	Summary
70	E13/10, m. 7	14 January 1283	Newburgh priory, North Riding Yorkshire (Augustinian)	James of Lissington and his wife, Agnes	123 sacks for delivery over 12 years 1283–1294
71	E13/10, m. 7d	21 January 1283	Roche abbey, Nottinghamshire (Cistercian)	Henry son of Robert le Veyl of Monyash, servant of Walter de Kancia	6 sacks of wool. The abbot claims that he is not bound to answer this plea in the Exchequer Court, as per Magna Carta.
72	E13/10, m. 8d	April 1283	Abbey Dore, Herefordshire (Cistercian)	John Doneden of Cahors	The wool of 800 sheep.
73	E159/57, rot. 11; E368/57, rot. 11d	Michaelmas 1283	Meaux abbey, Holderness (Cistercian)	Riccardi	11 sacks of wool for delivery over two years 1284–1285. The wool is to come from the best *collecta* lying between Bridlington, Kirkham and York. Each sack is to have 4 stones of wool pressed into it.
74	E159/57, rot. 13; E368/57, rot. 12d	Michaelmas 1283–4	Reginald Maniword, citizen of Hereford	John Donadeu and William Jon (Cahors)	8 sacks for delivery in the following year. 6 of these sacks are actually specified as lambswool, the remainder as ramswool, both though coming from the Welsh March.
75	E159/58, rot. 13	Michaelmas 1284	Biddlesden abbey, Buckinghamshire (Cistercian)	Riccardi	10 sacks for delivery in the following year
76	E159/58, rot. 14	Michaelmas 1284	Tilty abbey, Essex (Cistercian)	Frescobaldi	3 sacks for delivery in the following year. This contract represents the arrears owed by the abbot on a contract for the previous year.

No.	Reference	Date	Seller	Buyer	Summary
77	E159/58, rot. 14d	23 January 1285	Richard de Burgh, earl of Ulster and Nicholas de Segrave	Riccardi	50 sacks of wool for delivery over two years 1285–1286. Each sack is to be a 'great sack' of Ireland which is to contain 42 stones of wool at 13lb to the stone.
78	E159/58, rot. 16; E368/58, rot. 19	28 April 1285	St. Swithun's priory, Winchester (Benedictine)	Riccardi	Entire crop to a minimum of 240 sacks over six years 1287–1292
79	C54/102, m. 7d	20 May 1285	Robert Bozun, Derbyshire	Riccardi	16 sacks of wool
80	E159/59, rot. 1; E368/59, rot. 14	Michaelmas 1285	Biddlesden abbey, Buckinghamshire (Cistercian)	Merchants of Piacenza	28 sacks of wool
81	E13/12, m. 6	2 November and 7 December 1285	John son of Walter le Fleming of Stamford, Richard of Casterton, Robert le Fleming and Andrew Neye	William Servat (Cahors)	4 sacks and 4 stones of wool
82	E159/59, rot. 4 (schedules)	Hilary 1286	St. Swithun's priory, Winchester (Benedictine)	Riccardi	200 sacks for delivery over four years 1293–1296
83	E13/12, m. 21	Easter 1286	John son of Walter le Fleming of Stamford, Richard of Casterton, Robert le Fleming and Andrew Neye	William Servat (Cahors)	Satisfaction of contract (see 81)
84	E159/59, rot. 8d	Easter 1286	Bruern abbey, Oxfordshire (Cistercian)	Adam Blakeney, citizen of London	27 sacks of wool for delivery over three years 1286–1288. This is an 'either/or' contract: the abbot can satisfy the contract by the delivery of either 27 sacks of wool or £500 cash.

No.	Reference	Date	Seller	Buyer	Summary
85	E159/59, rot. 8d	Easter 1286	John de Columbariis, Berkshire	Riccardi	10 sacks for delivery later that year. Each sack is to weigh two weys or 48 stone with 14lb to the stone. The wool itself is to come from the good *colleta* of Newbury.
86	E159/59, rot. 9d; E368/59, rot. 19d	Easter 1286	Rievaulx abbey, North Riding Yorkshire (Cistercian)	Mozzi	168 sacks for delivery over nine years 1286–1293
87	E159/59, rot. 12d	Easter 1286	Lewes priory, Sussex (Cluniac)	Riccardi	23 sacks for delivery over two years 1287–1288. The wool is to be taken from the good *colleta* of Leicester, Grantham and Melton. It is to be weighed according to the weights and balance of the town of Leicester. The prior is to have the wool carried to Boston at his own costs and in his own sarpliers immediately after the end of each term.
88	E159/60, rot. 12d; E368/60, rot. 10d	Michaelmas 1286–7	Robert de Morteyn	William de Anarson and William Servat (Cahors)	1 sack of wool for delivery the following year
89	E159/60, rot. 12d; E368/60, rot. 10d	Michaelmas 1286–7	Robert of Warlingham, Surrey	Walter Herman and Master Peter de Guildeford	4 sacks for delivery over two years 1287–1288
90	E159/60, rot. 13d; E368/60, rot. 11d	Michaelmas 1286–7	Wroxton priory, Oxfordshire (Augustinian)	Peter de Mundenard of Spain	6 sacks for delivery over two years 1287–1288. The merchants, by this agreement, offer to acquit the prior of all debts owed in this manner on a contract entered into with one Walter Wyt of Banbury.

No.	Reference	Date	Seller	Buyer	Summary
91	E159/60, rot. 15; E368/60, rot. 13d	Hilary 1287	Jordan de Kendale, Chilterns	Riccardi	1½ sacks of wool for delivery later that year. Again, this is an 'either/or' contract; either the sacks or £10 at the pre-ordained date. The wool is to come from the good collecta of Dunstable.
92	E159/60, rot. 16d; E368/60, rot. 14d	Easter 1287	Rievaulx abbey, North Riding Yorkshire (Cistercian)	Riccardi	20 sacks for delivery later that year
93	E159/60, rot. 16d; E368/60, rot. 14d	Easter 1287	Fountains abbey, Yorkshire (Cistercian)	Mozzi	61 sacks for delivery later that year. The merchants acquitted the Abbey of all debts owing to them from the beginning of the world.
94	E159/60, rot. 17d	Easter 1287	Coxford priory, Norfolk (Augustinian)	Riccardi	4 sacks of wool for delivery later that year
95	E159/60, rot. 18	Easter 1287	Meaux abbey, Holderness (Cistercian)	Riccardi	11 sacks for delivery in 1289
96	E159/60, rot. 19d	Trinity 1287	John of Bulmer and Richard his son of Yorkshire	Riccardi	30 sacks for delivery in 1288
97	E159/60, rot. 20	Trinity 1287	Robert de Tateshale	Riccardi	19 sacks for delivery in 1288. 13 sacks are to be taken from the earldom of Richmond and the remaining six from Robert's Norfolk lands of Bambingle and Beckham or from any other good wool produced in the area.

No.	Reference	Date	Seller	Buyer	Summary
98	E159/60, rot. 2od	Trinity 1287	Reginald Maniword and William Brisebon, Herefordshire	Riccardi	2 sacks of lambswool
99	E159/61, rot. 11d	Michaelmas 1287	Rievaulx abbey, North Riding Yorkshire (Cistercian)	Riccardi	26 sacks for delivery over two years 1288–1289
100	E159/61, rot. 12	Michaelmas 1287	Coxford priory, Norfolk (Augustinian)	Riccardi	8 sacks of wool for delivery in 1288. The wool is to be weighed by the Lynn tron and carried in the convent's sarplers to Lynn.
101	E159/61, rot. 12d	Michaelmas 1287	John de Bosco, Leicestershire	Riccardi	Two separate contracts for 30 sacks and 10 sacks for delivery over four years 1288–1291
102	E159/61, rot. 13	Michaelmas 1287–8	Reginald Maniword of Hereford	Riccardi	5 sacks for delivery in 1288. Each sack is to be weighed by the tron of the fair of Winchester.
103	E159/61, rot. 14	Michaelmas 1287–8	Meaux abbey, Holderness (Cistercian)	Riccardi	65 sacks of wool for delivery over five years 1290–1294
104	E159/61, rot. 14	Michaelmas 1287–8	Lewes priory, Sussex (Cluniac)	Riccardi	400 sacks for delivery over five years 1288–1292
105	E159/61, rot. 17	Hilary 1288	Robert Bozon of High Peak	Riccardi	8 sacks for delivery later that year. The wool is to come from his own store or other good wool of the High Peak in Derbyshire and is to be weighed and treated as per the custom there.
106	E159/61, rot. 19	Easter 1288	Roger de Huntingefeld	Riccardi	1 sack of poor and white wool.

No.	Reference	Date	Seller	Buyer	Summary
107	C54/105, m. 3d	3 September 1288	Tilty abbey, Essex (Cistercian)	Bettori of Lucca	31 sacks of wool
108	E159/62, rot. 14	Michaelmas 1288–9	John de Bosco and Edmund Trussel, Leicestershire	Riccardi	6 sacks of wool for delivery over three years 1289–1291. The wool is to emanate from the pastures of Leicester.
109	E159/62, rot. 15	1288	Meaux abbey, Holderness (Cistercian)	Riccardi	11 sacks for delivery over three years 1289–1291
110	E159/62, rot. 4	12 November 1288	Pipewell abbey, Northamptonshire (Cistercian)	Arnald de Soliz, William Servat, Girard de Brolio (Cahors)	360 sacks for delivery over fifteen years 1289–1302
111	E159/62, rot. 4	20 January 1289	Minster Priory in Sheppey	Stephen de Cornhulle, citizen of London	The whole wool production for all of his life
112	E159/62, rot. 9d	5 July 1289	Pipewell abbey, Northamptonshire (Cistercian)	Arnald de Soliz (Cahors)	See 110 above
113	E159/62, rot. 16d	Michaelmas 1288–9	Robert Bozon of High Peak	Riccardi	3 sacks of wool for delivery later that year
114	E159/62, rot. 17d	Hilary 1289	Roger de Genny, Lincolnshire	Riccardi	2 sacks for delivery later that year. The wool is to come from his own store at Pickworth near Stamford.
115	E159/62, rot. 19	Easter 1289	Andrew de Basing, Ralph Sparwater and Richard Gamen of Ashbourne	Robert de Basing, citizen of London	21 sacks of wool for delivery over five years.
116	C54/106, m. 6d (schedule)	8 May 1289	Bruern abbey, Cotswolds (Cistercian)	Laurence, John and Thomas of Ludlow	5 sacks of wool. This small wool debt is associated with another larger pecuniary debt of 2000 marks owed by the abbot and later paid in full.

No.	Reference	Date	Seller	Buyer	Summary
117	E159/63, rot. 21; E368/61, rot. 26	Michaelmas 1289	John of Bulmer	Riccardi	7 sacks of wool
118	E159/63, rot. 25; E368/61, rot. 29	Hilary 1290	Gilbert of Birdsall, East Riding Yorkshire	Riccardi	2 sacks for delivery later that year. This wool is to come from Briddeshale and Huggate and each sack is to contain 30 stone by the weight of York. Delivery is to be at the merchants' costs.
119	E159/63, rot. 25d; E368/61, rot. 29	Hilary 1290	Robert le Baud and Michael Golosii, Burgesses of London	Riccardi	6 sacks of wool for delivery later that year. The wool is to come from his own store and the pasture of Rothwell (Northants.) Each sack is to contain 28 stones by the weight of Rothwell, each stone being 13lb.
120	E159/63, rot. 26d; E368/61, rot. 30d	Hilary 1290	John de Mohaut	Riccardi	2½ sacks of wool for delivery later that year. The wool is to come from his store on the manor of Mikelewet, each sack containing 30 stone with 12lb to the stone.
121	E159/64, rot. 1; E368/62, rot. 1	12 September 1290	Hugh de Brok	Cok son of Aaron the Jew	18 sacks of wool
122	E159/64, rot. 22d; E368/62, rot. 27	Michaelmas 1290–1	St. Swithun's Priory, Winchester (Benedictine)	Riccardi	30 sacks of wool for delivery over six years 1291–1296
123	E13/14, m. 8d	13–27 October 1290	Biddlesden abbey, Buckinghamshire (Cistercian)	Arnald de Soliz, John de Rodelegh, Arnold John (Cahors)	1½ sacks of wool
124	E13/14, m. 11	20–27 October 1290	Robert of Rothwell	Riccardi	5 sacks of wool
125	E13/14, m. 13d	2 and 12 November 1290	Merchants of Boston	Riccardi	9½ sacks of wool

No.	Reference	Date	Seller	Buyer	Summary
126	E13/14, m. 16d	25 November 1290	Biddlesden abbey, Buckinghamshire (Cistercian)	Riccardi	4½ sacks of wool for delivery over two years 1291–1291. The wool is to come from the good *collecta* of Brackley (Northants.)
127	E13/15, m. 5	14 and 21 January 1291	John son of Eudo, William son of Roger le Clerc, Peter son of William Godesone of Boston	Riccardi	9½ sacks of wool
128	E13/15, m. 5	14 and 21 January 1291	John son of Thomas son of Eudo of Boston and Conrad, his brother	Riccardi	2 sacks of wool
129	E159/64, rot. 6d	22 January 1291	Wardon and Pipewell abbeys	Arnold de Soliz (Cahors)	5 sacks of wool
130	E13/15, m. 4	27 January 1291	William Martyn of Tideswell, Nottinghamshire	Riccardi	3 sacks and three stones of wool
131	E13/15, m. 4	27 January 1291	William of Stoke, Gilbert of Barwell of Higham and William le Mareschal of Upton, Warwickshire and Leicestershire	Riccardi	1½ sacks of wool
132	E13/15, m. 4	27 January 1291	William of Stoke, Ralph of Sutton, Herbert Bate of Stoke and John de Hurley, Warwickshire and Leicestershire	Riccardi	3 sacks of wool

No.	Reference	Date	Seller	Buyer	Summary
133	C54/108, mm. 8d–9d; E159/64, rot. 10; E368/62, rot. 14	28 February 1291	Pipewell abbey, Northamptonshire (Cistercian)	Arnald de Soliz, William Servat, Girard de Brolio and John de Redole (Cahors)	The entire crop of wool over 13 years 1291–1303. This contract appears as a result of litigation between the parties in a local eyre. A dresser is to be employed at the convent's costs and he is to receive 5 stones of common-grade wool a year for his work. Conditions are set down for the construction and layout of the wool sheds and the methods of storing therein. 900 sheep are to be set aside and marked with the signs of both parties, the intention being to create a constant flock of 2000 sheep so that this and other contracts might be met.
134	E159/64, rot. 25d; E368/62, rot. 29	Easter 1291	Robert Bozon of High Peak	Riccardi	1 sack of wool
135	E159/64, rot. 26; E368/62, rot. 30d	Trinity 1291	Tilty abbey, Essex (Cistercian)	Riccardi	9 sacks of wool
136	E159/64, rot. 27	Trinity 1291	Fountains abbey, Yorkshire (Cistercian)	Baldwin de Lacre and John del Court, burgesses of Ghent	Arrears of 41 sacks of wool
137	E159/65, rot. 27; E368/63, rot. 20	8 October 1291	Rievaulx abbey, North Riding Yorkshire (Cistercian)	Riccardi	1 sack of wool for delivery in 1294. This wool is to come from the good *collecta* of the abbey and is to be taken from the woolsheds.
138	E159/65, rot. 27; E368/63, rot. 20	9 October 1291	Adam Cokerel and Robert le Venour, Lincolnshire	Riccardi	6 sacks of wool
139	E13/17, m. 16d	14 and 21 January 1292	Master William de Bosco	Merchants of Lucca	1 sack of wool

No.	Reference	Date	Seller	Buyer	Summary
140	E159/65, rot. 33; E368/63, rot. 26d	Easter 1292	John fitz Thomas, knight of Ireland	Riccardi	15 sacks for delivery in 1293.
141	E159/65, rot. 33d; E368/63, rot. 26d	Easter 1292	Master Ralph de Halton, parson of Halton in the diocese of Lincoln	Ammanati of Pistoia	2 sacks for delivery in 1292
142	E159/65, rot. 36d	10 July 1292	Nicholas of Winchester, Bindon abbey, Dorset (Cistercian)	Riccardi	39 sacks of wool
143	E159/66, rot. 43; E368/64, rot. 35	October 1292	Forde abbey, Dorset (Cistercian)	Riccardi	12 sacks of wool over two years 1293–1294. This wool is to come from the abbey's woolsheds and four stones are to be pressed into every sack, at 12lb to the stone.
144	E159/66, rot. 43d; E368/64, rot. 35d	20 October 1292	Roger de Huntingfeld, Lincolnshire	Frisoto and Galterio de Monte Claro (Lucca)	6 sacks for delivery the following year 1293
145	E159/66, rot. 44; E368/64, rot. 36	29 October 1292	Vaudey abbey, Lincolnshire	Riccardi	10 sacks for delivery in the following year 1293. The wool is to come from the abbot's woolsheds on his pastures within two or three leagues from the abbey and is to be prepared in the custom of South Grange. The merchants are to contribute 10s to the costs of carriage.
146	E159/66, rot. 48; E368/64, rot. 41	Easter 1293	Tickford priory by Newport Pagnell, Chilterns (Benedictines)	Riccardi	12 sacks for delivery over two years 1293–1294
147	E13/18, m. 27	19 and 26 April 1293	Henry of Mapelton	John de Brylaunde	1 sack of wool falsely claimed
148	E13/18, m. 31	19 and 26 April 1293	Richard de Farford', Merchant of Louth	William de Hereford, citizen of London	10 sacks of wool

No.	Reference	Date	Seller	Buyer	Summary
149	E13/18, m. 32	26 April and 3 May 1293	Robert de Henneye and Thomas de Bereford	Merchants of Lucca	1 sack of wool
150	E13/19, m. 83d	30 September 1293	Nicholas de Norff' of York	Merchants of Lucca	1 sack and 3 stones of wool
151	E13/19, m. 76d	12 and 19 November 1293	John son of Henry Pychard	Edmund, the King's brother	10 sacks of wool
152	E159/68, rot. 30d	Hilary 1295	Roger and Henry, sons of Blak de Gatesby	Nicholas de Loo, merchant	5 sacks of wool
153	E159/69, rot. 62	15 February 1296	St Swithun's priory, Winchester	Riccardi	Wool taken by the King
154	E13/21, m. 59d	24 May 1297	Henry de Medugh'	Walter de Goushull'	26 sacks of wool
155	E159/71, rot. 56d	Easter 1298	Temple Dinsley	Luke le Vineter of Hitchin	144 m. of wool
156	E159/72, rot. 45	29 September 1298	Combermere abbey, Cheshire (Cistercian)	Frescobaldi	140 sacks for delivery over twenty years 1299–1318. This is an exclusive contract and the monks are not to sell any wool to any other party before this contract is fulfilled.
157	E159/72, rot. 45	18 March 1298	Byland abbey, North Riding Yorkshire (Cistercian)	Frescobaldi	245 sacks for delivery over seven years 1299–1305
158	E13/22, m. 13	13 October 1298	Quarr Abbey	Frescobaldi	All the wools of his house
159	E13/22, m. 27	14 January 1299	Newstead in Sherwood priory, Nottinghamshire (Augustinian)	Frescobaldi	This plea records a contract for 25 sacks which the prior is alleged to have reneged upon. A renegotiation structures new terms for the delivery of 48 marks and one sack over three years, the prior having been placed in mercy for unjust detention.

No.	Reference	Date	Seller	Buyer	Summary
160	E13/22, m. 31	27 January and 3 February 1299	John de Redmar, Lincolnshire	Riccardi	John is found guilty of reneging on an earlier deal for 20 sacks. The restructured agreement sets out repayment of 100s, over two instalments on 9 July and 13 October 1299.
161	E13/22, m. 37	17 February 1299	Basingwek abbey, Flintshire (Cistercian)	Frescobaldi	In another plea of debt the Frescobaldi claim a debt of 130 marks from the abbot. In the renegotiated agreement, the abbot was to pay 50 marks and a sack of good wool at the Boston fair in the next two years and 30 marks and a sack of middle-grade wool in the third year. Ultimately the abbot acquitted himself.
162	E13/22, m. 70d	16 July 1299	William Cause of Lincoln	James Pilate, Everard de sancto Venancio, Bernard Pilate of Douai	This plea refers to a contract of 1287. This was for the entire crop for seven years 1290–1296. William claimed that the merchants took the wool for the first three years, but thereafter did not appear as promised, whereby the wool deteriorated and could not be sold. They reply that they could not enter the kingdom in the fourth year due to the trade embargo and the blockade of the North Sea. No verdict is recorded.

No.	Reference	Date	Seller	Buyer	Summary
163	E159/73, rot. 35	Michaelmas 1299–1300	Flaxley abbey, Gloucestershire (Cistercian)	James Pilate of Douai	5 sacks for delivery over two years 1300–1301
164	E13/24, m. 9d	30 September 1300	Stoneleigh abbey, Warwickshire (Cistercian)	Brachius Gerardi (Florence)	This is a plea brought against the abbot for detention of 5 sacks and 132.5 marks. The abbot is out of the country en route to the Curia and so no progress is made in the case.
165	E159/74, rot. 41d	Michaelmas 1300	Robert Ughtred	Frescobaldi	6 sacks and 6 stone for delivery in the following year 1301. The only details recorded are that for each sack sold the merchants are to receive one extra stone of wool as profit ('de avantagio') for nothing. 100 marks and 6 sacks.
166	C54/118, m. 17d	27 January 1301	Rievaulx abbey, North Riding Yorkshire (Cistercian)	Cerchi Negri	
167	C54/118, m. 8d	2 June 1301	Stoneleigh abbey, Warwickshire (Cistercian)	Pulci-Rembertini	12 marks and 5 sacks
168	E13/25, m. 15	18 November 1301	Abbey of St Osyth, Essex (Augustinian)	Frescobaldi	Original contract for 5 sacks of wool. Upon acknowledging his debt, the abbot agreed to repay 60 marks for the wool and 60s in damages.
169	E13/25, m. 27	29 January 1302	Newminster abbey	Frescobaldi and Riccardi	1 sack of wool
170	E13/25, m. 47d	14 May 1302	Newminster abbey	Frescobaldi and Riccardi	All the wool of the house for three years

No.	Reference	Date	Seller	Buyer	Summary
171	E13/26, m. 23	1 December 1303	Margaret (prioress), Arden priory, North Riding Yorkshire (Benedictine)	Frescobaldi	This plea arises as an attempt to broker compromise between the current prioress and the Frescobaldi because the merchants claim the wool mentioned in the contract was not delivered after the fourth year as it had not been prepared or dressed as agreed, wherefore they refused to make payments. The nuns, meanwhile, argue that until this point the merchants had sent their attorney, but that after this year they no longer turned up or paid any money for the wool. The original contract was for the entire crop of the priory for ten years 1291–1300. The wool was to be carried at the convent's costs to Thorpe, a wool-shed of Byland abbey. Ultimately agreement was brokered to the effect that the nuns would provide 2 sacks of wool worth 8 marks each, one sack at 24 June 1304 and the other a year later.
172	E13/26, m. 69	25 June 1304	Selby abbey	William Servat Merchants of Lucca	One poke of wool
173	E13/27, m. 5d	30 September 1304	Baroncino Gualteri and Brunetto, his Son		261/2 sacks of wool
174	E13/27, m. 69	14 June 1305	Sawtry abbey	Frescobaldi	Debt and 7 stones of wool
175	E159/79, rot. 46d	Michaelmas 1305–1306	Stephen de Stannham	Walter Langton, bishop of Coventry and Lichfield	27 sacks for delivery in the following year 1306

No.	Reference	Date	Seller	Buyer	Summary
176	E159/80, rot. 62	Michaelmas 1306–1307	Thomas le Latimer de West Wardon'	John de Triple	4 sacks for delivery in the following year 1307
177	E13/29, m. 40	3 April 1307	Henry le Teynturer of Hereford	John de London'	4 sacks of wool
178	E13/29, m. 42d	Easter 1307	Jervaulx abbey, North Riding Yorkshire (Cistercian)	Frescobaldi	12 sacks for delivery over three years 1307–1309. This contract is the result of a plea before the Exchequer. In return for a remittance of a debt to the merchants of 90 marks and 2 sacks of wool, which had gone unpaid, the abbot agrees to this deal.
179	E159/81, rot. 43d	28 February 1308	Temple Bruer, Eagle and Willoughton	Bardi and Portenare	The wool of these houses. The debt passed to the Bellardi of Lucca in part payment of the King's own debt.
180	E159/81, rot. 59	Hilary 1308	Tilty abbey, Essex (Cistercian)	Frescobaldi	2 sacks for delivery over two years 1308–1309
181	E159/81, rot. 60d	Easter 1308	William de Wantyng, Berkshire	Bellardi	6 sacks for delivery later that year. The wool is to come from the area of Lambourn and Aldbourne (Berkshire).
182	E159/82, rot. 81	Michaelmas 1308–1309	Combermere abbey, Cheshire (Cistercian)	Frescobaldi	110 sacks for delivery over twenty years 1309–1328
183	E13/33, m. 23d	26 November 1309	Waverley Abbey	Frescobaldi	All of the wool of the house for five years
184	E13/33, m. 51d	4 May 1310	Jervaulx abbey, North Riding Yorkshire (Cistercian)	Frescobaldi	4 sacks of wool
185	E159/83, rot. 73	24 July 1310	Bruern abbey, Oxfordshire (Cistercian)	Frescobaldi	2 sacks for delivery in 1311
186	E13/34, m. 28	19 April 1311	Richard le Faytour of Chipping Norton	Frescobaldi	4 sacks of wool

No.	Reference	Date	Seller	Buyer	Summary
187	C54/130, m. 30d	30 July 1312	Gerard Salveyn, Yorkshire	Bellardi	14 sacks of wool
188	C54/131, m. 26d	10 August 1313	Combermere abbey, Cheshire (Cistercian)	John de Wyndeloke of Ypres	11 sacks of wool
189	E159/87, rot. 49d	29 October 1313	Lewes priory, Sussex (Cluniac)	John de Triple	100 sacks for delivery over four years 1314–1318
190	E159/87, rot. 70	11 June 1314	Pipewell abbey, Northamptonshire (Cistercian)	William Servat, Arnold de Soliz, John de Redole (Cahors, now citizens and merchants of London)	The Abbey is quit of all money, sheep and wool
191	E13/36, m. 45d	25 June 1314	John son and heir of Ranulph de Ry	Dyno Reyneri	5 sacks of wool
192	E159/87, rot. 70	27 June 1314	Pipewell abbey, Northamptonshire (Cistercian)	William Servat, Arnold de Soliz, John de Redole (Cahors, now citizens and merchants of London)	Entire crop over eight years 1315–1322. The monks are to carry the wool to Boston at their own costs, but the merchants will acquit them of toll and any other customs charges. They will also give the monks a tun of wine each year for the celebration of mass. The monks, on the other hand, will give William Servat 5 stones of wool each year for his robe. Before 14 April 1315 the merchants will find 1000 sheep, half male, half female, which will be kept on their pastures and marked with the marks of both parties. The wool arising each year from such sheep will be divided equally, while the fells will likewise be sold each year to joint profit.

No.	Reference	Date	Seller	Buyer	Summary
193	E159/88, rot. 140	Hilary 1315	Combermere abbey, Cheshire (Cistercian)	Frescobaldi	110 sacks of wool. Reorganisation of debt.
194	E159/89, rot. 73	1 March 1316	Lewes priory, Sussex (Cluniac)	John de Triple	40 sacks of wool over four years
195	E159/91, rot. 91	10 May 1318	Combermere abbey, Cheshire (Cistercian)	Bardi	The Abbey of Burton upon Trent paying the debt of Combermere abbey (see 193)
196	E159/91, rot. 105d	Michaelmas 1317–1318	Tilty abbey, Essex (Cistercian)	Riccardi	8 sacks being recovered by the King
197	E159/92, rot. 62d	26 October 1318	Kingswood Abbey, Gloucestershire	Peruzzi	8 sacks of wool
198	E159/92, rot. 26	20 January 1319	John de Halton, Bishop of Carlisle	Spini	50 sacks of wool
199	E159/92, rot. 70	10 February 1319	Lewes priory, Sussex (Cluniac)	John de Triple	160 sacks over eight years
200	E159/95, rot. 39d	31 October 1321	Abingdon abbey, Berkshire (Bendictine)	Richard de Shipene and Ingram le Spicer of Abingdon	120 sacks for delivery over four years 1322–1325
201	E159/95, rot. 43	4 December 1321	Lewes priory, Sussex (Cluniac)	John de Triple	140 sacks over seven years
202	E159/97, rot. 16	2 July 1324	Thornton Abbey and Newsham Abbey	Gotele	All the wool of Thornton for four years and Newsham for five years granted to the Bardi
203	E159/100, rots. 43d., 114d	Trinity 1325	Rievaulx abbey, North Riding Yorkshire (Cistercian)	Riccardi	1 sack of wool

Bibliography

MANUSCRIPT SOURCES

British Library, London
Additional MS 37022 – Thirteenth-century cartulary of Pipewell abbey (fragment)
Cotton MS Caligula A XII, ff. 2–159v. – Thirteenth-century cartulary of Pipewell abbey
A XIII – Thirteenth-century register of Pipewell abbey
Cotton MS Otho B xiv, ff. 150r–205r – *Speculum Willelmi de Lalleford*. Fourteenth-century chronicle of Pipewell abbey
BL Stowe MS 937 – Register of Pipewell abbey, thirteenth–fourteenth centuries

The National Archives, Kew
Chancery
Close Rolls (C 54)
Certificates of Statute Merchant and Statute Staple (C 241)

Court of Common Pleas
Plea Rolls (CP 40)

Exchequer
Plea Rolls (E 13) Ancient Deeds (E 210, E 326, 327, 329)
Exchequer Miscellanea (E 101)
King's Remembrancer: Memoranda Rolls (E 159)
Augmentation Office: Ancient Deeds, Series B (E 326)
Lord Treasurer's Remembrancer: Memoranda Rolls (E368)

Justices in Eyre
Assize Rolls (JUST 1)

King's Bench
Coram Rege rolls (KB 26)

Special Correspondence
Ancient Correspondence (SC 1)

PRINTED PRIMARY SOURCES

Bell, A. R., C. Brooks and P. Dryburgh, *Advance Contracts for the Sale of Wool c. 1200–1327* vol. 315 (List and Index Society, 2006) also accessible at the UK Data Archive, study number 5325: www.data-archive.ac.uk

Calendar of the Charter Rolls preserved in the Public Record Office, 1226–57 (London, 1903)

Calendar of the Close Rolls preserved in the Public Record Office, 1288–96 (London, 1904)

Calandar of Fine Rolls preserved in the Public Record Office, 1272–1307 (London, 1911)

Calendar of the Liberate Rolls preserved in the Public Record Office, 1251–60 (London, 1959)

Calendar of Patent Rolls preserved in the Public Record Office, Edward I–Edward II, 10 vols. (London, 1893–1904)

The Cartulary of Newnham Priory, ed. J. Godber (Bedfordshire Historical Record Society Publications 43, 1963)

The Coucher Book of Furness Abbey, III, ed. J. C. Atkinson (Chetham Society, 1919)

Della Decime e delle altre gravezze imposte dal Commune de Firenze, della moneta, e della mercatura dei Fiorentini fino al secola XVI, ed. G-F Pagnini, III (Lisbonne-Lucques, 1766)

Jenks, S. *The Enrolled Customs Accounts (TNA: PRO E 356, E 372, E 364), 1279–80 – 1508–09 (1523/1524)*, Part I (Kew: List and Index Society, 2004)

La Pratica della Mercatura, ed. Allan Evans (Cambridge, MA., 1935)

Lay Taxes in England and Wales, 1188–1688, ed. M. Jurkowski, C. L. Smith and D. Crook (Richmond, 1998)

Memorials of the abbey of St Mary of Fountains, ed. J. R. Walbran (Durham: Surtees Society volume XLII, 1867)

Rotuli Parlamentorum, V, ed J. Strachey et al (London, 1787)

Select Cases Concerning the Law Merchant, 1239–1633, II, ed. H. Hall (London: Selden Society, 1930)

Statuta Capitulorum Generalium Ordinis Cisterciensis ab anno 1116 ad annum 1786, ed. J. Canivez (Louvain, 1934)

Taxatio Ecclesiastica Angliae et Walliae Auctoritate P. Nicholai IV circa A.D. 1291, ed. J. Caley (London: Record Commission, 1802)

Wellingborough Manorial Accounts, AD 1258–1323, ed. F. M. Page (Kettering: Publications of the Northamptonshire Record Society VIII, 1936)

SECONDARY SOURCES

Albe, E., 'Les Marchands de Cahors a Londres au XIIIe siècle,' *Bulletin de la Société des Etudes du Département de Lot* (Cahors, 1908), pp. 5–29

Arens, F., 'Wilhelm Servat von Cahors als Kaufmann zu London (1273–1320), *Vierteljahrsschrift für Sozial- und Wirtschaftsgeschichte* 11 (1913), pp. 477–514

Barnes, G. *Kirkstall Abbey, 1147–1539: An Historical Study* (Leeds: Publications of the Thoresby Society, LVII, no. 128, 1984)

Barratt, N., 'Finance on a Shoestring: The Exchequer in the Thirteenth Century', in A. Jobson (ed.), *English Government in the Thirteenth Century* (Woodbridge, 2004)

Bell, A. R., C. Brooks and P. Dryburgh, 'Modern Finance in the Middle Ages? Advance Contracts with Cistercian Abbeys for the Supply of Wool *c.* 1270–1330: A Summary of Findings', *Cîteaux: Commentarii cistercienses*, vol. 55, fasc. 3–4 (2004), pp. 339–343

Bell, A. R., C. Brooks and P. Dryburgh, 'Why Forwards Really Came from the Past', *Professional Investor* (April 2005), pp. 21–26

Bell, A. R., C. Brooks and P. Dryburgh, ' "*Leger est aprendre mes fort est arendre*" ': Wool, Debt and the Dispersal of Pipewell Abbey, 1280–1328,' *Journal of Medieval History* vol. 32, no. 3 (2006), pp. 187–211.

Bell, A. R., C. Brooks and P. Dryburgh, 'Interest Rates and Efficiency in Medieval Wool Forward Contracts', *Journal of Banking and Finance* vol. 31, 2 (2007), pp. 361–380.

Bigwood, G., 'Un marché de matières premières: laines d'Angleterre et marchands italiens vers la fin du XIIIe siècle', *Annales d'histoire économique et sociale* 2 (1930), pp. 196–211

Bischoff, J. P., 'Pegolotti: An Honest Merchant?', *Journal of European Economic History* 6 (1977), pp. 103–108

Bouchard, C. B. *Holy Entrepreneurs: Cistercians, Knights, and Economic Exhange in Twelfth-Century Burgundy* (Ithaca, 1991)

Bowden, P. J. 'Wool Supply and the Woollen Industry', *Economic History Review* 9 (1956), pp. 44–58

Britnell, R., *Britain and Ireland 1050–1530: Economy and Society* (Oxford, 2004)

Burton, J. E., *Monastic and Religious Orders in Britain, 1000–1300* (Cambridge, 1994)

Campbell, B. M. S. (ed.) *Before the Black Death: Studies in the 'Crisis' of the Early Fourteenth Century* (Manchester, 1991)

Carus-Wilson, E. M., and O. Coleman, *England's Export Trade, 1275–1547* (Oxford, 1963)

Chorley, P., 'English Cloth Exports during the Thirteenth and Early Fourteenth Centuries: the Continental Evidence', *Historical Research*, vol. 60, no. 144 (1988), pp. 1–10

Chorley, P., 'The Evolution of the Woolen, 1300–1700' in N. B. Harte (ed.), *The New Draperies in the Low Countries and England, 1300–1800* (Oxford, 1997)

A Commercialising Economy: England 1086 to 1300, ed. R. H. Britnell and B. M. S. Campbell (Manchester, 1991)

Deighton, H. S., 'Clerical Taxation by Consent, 1279–1301', *English Historical Review* 68 (1953), pp. 161–192

Denholm-Young, N., *Seigneurial Administration in England* (London, 1937)

Denholm-Young, N., 'The Merchants of Cahors,' *Medievalia et Humanistica* 4 (1946), 37–44

Donkin, R. A., 'The Disposal of Cistercian Wool in England and Wales during the Twelfth and Thirteenth Centuries', *Citeaux in den Nederlanden* 8 (1957), pp. 115–20.

Donkin, R. A., 'Bercaria et Lanaria', *Yorkshire Archaeological Journal* 39 (1958), pp. 447–50

Donkin, R. A., 'Cistercian Sheep-Farming and Wool-Sales in the Thirteenth Century', *Agricultural History Review* 6 (1958), pp. 2–8

Donkin, R. A., *The Cistercians: Studies in the Geography of Medieval England and Wales* (Toronto, 1978)

Donnelly, J. S., 'Changes in the Grange Economy of English and Welsh Cistercian Abbeys, 1300–1540', *Traditio* 10 (1954), pp. 399–458

Duby, G., *Rural Economy and Country Life in the Medieval West*, trans C. Postan (Columbia, 1990)

Eldridge, R. M., and R. Maltby, 'On the Existence and Implied Cost of Carry in a Medieval English Forward/Futures Market', *Review of Futures Markets* 11 (1992), pp. 36–49

Foard, G., 'Medieval Woodland, Agriculture and Industry in Rockingham Forest, Northamptonshire,' *Medieval Archaeology* 45 (2001), pp. 41–97

Fryde, E. B., *Studies in Medieval Trade and Finance* (London, 1983)

Fryde, E. B., *William de la Pole, Merchant and King's Banker* (London, 1988)

Fryde, N. M., *Tyranny and Fall of Edward II, 1322–6* (Cambridge, 1979)

Fryde, N. M., 'Die Kaufleute aus Cahors im England des 13. Jahrhunderts', in *Kredit im Spätmittelalterlichen und Frühneuzeitlichen Europa: Quellen und Darstellungen zur Hansischen Geschichte* 38 (1991), pp. 25–38

Gilchrist, J., *The Church and Economic Activity in the Middle Ages* (London, 1969)

Goddard, R. M., *Lordship and Medieval Urbanisation: Coventry, 1043–1355* (Woodbridge, 2004)

Goldthwaite, R. A., 'Local Banking in Renaissance Florence', *Journal of European Economic History* 14 (1985), pp. 5–55

Goodfellow, P., 'Medieval Markets in Northamptonshire', *Northamptonshire Past and Present* 7 (1989), pp. 305–324

Goodhart, C. A. E., P. C. McMahon. and Y. L. Ngama, 'Does the Forward Premium/Discount Help to Predict the Future Change in the Exchange Rate?', *Scottish Journal of Political Economy* 39 (1992), pp. 129–139

Goss, B. A., 'The Forecasting Approach to Efficiency in the Wool Market', *Applied Economics* 22 (1990), pp. 973–993

Graham-Higgs, J., A. Rambaldi and B. Davidson, 'Is the Australian Wool Futures Market Efficient as a Predictor of Spot Prices?', *Journal of Futures Markets* 19 (1999), pp. 565–582

Graves, C. V., 'The Economic Activities of the Cistercians in Medieval England (1128–1307)', *Analecta Sacri Ordinis Cisterciensis* 13 (1957), pp. 3–60

Haines, R. M., *King Edward II: His Reign and its Aftermath, 1284–1330* (Montreal, 2003)

Hall, S. G., and M. P. Taylor, 'Modeling Risk Premia in Commodity Forward Prices: Some Evidence from the London Metal Exchange', *Review of Futures Markets* 8 (1989), pp. 200–217

Hansen, L. P., and R. J. Hodrick, 'Forward Rates as Optimal Predictors of Spot Rates: An Econometric Analysis', *Journal of Political Economy* 88 (1980), pp. 829–853

Harvey, B., 'Introduction' in B. M. S. Campbell (ed.), *Before the Black Death*, pp. 1–16

Hill, J. F., *Medieval Lincoln* (Cambridge, 1948)

Hoshino, H., 'The Rise of the Florentine Woolen Industry in the Fourteenth Century' in N. B. Harte and K. G. Ponting (eds.), *Cloth and Clothing in Medieval Europe: Essays in Memory of Professor E. M. Carus Wilson* (1983), pp. 184–204

Hunt, E. S., 'A New Look at the Dealings of the Bardi and Peruzzi with Edward III', *Journal of Economic History* 50 (1990), pp. 149–162

Hunt, E. S., *Medieval Super Companies* (Cincinnati, 1995)

Hunt, E. S., and J. M. Murray, *A History of Business in Medieval Europe 1200–1550* (Cambridge, 1999)

Jamroziak, E., 'Rievaulx Abbey as a Wool Producer in the Late Thirteenth Century: Cistercians, Sheep and Debts', *Northern History* 50 (2003), pp. 197–218

Jenkinson, H., 'William Cade, a Financier of the Twelfth Century', *English Historical Review* 28 (1913), pp. 209–227

Jordan, W., *The Great Famine: Northern Europe in the Early Fourteenth Century* (Princeton, 1996)

Kaueper, R. W., *Bankers to the Crown: The Riccardi of Lucca and Edward I* (Princeton, 1973)

Kairys Jr., J. P., and N. Valerio III, 'The Market for Equity Options in the 1870s', *Journal of Finance* 52 (1997), pp. 1707–1723

Keen, M., *England in the Later Middle Ages: A Political History*, 2nd edn (London, 2003)

Kershaw, I., 'The Great European Famine and Agrarian Crisis in England, 1315–22', *Past and Present* 59 (1973), pp. 3–50

Knoll, M. S., *The Ancient Roots of Modern Financial Innovation: The Early History of Regulatory Arbitrage* (2004) Mimeo. Wharton School, University of Pennsylvania, published online

Knowles, D., *The Religious Orders in England*, II (Cambridge, 1948)

Kohn, M., 'Risk Instruments in the Medieval and Early Modern Economy', Department of Economics, Dartmouth College (1999), Working paper 99–107

Kowaleski, M., *Local Markets and Regional Trade in Medieval Exeter* (Cambridge, 1995)

Kroll, S., and M. J. Paulenoff, *The Business One Irwin Guide to the Futures Markets* (Homewood, IL: Business One Press, 1993)

Lekai, L. J., *The Cistercians: Ideals and Reality* (Dallas, 1977)

Lekai, L. J., 'Ideals and Reality in Early Cistercian Life and Legislation', in *Cistercian Ideals and Reality*, ed. J. R. Summerfeldt (Kalamazoo, 1978), pp. 4–29

Lloyd, T. H., 'The Movement of Wool Prices in Medieval England', *Economic History Review Supplement 6* (Cambridge, 1973)

Lloyd, T. H., *The English Wool Trade in the Middle Ages* (Cambridge, 1977)

Lloyd, T. H., *Alien Merchants in England in the High Middle Ages* (Brighton, 1982)

Lopez, R. S., and I. W. Raymond, *Medieval Trade in the Mediterranean World* (New York, 1955)

Lunt, W. E., *Financial Relations of the Papacy with England to 1327* (Cambridge, MA, 1939)

McNamee, C., *The Wars of the Bruces: Scotland, England and Ireland, 1306–28* (East Linton, 1997)

Madden, J. E., 'Business Monks, Banker Monks, Bankrupt Monks: The English Cistercians in the Thirteenth Century', *Catholic Historical Review* 49 (3) (1963), pp. 341–364

Martines, L., *Power and Imagination: City-States in Renaissance Italy* (Baltimore: Johns Hopkins, 1988)

Masschaele, J., *Peasants, Merchants and Markets: Inland Trade in Medieval England, 1150–1350* (Basingstoke, 1996)

Mate, M., 'The Indebtedness of Canterbury Cathedral Priory 1215–1295', *Economic History Review, Second Series* 26 (1973), pp. 183–197

Miller, E., and J. Hatcher, *Medieval England: Rural Society and Economic Change, 1086–1348* (Cambridge, 1990)

Miller, E. (ed.), *Agrarian History of England and Wales*, vols. II, 1086–1348 and III, 1348–1500 (Cambridge, 1991)

Moore, E. W., *The Fairs of Medieval England* (Toronto, 1985)

Munro, J. H., 'Bruges and the Abortive Staple in English Cloth: An Incident in the Shift of Commerce from Bruges to Antwerp in the Late Fifteenth Century', *Revue belge de philologie et d'histoire* 44 (1966), pp. 1137–1159

Munro, J. H., 'Wool Price Schedules and the Qualities of English Wools in the Latter Middle Ages c. 1270–1499', *Textile History* 9 (1978), pp. 118–169

Munro, J. H., 'Urban Regulation and Monopolistic Competition in the Textile Industries of the Late-Medieval Low Countries', in Erik Aerts and John Munro (eds.), *Textiles of the Low Countries in European Economic History*, Proceedings of the Tenth International Economic History Congress: Session B-15, Studies in Social and Economic History 19 (Leuven: Leuven History Press, 1990)

Munro, J. H., 'Industrial Transformation in the North-west European Textile Trades, c. 1290–c. 1340: Economic Progress or Economic Crisis?', in B. M. S. Campbell (ed.), *Before the Black Death: Studies in the 'Crisis' of the Early Fourteenth Century* (Manchester, 1991), pp. 110–148

Munro, J. H., 'The International Law Merchant and the Evolution of Negotiable Credit in Late-Medieval England and the Low Countries', in D. Puncuh (ed.), *Banchi pubblici, banchi privati e monti di pietà nell'Europa preindustriale: amministrazione, tecniche operative e ruoli economici*, Nouva Serie, Vol. xxi (Genoa: Società Ligure di Storia Patria), 49–80; reprinted in Munro, *Textiles, Towns, and Trade: Essays in the Economic History of Late-Medieval England and the Low Countries*, Variorum Collected Studies series CS 442 (Aldershot and Brookfield: Ashgate Publishing Ltd, 1994)

Munro, J. H., 'Anglo-Flemish Competition in the Internatiopnal Cloth Trade, 1340–1520', *Publication du centre européen d'études bourguigonnes*, 35(1995), pp. 37–60

Munro, J. H., 'The 'Industrial Crisis' of the English Textile Towns, 1290–1330', in Michael Prestwich, Richard Britnell and Robin Frame (eds.) *Thirteenth Century England: VII* (Woodbridge, 1999), pp. 103–141

Munro, J. H., 'The Symbiosis of Towns and Textiles: Urban Institutions and the Changing Fortunes of Cloth Manufacturing in the Low Countries and England, 1270–1570', *Journal of Early Modern History: Contacts, Comparisons, Contrasts* 3 (1999), pp. 1–74

Munro, J. H., 'The "New Institutional Economics" and the Changing Fortunes of Fairs in Medieval and Early Modern Europe: The Textile Trades, Warfare, and Transactions Costs', *Vierteljahrschrift für Sozial-und Wirtschaftsgeschichte* 88 (2001), pp. 1–47

Munro, J. H., 'Medieval Woollens: Textiles, Textile Technology, and Industrial Organisation, c. 800–1500', in David Jenkins (ed.), *The Cambridge History of Western Textiles* (Cambridge, 2003), pp. 181–227

Munro, J. H., 'Medieval Woollens: The Western European Woollen Industries and their Struggles for International Markets, c. 1000–1500', in David Jenkins (ed.), *The Cambridge History of Western Textiles* (Cambridge, 2003), pp. 228–324

Murray, J. M., *A History of Business in Medieval Europe 1200–1550* (Cambridge, 1999)

Nightingale, P., 'Knights and Merchants: Trade, Politics and the Gentry in Late Medieval England', *Past and Present* 169 (November 2000), pp. 36–62

Nightingale, P., 'Norwich, London, and the Regional Integration of Norfolk's Economy in the First Half of the Fourteenth Century', in *Trade, Urban Hinterlands and Market Integration c. 1300–1600*, ed. James Galloway (London: Centre for Metropolitan History Working Paper Series 3, 2000)

Ormrod, W. M., 'The Crown and the English Economy, 1290–1348', in B. M. S. Campbell (ed.), *Before the Black Death: Studies in the 'Crisis' of the Early Fourteenth Century* Manchester, 1991), pp. 149–183

Pirenne, H., *The Economic and Social History of Medieval Europe* (New York, 1937)

Platt, C., *The Monastic Grange in Medieval England: A Reassessment* (London, 1969)

Postan, M. M., *Medieval Trade and Finance* (Cambridge, 1973)

Power, E., *The Wool Trade in English Medieval History* (Oxford, 1941)

Power, E., and M. M. Postan, *Studies in English Trade in the Fifteenth Century* (London, 1933)

Prestwich, M., 'Italian Merchants in Late Thirteenth and Early Fourteenth Century England', in *The Dawn of Modern Banking* (Yale, 1979), pp. 77–104

Prestwich, M., *Edward I* (New Haven and London, 1997)

Raftis, J. A., 'Western Monasticism and Economic Organization', *Comparative Studies in Society and History* 31 (1960–1), pp. 452–469

Roon-Basserman, E. von, 'Die Handelsperre Englands gegen Flandern 1270–1274 und die lizenzierte englische Wollausfuhr', *Vierteljahrsschrift für Sozial- und Wirtschaftsgeschichte* 50 (1963), pp. 71–82

Ryder, M. L., 'Medieval Sheep and Wool Types', *Agricultural History Review* 32 (1984), pp. 14–28

Snape, R. H., *English Monastic Finances in the Later Middle Ages* (Cambridge, 1926)

Spufford, P., *Handbook of Medieval Exchange* (London, 1986)

Spufford, P., *Power and Profit: The Merchant in Medieval Europe* (London, 2002)

Stephenson, M., 'Wool Yields in the Medieval Economy', *Economy History Review* 41 (1988), pp. 368–391

Stoll, H. R., 'The Relation between Put and Call Prices', *Journal of Finance* 44 (1969), pp. 801–824

Swan, E. J., *Building the Global Market: A 4000 Year History of Derivatives* (Dordrecht, 2000)

Varenbergh, E., *Relations Diplomatiques entre le Comte de Flandre et l'Angleterre* (Brussels, 1874)

Waites, B., 'Monasteries and the Wool Trade in North and East Yorkshire during the 13th and 14th Centuries', *Yorkshire Archaelogical Journal* 52 (1980), pp. 111–121

Whitwell, R. J., 'Italian Bankers and the English Crown', *Transactions of the Royal Historical Society* (n. s.) 17 (1903), pp. 175–233

Whitwell, R. J., 'English Monasteries and the Wool Trade in the 13th Century', *Vierteljahrsschrift für Sozial- und Wirtschaftsgeschichte* 2 (1904), pp. 1–33

Wright, R., ' "Casting Down the Altars and Levelling Everything before the Ploughshare"? The Expansion and Evolution of the Grange Estates of Kirkstall Abbey', in M. Prestwich, R. Britnell and R. Frame (eds.), *Thirteenth Century England IX* (Woodbridge, 2003)

Zell, Michael, 'Credit in the Pre-Industrial Woollen Industry', *Economic History Review* 49 (1996), pp. 667–691

Index

Abbreviations for Religious Orders mentioned in the text:

Aug.   Augustinian canons
Ba.   Benedictine monks (alien houses)
Ben.   Benedictine monks
Cist.   Cistercian monks
Clun.   Cluniac monks
Gilb.   Gilbertine (double order)
NB   Benedictine nuns
NC   Cistercian nuns
Prem.   Premonstratensian canons

Abbey Dore (Herefords; Cist.), 52, 78, 82
   abbot of, *see* William
   brethren, *see* Sautebroyl
Adam, abbot of Byland, 30
Adam, abbot of Combermere, 98, 119
Adam, abbot of Vaudey, 62
adjusted prices, 133
agents, 18, 22, 41, 42, 43, 45, 46, 47, 54, 76, 91,
   117, 147
Aldbourne (Wilts.), 53 n.179
Alvingham priory (Lincs.; Gilb.), 57 n.208, 61
Alzun, Robert, of Pontefract, 38 n.109
Amaduri, Guido, 32, 39, 128
Ammanati of Pisa, 20
Ancholme, River, 62
Ancient Deeds, series of, 17
Andover (Hants),
   merchants of, 59, 64
Anglo-Flemish trade disputes (1270–4), 13, 79,
   80, 81, 117
Appleby (Lincs.), 62
Arden priory (Yorks.; NB), 66
   prioress of, 49, 62 n.233; *see also* Margaret
Ardingelli, Roger, 102
asset pricing techniques, 9
attorneys, 28, 36, 39, 43, 44, 53, 64, 86 n.113
Aumale, counts of, 60
Averson, William de, 82, 83
Avignon, John of, prior of Lewes, 24

Avon, River, 74
Aylesford, William de, prior of Wroxton, 44
Ayre, Giles de, 28, 36, 39, 40–41, 43, 53, 64,
   138, 147

bailiffs, 41
Baldock (Herts.), 59
Banbury (Oxon), 37, 49, 53 n.179, 59, 79
   burgesses of, 58
   liberty of, 38
   merchants of, 47, 49, 129
bankruptcy, 9, 29, 30, 108, 116, 124, 125, 136, 137,
   147, 151
Bannockburn, battle of (1314), 102
Bar; *see* wool, fairs
Bardi of Florence, 7, 18, 20, 46, 63, 65, 76, 101,
   102, 103, 104, 107, 109, 117, 133
Bardney abbey (Lincs.; Ben.), 57 n.208, 61
Barford (Warks.), 74 n.35
Barlings abbey (Lincs.; Prem.), 57 n.208, 61,
   63, 78
Barons' Wars, 74, 80
Barton, Richard de, abbot of Meaux, 115
Basing, William de, prior of St Swithun,
   Winchester, 28, 33
Basinges, Thomas de, of London, 34, 35, 41, 50,
   53, 118, 124
Basingwerk abbey (Flints.; Cist.), 57 n.208
Baston (Lincs.), 82

Printed in Great Britain
by Amazon